To most Americans today, the Civil War is known through popular culture, not through the professional historical literature. In this book Jim Cullen examines popular renderings of the war—from books and films to songs and drama—showing how they have come to represent various truths about the war to certain groups, precisely because they resonate with contemporary points of division and struggle.

Cullen takes specific examples from twentieth-century popular culture, including Carl Sandburg's biography of Abraham Lincoln, Margaret Mitchell's *Gone with the Wind* and its film adaptation, southern rock 'n' roll of the 1970s, the film *Glory*, and historical reenactors. For each, the recollection of the Civil War serves and is shaped by current concerns. Sandburg, writing during the Depression, saw in Lincoln a powerful, mythic leader of the sort needed to push through New Deal reforms. Cullen argues that Mitchell's epic reflected her (and her readers') ambivalence about feminism. Linking the rock group Lynyrd Skynyrd with southern reactions to the Civil Rights movement of the 1960s and the imagery of *Glory* with other post-Vietnam films, Cullen shows how each rendering—especially those of reenactors— creates communal emotions and memories responsive to current concerns.

The CIVIL WAR in
POPULAR CULTURE

The CIVIL WAR in POPULAR CULTURE

A Reusable Past

JIM CULLEN

SMITHSONIAN INSTITUTION PRESS

WASHINGTON AND LONDON

Copy Editor: Sally Bennett
Supervisory Editor: Duke Johns
Designer: Kathleen Sims

Library of Congress Cataloging-in-Publication Data
Cullen, Jim, 1962–
    The Civil War in popular culture : a reusable past / Jim Cullen.
      p. cm.
    Includes bibliographical references and index.
    ISBN 1-56098-459-7 (alk. paper)
      1. United States—History—Civil War, 1861–1865—Influence.   2. United States—
History—Civil War, 1861–1865—Literature and the war.   3. United States—History—
Civil War, 1861–1865—Motion pictures and the war.   4. United States—History—Civil
War, 1861–1865—Historiography.   5. Historical fiction, American—History and
criticism.   6. Historical fiction, American—Film and video adaptations.   I. Title.
E468.9.C97   1995
973.7—dc20   94-25072

British Library Cataloguing-in-Publication Data is available

Manufactured in the United States of America
02 01 00 99 98 97 96 95   5 4 3 2

♾ The paper used in this publication meets the minimum requirements of the American
National Standard for Permanence of Paper for Printed Library Materials Z39.48-1984.

For my PARENTS
and the complexities of the American Dream

For my WIFE
and the rigors of a happy marriage

For my SON
and his promise in an uncertain future

The idea of history itself, special kinds of historical studies, and various attitudes toward history always play—whether intelligently conceived or not—a major role within a culture. That strange collection of assumptions, attitudes, and ideas we have come to call "a world view" always contains a more or less specific view of the nature of history. Attitudes toward the past frequently become facts of profound consequences for the culture itself.

Warren Susman,
in a joint address to the
American Historical and American
Studies Associations, 1960

Contents

Acknowledgments

Now that my labors on this project are at an end (though like many first-time authors, I have had my doubts that this book would *ever* be finished), it is my great pleasure to thank some of the people who made it possible.

The roots of this project date back to the winter of 1988, when I had the privilege of enrolling in the history seminar taught by John L. Thomas in my first year of graduate school at Brown University. The paper I wrote for him on Carl Sandburg was the seed for the dissertation on which this book is based. I am in Professor Thomas's debt not only for his having served as a reader for this dissertation, but also for the warmth, humor, and generosity that have endeared him to so many students for so many years.

Susan Smulyan of Brown's American Civilization Department was also a reader of this dissertation and contributed many insightful suggestions. I am even more grateful for her friendship, which has taken many different forms in the years since.

My dissertation was directed by Mari Jo Buhle. Besides serving as my primary teacher, she was the most careful editor for which any student could ever hope. In her teaching and scholarship, she has decisively shaped a generation of students, and I consider myself lucky to be one of them. I would also like to thank Paul Buhle for years of sage advice and illuminating conversation.

A number of colleagues have read and commented upon various parts of this project. Among those I would like to thank specifically are Bruce Dorsey, Dorothee Kocks, and David Moore. I am especially indebted to the anonymous readers who evaluated my manuscript for the Smithsonian Institution Press, whose incisive observations and suggestions have made a vast difference.

I would also like to express my gratitude to a number of people who facilitated my work with aid in gathering pictures, permissions, and information. Among them are Joanna C. Britto of the National Portrait Gallery of the Smithsonian Institution in Washington, D.C.; Diana R. Hellyer of the Turner Entertainment Co., Los Angeles; Helen Ashford and Lynn Richardson of the Michael Ochs Archive of Venice, California; Cassandra Barbour of Tri-Star Pictures of Culver City, California; Sharon Cavileer of the Prince William County Park Authority in Manassas, Virginia; and Civil War reenactor Paul Oliveria of the 2d Rhode Island Infantry in Rehoboth, Massachusetts. I also wish to single out the remarkable woman that readers of Chapter 6 will know as Jonathan Clarke, who despite some initial reservations agreed to share her vision of U.S. history with me. She, in turn, has asked that I acknowledge her mother, Barbara Clarke, a request with which I will happily comply.

My acquisitions editor at the Smithsonian, Mark Hirsch, stepped in at a low moment in my fortunes in 1992 and shepherded my manuscript through to acceptance. I appreciate his tact, humor, patience, and above all the confidence he showed in my work and the willingness of his colleagues at the Press to take me aboard. I feel privileged to have my book published by this great national institution. My thanks also go to Sally Bennett, who copy edited the manuscript with intelligence and sensitivity, and to supervisory editor Duke Johns, who offered valuable aid and advice throughout.

On a more personal note: My cherished friend Gordon Sterling provided valuable computing services and a willing ear. Robert Falvo and Jaime Silverman remained lifelong comrades in comparable enterprises. My in-laws, Theodore and Nancy Sizer, were helpful in countless ways, from the home they lent me in 1990–91 (Chapters 2 through 5 were drafted there) to less tangible forms of support.

I would also like to acknowledge my parents. My father, a New York City fireman, gave me a model of a man who loved his work and brought to it a devotion exceeded only by his commitment to his two children. My mother, the daughter of an immigrant taxicab driver who was a passionate supporter of Franklin Delano Roosevelt, realized her ambition of giving my sister and me something neither she nor my father ever had—a college education—and the means to a better life. This book can pay only the most slender homage to the great traditions embodied by these people.

My final debt is to my wife, Lyde Cullen Sizer, my companion in every sense of the word. It was she who allowed me to see that I could combine my interests in the Civil War and in popular culture into a viable project. This work is immeasurably better for her role in it, and I consider myself extraordinarily lucky to have married her and collaborated with her on our most important work to date: our son.

Introduction

History
as
Culture

> History, I am convinced, is not just
> something to be left to the historians.
>
> Warren Susman,
> *Culture as History*[1]

This book shows how novelists, moviemakers, musicians, and creators of other forms of popular culture have portrayed the Civil War throughout the twentieth century. It compares their efforts with those of academic scholars and explores the ways histories tell us something about their times—and ours.

The Civil War is an especially good focus for this kind of inquiry. The war wrought enormous changes in society, changes that can still help explain who we are: black or white, rich or poor, man or woman. Indeed, people who have no apparent connection with the Civil War have been affected by it. The issue of slavery split the Cherokee nation, for example, and it is unlikely that the transcontinental railroads that employed and exploited thousands of Asian Americans would have been built where they were—or when they were—had there been no war or had the South won it. Industrialization, immigration, and nationalism all affected the origins, progress, and aftermath of the conflict. It is doubtful that any single event in U.S. history can encompass everyone in a society as pluralistic as this one. But the Civil War has come as close as any to being what Shelby Foote called "the crossroads of our being."

Shelby Foote made this comment on the public television series *The Civil War*, first broadcast in the fall of 1990. He is a novelist and the author of a three-volume narrative of the war,[2] and the series on which he spoke was produced by Ken Burns, a documentary filmmaker. Neither man is a professional historian. Yet their work on the war probably reached more people than that of any contemporary academic, even Princeton historian James McPherson, author of the 1988 best-seller *Battle Cry of Freedom: The Civil War Era*. Similarly, the images and implicit interpretations of the war made in Margaret Mitchell's *Gone with the Wind* in 1936 continue to shape historical understanding more widely than do academic studies of the war. Works such as hers have received plenty of attention as works of art (or artlessness), as commerce, as sociological phenomena. Remarkably, however, they have received scant assessment as works of history.

In one sense, this silence is hardly surprising: Margaret Mitchell wrote a novel, not a monograph. Yet such an explanation assumes an ahistorical notion of what history has been and continues to be. The first historians, after all, were poets, and history, as we currently know it, is the product of specific developments in the late nineteenth century, including the rise of specialization, the growing prestige of the scientific model of objectivity, and the organizational revolution that allowed some people to make careers out of the discipline at colleges and universities.[3] At the same time, however, many people in the United States continued to learn about the past from other sources. A *Tale of Two Cities* informed countless understandings of the causes and effects of the French Revolution, *War and Peace* the follies of Napoleon's invasion of Russia, and *Gone with the Wind* the costs of the Civil War (all these novels received new audiences in film versions). However familiar we may be with the work of academic historians, our images and interpretations of the historical events portrayed in these or other works continue to exert an important, even decisive influence.

This study is an attempt to understand the intellectual and cultural currents that shape particular images and interpretations. I am less interested in formulating tightly reasoned arguments or documenting previously unknown aspects of human experience—two traditional and still valuable methods of practicing academic history—than I am in making revealing juxtapositions and suggestive observations that can enrich our sense of past and present. At the same time, however, I do have some overarching objectives, which I will try to lay out as concisely as I can at the outset.

The subtitle of my study, *A Reusable Past*, is an allusion to "On Creating a Usable Past," a famous 1918 essay by literary critic Van Wyck Brooks. Lamenting the crass, individualistic, commercial culture of the masses ("lowbrow") and the cramped, unadventurous culture of academic scholarship ("highbrow"), Brooks here and elsewhere sought the recovery of indigenous national traditions that would bridge and improve both. He remains a notable example of the free-lance intellectual who roamed the intellectual landscape before the expansion of the nation's university system after the Second World War.[4]

Brooks's insights notwithstanding, this book is based on the premises that U.S. culture was more dynamic, even synergetic, than he recognized and that far from lying dormant, the Civil War past was being used even as he wrote and has been reused for the rest of the century. With that in mind, my most basic and perhaps most important goal is to provide relatively vivid and detailed examples of the ways history has been rewritten (or refilmed, rerecorded, etc.) to reflect the concerns of different constituencies in U.S. society.

The case studies that form the core of the book—Carl Sandburg's Lincoln biography, the fictional and cinematic versions of *Gone with the Wind*, a selection of rock songs about the Civil War, the 1989 film *Glory*, and the worlds of Civil War reenactors—are unabashedly idiosyncratic. I chose these subjects because I consider them unusually apt and important embodiments of the questions, tensions, and ideological solutions of their time. They represent invitations to seek out—or create—other uses for the Civil War and perhaps other areas of U.S. history as well.

To summarize the chapters that follow: The key issue informing Sandburg's work was the dramatic expansion of the federal government into many new areas in everyday life, the uncertainties surrounding Franklin Roosevelt's New Deal, and the role of political leadership in preparing for the Second World War. The crisis of capitalism ushered in by the Great Depression led to a widespread desire for new measures, which Roosevelt supplied. Carl Sandburg was one of a number of people who soothed the resulting unease over the New Deal by turning to history and pointing out another occasion of unease: Abraham Lincoln's vast expansion of federal power during the Civil War. Sandburg demonstrated how it had been used for morally compelling purposes, just as, he believed, Roosevelt would do as well.

The key issue looming over the novel *Gone with the Wind* (1936) was the women's movement. It emerged in a recognizably modern form at the turn of the century, when the New Woman on college campuses and in large cities provoked constant comment from admirers and detractors alike. Born in 1900, Margaret Mitchell grew up with the model of the New Woman in the segregated South and struggled with it her whole adult life. Her ambivalence is vividly captured in *Gone with the Wind,* and one measure of the persistence of ambivalence about women's roles in the twentieth century is the continuing power Scarlett O'Hara exerts on men and women alike all over the world. For all its seemingly universal appeal, however, *Gone with the Wind* is also the distillation of a very specific white Southern experience and memory of the Civil War. One can sense this by comparing Mitchell's book with the 1939 movie vis-à-vis race and class as well as gender. In so doing, I hope to show how both were products of their time and perhaps to illuminate some characteristics of our own.

The backdrop for my discussion of Confederate iconography in rock 'n' roll is the impact of the Civil Rights movement and the effects this struggle for equality has had on the psyches of some whites. Rock 'n' roll music provides a unique window on the subject because it began as a genuinely interracial music in the South at a time when the region was finally confronting Civil War issues that had been ignored or resisted for a century. Rock musicians did not develop a sense of thematic self-consciousness until the 1960s and 1970s and have dealt only fleetingly with the war as a subject ever since; nevertheless, some of those occasions have been extraordinarily revealing of the dilemmas, resentments, and ironies that surround Southern—as well as Northern—attempts to reckon with the past.

To greater or lesser degrees, race looms over the whole book and is crucial to my analysis of *Glory*. Central to this chapter, however, is the legacy of

Vietnam and the burden it has imposed on anyone who wishes to overcome the corrosive cynicism that it engendered. The makers of *Glory* attempted to do this by depicting the Civil War as a just struggle in the name of freedom, secured in part by African Americans who have so often been described as passive (or marginal) figures in the great national struggle. As such, the movie suggests a yearning for "the good fight" even on the part of those who have viewed recent wars with skepticism.

The last chapter examines the culture of Civil War reenactors. Although never referred to directly by its participants, pluralism, I believe, is the key issue looming over those who participate in this hobby. In a multicultural society where minorities are showing a new awareness of their own pasts and the elements that distinguish their histories from that of the European American majority, the Civil War serves as a vital center for that majority to affirm the centrality of its own past. In some ways, this is a perfectly legitimate enterprise (and one that has a long history); in others, it raises troubling questions and evokes dark precedents. In either case, reenacting illustrates the continuing power of the Civil War as a vehicle for embodying sentiments and politics in our day.

Reenactors provide an especially vivid example of a motif that runs through this study: the concept of history as a form of communion. In this context, the term *communion* does not really carry religious connotations (although it can; see Carl Sandburg's description of Abraham Lincoln as an American Christ in Chapter 2). Rather, it suggests the shared feelings certain characters or events evoke for producers—and, one tentatively surmises, the audiences—of popular culture. Professional scholars tend to avoid partaking of this aspect of history themselves, rooted as they are in the culture of social science. A reevaluation of this stance lies at the heart of this project. I realize that professional scholars have some very good reasons for having avoided history as communion. In many cases, this sensibility lapses into a sentimental view of the past that conceals more than it reveals, or a truculent one that excludes more than it includes. I try to show in every chapter of the book how this happens. At the same time, however, history as communion has unique strengths that have been too often overlooked or denigrated by academic historians—even when they unconsciously embrace it. A frank acceptance of these dimensions of history can be used to contest or revise some of the more dangerous or repugnant configurations of the past.

In historiographic terms, my work falls within the purview of the emerging subdiscipline of history of memory. I consider myself a member of this "school," a term I use rather loosely, and participate in it with some excitement. Some of the established historians who have inspired and provoked me have had relatively little to say about the Civil War but have influenced the way I approach it.[5] Others share my sensibility and do explore the legacy of the Civil War but tend not to focus on popular culture or the twentieth century.[6] Still others continue to use the methods of social history in studying the Civil War but infuse them with the kinds of analysis used by cultural historians generally and students of memory specifically.[7]

Popular culture has a special role to play in the study of memory. In his introduction to a 1989 issue of the *Journal of American History* devoted to the study of memory, editor David Thelen notes that "by connecting history with its origins in the narrative form of everyday communication, attention to memory transcends specialization by speaking the language of face-to-face association and firsthand experience."[8] Attempting to reach large numbers of people, if only to make money (which they do with only fitful success), the creators of popular cultural documents rely on vernacular words and ideas, even when they communicate in the most impersonal settings.

I see my work as an attempt to affirm what I regard as the most attractive aspect of much recent historical scholarship: its focus on the minds and lives of those who have been traditionally overlooked and on the issues and artifacts that matter to them most. But I wish to do so in as simple a way as I know how. In doing this, I realize that I risk oversimplifying matters, for in the context of cultural studies in the last two decades, concepts such as "shared feelings" have been the subject of intense scrutiny and skepticism. Theoretically minded scholars have focused considerable attention on the complex negotiations between producers and audiences of popular culture and have argued that particular works of art, by drawing on common stories (myths) or points of view (ideologies), deny alternatives by making what is depicted seem realistic or natural. In contrast to mythological popular culture, which seeks to conceal its ideology (often an affirmation of the status quo), this scholarship seeks to unmask such power relations in an effort to liberate readers from epistemological domination.[9]

The degree of my acceptance of this critique should be clear in what follows, where I repeatedly plumb silences, note ambiguities, and explore contradictions. At the same time, however, I see clear limits in the utility of such an approach—not only because some cultural studies at least implicitly posit a false dichotomy between myth and theory, as if the act of theorizing itself is not a matter of trying to naturalize worldviews, but also because I believe our indigenous stock of myths (myths that include, for example, a series of variations on the life of Abraham Lincoln) remain vital and can, despite their omissions, ironies, or frankly repressive tendencies, at least potentially express what Lincoln called "the better angels of our nature." So in an effort to be as honest as I can about where I stand, I hereby pledge my allegiance to representative—and representational—democracy.

A similar pragmatism governs my stance toward the question of audience. This has become perhaps the single most vexing problem in contemporary cultural studies, because no one can be altogether sure of how any given person or group understands a particular document. In an effort to circumvent this problem, some scholars have devised imaginative means for gauging audience response. [10] Although such work is useful, and has a place in cultural study, it can never really succeed on the empirical terms it seeks to emulate. Findings take on significance only when they are interpreted; when larger meanings are at least implied; when we move beyond the realm of quantified certainty into one of imaginative speculation.

Placing faith in an older American studies tradition, this book relies on textual analysis and imaginative speculation. [11] However, I am trying to do more than make educated guesses about perceptions of particular well-known works (a term roughly measured by sales figures, references in the culture at large, etc.). I am also trying to argue how they *should* be seen, what *you* stand to gain by reading—and then accepting, adapting, or rejecting—my interpretations in the chapters that follow.

Ultimately, my goal is to evaluate elements of twentieth-century popular culture of the Civil War not as a series of specimens to be dissected in the academic laboratory but as works that deserve to be examined on their own terms as well on more critical ones. Although I cannot expect my work to reach many of those whose aspirations and fears seem crystallized in the works I study, I labor in the faith that it is possible to bring together the expert and the citizen in a mutually satisfactory way. It seems to me that whether in history, public policy, or any other form of writing, this faith is part of a venerable national tradition, and democracy itself depends on it.

Chapter 1

The Past Keeps Changing

The Civil War in Popular Culture and Academic History, 1830–1930

Any understanding of this nation has to be based, and I mean really based, on an understanding of the Civil War. I believe that firmly. It defined us. The Revolution did what it did. Our involvement in European wars, beginning with the First World War, did what it did. But the Civil War defined us as what we are, and it opened us to what we became, good and bad things. And it is very necessary, if you're going to understand the American character in the twentieth century, to learn about this enormous catastrophe of the nineteenth century. It was the crossroads of our being, and it was a hell of a crossroads.

Shelby Foote, in *The Civil War*,
a film by Ken Burns[1]

During one week in the fall of 1990, an estimated fourteen million television viewers tuned in to watch Ken Burns's eleven-hour film *The Civil War* on public television—more than the entire population of the seceded Confederate states. Countless more taped the series for later viewing, saw its rebroadcast by individual stations during the 1990–91 season, or watched it in classrooms (seven thousand schools and libraries inquired about ordering the series and teaching materials).[2] The companion volume spent six months on the *New York Times* best-seller list, Time-Life sold videocassettes of the series, and record stores featured its sound track. In living rooms, corporate offices, and local newspapers, the series—and its subject—became a matter of widespread discussion. "I've had more Civil War conversations in the last three days in elevators and waiting in line than I've had in the last ten years," a self-described war buff told *Time* magazine in the week following the broadcast of the series.[3] *Time*'s rival *Newsweek* put the war on its cover.

The Civil War is a documentary shot on film, not video, and its broadcast on relatively highbrow but low-funded public television, not one of the major networks, made it an unlikely hit program. Yet at a more fundamental level it was a quintessential television experience. In projecting images instantly across space and time to an entire nation, if not the world, television reigns as the supreme form of contemporary popular culture; indeed, simultaneity itself becomes an experience along with whatever is shown on the screen. The advent of cable, video, and new networks has fractured this power somewhat, though broadcasts of the Persian Gulf War on television suggest its continuing power. Coincidentally, *The Civil War* was shown during the early stages of the Persian Gulf War, which in itself can partly explain the appeal of the series: As the nation's most costly war in terms of national mobilization and human life, the Civil War has become a point of reference for all those that followed.

It has not been the focus of television programming, however. For the most part the Civil War has been marginalized, most notably in the Western, which used it as a point of departure in series such as *The Rebel* (1959–62), *Branded* (1966–69), and many others (and, for that matter, in movies). One possible explanation for this underrepresentation is the unwillingness on the part of the networks to offend their broad national audience by dealing with sectional issues during the Civil Rights years; another is the difficulty of handling the narrative complexities of the war in television's tightly segmented commercial format. In any case, with the rise of the miniseries (beginning with *Roots* in 1977), the medium has shown more flexibility, and in recent years the war has been featured in a number of miniseries, including

Love's Savage Fury (1980), *North and South* (1986), and *Gore Vidal's Lincoln* (1987). In this context, *The Civil War* can be seen not only as a kind of miniseries—in the wake of its success, *Roots* producer David Wolper asserted that the costly and increasingly infrequent format "is not dead"[4]—but also as the most sophisticated attempt to date to come to grips with the conflict.

The *Civil War* can also be seen as the culmination of roughly a quarter-century of scholarly thinking on the subject. Indeed, some of the most respected historians in the field contributed to the project, a sign of an increased willingness on the part of professionals to participate in the making of public culture. The emphasis on individual soldiers, the attention given to everyday life in the North and the South, the effort (however compartmentalized) to include the contributions of women: All these accents reflect new or increased interest on the part of historians who came of age during or after the 1960s.

Above all, the film emphasizes the slavery issue and the racial dimension of the war. "If there's one political theme in this film, it's this: *The Civil War* is a chronicle of making permanent that which was promised, but not delivered, in the Declaration of Independence and the Constitution," director/producer Burns is quoted as saying in the press kit for the series. "Our Constitution starts off 'We the People,' yet it ultimately made four million [African Americans] only 3/5ths of a person, without voting rights, held in chattel slavery. The Civil War corrected that, or at least began to correct that." Elsewhere in the press release, he emphasizes his determination to report "the true and heroic story of American blacks—not as mere passive bystanders to the struggle, but [as] active, dedicated, self-sacrificing soldiers in the personal drama of self liberation."

This said, there are also elements in *The Civil War* that strike more traditional notes. The heart of the series remains military history, "the narrative-driving engine of this machine," according to Burns.[5] As such, the viewer sees the conventional diagrams of Gettysburg and Antietam, profiles of Abraham Lincoln and Jefferson Davis, and political and economic tallying.

An 1897 poster for Harriet Beecher Stowe's Uncle Tom's Cabin *by the Erie Lithography Company. By the turn of the century, Stowe's novel—which proliferated in a series of minstrel, dramatic, and even cinematic versions—had become a virtual symbol of the Civil War itself, taking on associations far beyond what was portrayed or discussed in the original novel. (Photo courtesy of the National Portrait Gallery, Smithsonian Institution, Washington, D.C.)*

This focus on battles and leaders includes the usual portraits of the slovenly Grant and gallant Lee, whose ability to escape lasting criticism in the last 125 years has begun to seem more impressive than any of his military achievements. The film also cultivates the customary sympathy for the Confederate people, if not their cause. The pathos of scenes such as that of Union and Confederate veterans charging to embrace each other at the fiftieth anniversary of Gettysburg competes with, if it does not overwhelm, the viewer's sense of fiercely contested political issues whose legacy affects us still.

Although Burns's narrative strategy won him wide acclaim, he was not without his critics on either end of the political spectrum. A front-page story in the *Charlotte Observer* reported that some North Carolinians felt the series was "all blue and no gray," whereas political scientist Jeffrey Abramson of Brandeis University believed it had a "Southern spin." Historian Jacqueline Jones lamented both the dearth of black women in the series and its military emphasis, and Charles Lunsford, spokesman for the Sons of the Confederate Veterans, argued that secession was the primary cause of the war and that the war had a variety of origins independent of racial issues. "This overemphasis on the slavery issue really rankles us," he said. For Daughter of the Confederacy Sarah Dunaway of Atlanta, the series demonstrated the need for more Southern historians.[6]

It would be easy to conclude from these remarks that *The Civil War* strikes a classic middle-of-the-road stance in its politics. However, such a view overlooks not only the way the middle of the road keeps shifting, but also the very distinctive flavor of the series and its place as a late twentieth-century interpretation of the war. At a time of increasing awareness of the diversity of U.S. culture, *The Civil War* represents an attempt at pluralism on the part of its white producer/director, an effort to provide a coherent vision of the past that integrates a variety of elements in the culture into a single master narrative. Burns undertook this enterprise at a time when many professional historians had abandoned it.

This pluralism, and the implicit tension it involves, is embodied in commentators Shelby Foote and Barbara Fields, the white man and the black woman. Mississippi-born Foote, as *Newsweek* noted, "humanizes the Southerners; he emphasizes their underdog status, pays tribute to their great leaders and in general distracts from what black historians consider the single salient fact about the South: that it was fighting to preserve slavery." Fields, by contrast, used her screen time to stress emancipation as the only redeeming factor in an otherwise senseless and brutal struggle. Burns admitted that he "had a problem convincing Barbara about our motives," saying he thought she suspected "we might give it an old-folks-down-home treatment." Although this description is exaggerated, Foote did get the last word more often than not, and *Newsweek* reported rumors that Fields was unhappy about the final product. At the very least, her refusal to confirm or deny the rumors is not exactly a ringing endorsement of the series.[7]

However one views the series, Ken Burns was not simply *describing* the Civil War; he was also *using* it to make statements about the present. These statements range from the active role African Americans played in their history to the pivotal place the Civil War should occupy in the history of the United States. (I will return to the latter point at the end of Chapter 6.) Hence the decisive image at the end of the series is the unifying embrace of Federal and Confederate soldiers at the Gettysburg reunion—footage of reunions dominates the conclusion of the last episode—and not, for example, the founding of the bitterly divisive Ku Klux Klan. One image suggests the healing of scars; the other those to come. When Burns received praise or criticism for his work, it was those perceived uses of the war, and their contemporary implications, that were really provoking comment. They were important because they were offered so appealingly on a mass basis from coast to coast.

This is the power of popular culture: to offer large numbers of people explanations of why things are the way things are—and what, if anything, can be done about it. Infuse this power with history—explanations of how things came to be the way they are—and you have a potent agent for influencing the thinking, and thus the actions, of millions of people. That is why popular culture with historical subjects demands careful attention from scholar and nonscholar alike. That is also why the Civil War is so important: As "the crossroads of our being," it has become a key battleground in struggles to envision the possibilities and limits of U.S. society.

Viewed in this light, Ken Burns's series is the latest chapter in an ongoing story. Popular culture has played a critical role in preparing for, fighting, and remembering the Civil War; the two were entwined long before the war and long after it. The technological, economic, and social developments that made possible so many forms of popular culture—from religious tracts and dime novels to recorded music and film—were also the source of an often sharp debate over the nature, and future, of the nation.

In this book I will examine some of the ways that debate was conducted during the twentieth century. Before doing so, however, it would be useful to trace the roots of these debates and a few of the forms that participants used to mobilize opinion. What follows is far from a comprehensive survey of Civil

War culture, but it will suggest many of the structural, rhetorical, and political strategies that surfaced repeatedly in the decades that preceded and followed the war.

The following story has never been independently verified but resonates with
the ring of truth nonetheless. "I mean to have a talk with 'Father Abraham,'"
a skeptical Harriet Beecher Stowe wrote publisher James T. Fields in November of 1862. The author of Uncle Tom's Cabin, who said she was making the
trip to "satisfy myself that I may refer to the Emancipation Proclamation as a
reality and a substance not to fizzle out like the little end of a horn," went to
Washington with her son and daughter and was greeted by the president, who
strode toward her with outstretched hands and said, "So this is the little lady
who made this great war."[8]

Lincoln was indulging in some hyperbole, of course; no one single-
handedly "made" the Civil War. But if Stowe's role remains impossible to
quantify, verify, or otherwise fix, most observers then and since would agree
that her novel had an enormous impact in crystallizing the perceptions that
made the war possible. In writing a novel (the supreme form of popular
culture in the nineteenth century), Stowe played a role comparable to the
oratory of John Calhoun or the actions of John Brown.

Even before the first shot was fired, issues intrinsic to the Civil War were
being mediated by popular culture, especially in the varied forms of publishing that technological and demographic changes had made possible in the
first half of the nineteenth century.[9] Stowe's immediate motive for writing
Uncle Tom's Cabin was the fugitive slave provision in the Compromise of
1850. The story was serialized in 1851 and published in book form in 1852.
By the standards of what followed, Uncle Tom's Cabin was a moderate document, almost as harsh on the North as on the South and notable in that the
evil Simon Legree was a Northerner while the slave-owning Augustus St.
Clare was meant to be seen at least somewhat sympathetically. The power of
Stowe's moral indictment was unmistakable, however, as was the trend in her
politics. A storm of criticism, denial, and censorship of her graphic portrayal
of slavery followed, and the argument of Uncle Tom's Cabin was rebutted in
an ensuing flurry of "anti-Tom" novels such as Aunt Phyllis's Cabin; or Southern Life as It Is (1852) and The Planter's Northern Bride (1854). Stowe herself
amplified her polemic with The Key to Uncle Tom's Cabin (1853), which
attempted to prove that the scenes she depicted were, if anything, too mild.
"Tom" literature, pro and con, became a kind of subgenre of its own in the
years preceding the Civil War, though no work came as close as Stowe's book

in articulating a political critique that drew on—and reconfigured—the conventions of what is now known as domestic fiction.[10]

One can also trace growing sectional tension between North and South in
the development of the slave narrative, a cultural form that influenced domestic fiction and was important in its own right. The slave narrative dates
back to 1701, when Judge Samuel Sewall of Boston published *The Selling of
Joseph*, launching the literature of abolitionism in this country. Starting in
the 1830s, a perceptible quickening of tone and visibility of the slave narrative became discernible as the abolitionist movement received new momentum and the stigma of slavery began to shift from enslaved to enslaver.
Focusing less on success stories of exceptional African Americans than on
moral indictments of those who upheld the peculiar institution, slave narratives sought to persuade the politically indifferent of the need for emancipation. Stowe drew on the conventions of the form in her work, and a number
of scholars have noted its impact on other antislavery novels.[11]

The cultural project of the abolitionists did not go unanswered, as white
Southern writers mobilized popular culture to affirm the Southern way of life
in general and the proslavery point of view in particular. Southern fiction,
usually given a plantation setting that drew heavily on the Romantic style of
the popular Sir Walter Scott, grew increasingly defensive in the decades
following the publication of George Tucker's *Valley of the Shenandoah* in 1824.
John Pendleton Kennedy's *Swallow Barn* (1832) was notable for its portrayal
of the "happy darky," an archetypal figure that persisted straight through to
Gone with the Wind. As the debate over slavery intensified, the figure of the
plantation slave moved from a marginal figure on the plantation to an increasingly important, if uncomfortable, subject of examination in Southern
fiction. To meet the challenge posed by the abolitionists, Southern writers
found themselves vacillating between one extreme that slaves were animals
that required no special sympathy and another that slaves were childlike
humans who benefited from the beneficent care of their owners, depending
on which strategy seemed more rhetorically effective at any given time.[12]

Southerners were not without their Northern allies, especially in the cities.
As cultural and political historians have long noted, a Democratic party
alliance between Southern planters and the white Northern working class in
the 1830s, 1840s, and 1850s checked the rising power of industrialists and
abolitionists who increasingly turned to the Whig, Free Soil, and (eventually) Republican parties as vehicles for their programs. For all their considerable differences, some agrarian aristocrats and urban workers believed they
shared an interest in white supremacy: the planters to secure their labor

system and the workers to foreclose competition in their own. The most vivid cultural expression of this political coalition could be seen in Jacksonian theater and especially in the rise of blackface minstrelsy, in which actors in blackface enacted sentimental plantation scenes for enthusiastic city audiences. Ironically, the most important figures in the making of minstrel shows had largely Northern backgrounds.[13]

Uncle Tom's Cabin itself was quickly absorbed into this theatrical culture, usually for racist purposes, and remained a fixture of it for the next half-century.[14] Nevertheless, whether playing on white fears of massive black migration into nonslaveholding areas, persuading Northerners that the slave system impeded economic development, or simply arguing for abolitionism on moral grounds, the Republican party was able to win enough support to take on the Southern system directly.[15] By the time Abraham Lincoln was elected to the presidency in 1860, popular culture could no longer mediate or contain sectional differences, which, at least temporarily, eclipsed all others.

When the war came, so did even more insistent declarations of war aims in fiction, poetry, and other forms of popular culture. Depending on who was speaking—or what was being sought—the Civil War was presented as a means of realizing religious aspirations, as a necessary astringent for Anglo-Saxon stock, or as a quest for freedom.[16] At the same time, the war also offered pretexts for other agendas. For some women writers, for example, the home became a battlefield as Northern armies swept south, while in others the battlefield became home as women worked as nurses, spies, and even combatants in fact and fiction. Their stories, which carried latent messages about the role of women in the North and South, flooded newspapers, magazines, and publishing houses during and immediately following the war.[17]

Officially, the Civil War ended in 1865, but culturally, it was just beginning. At stake was the war's meaning and how that meaning would be applied to new social conditions in the years following the war. Perhaps the most striking uses of the war in the decades that followed were made by Southern writers, seeking to secure ideologically what could not be achieved militarily. Many Southern writers who came of age after 1865 drew on the conventions of the antebellum plantation novel and their residual affection for Scott's romances, which Mark Twain dubbed "Sir Walter's Disease."[18] Thomas Nelson Page and Joel Chandler Harris, whose short stories and novels won them national audiences at the end of the nineteenth century, extended the tradition of the faithful slave in novels such as Page's *Meh Lady* (1893) and Harris's Uncle Remus stories, whose popularity later provided fodder for

Disney movies. These writers portrayed the Old South as a lost eden, a convention that reached its zenith in *Gone with the Wind*.

Other Southern voices sought to emphasize the future over the past. The journalists, politicians, merchants, and other prophets of the so-called New South who came into vogue in the 1870s and 1880s tended to see the Civil War as a tragic mistake, brought on by an understandable but mistaken belief in the necessity of secession by the South and a less understandable abolition-ist zeal in the North. Still, the argument ran, the South was better off without its peculiar institution, and it was time to let bygones be bygones—and to bring Northern capital into the region. This bid for reconciliation, which became increasingly successful as the nineteenth century drew to a close (and was widely noted at the outbreak of the Spanish-American War in 1898), was accomplished at the expense of African Americans, who suffered from increasing neglect in the North and more overt hostility in the South.

The cultural logic infusing the strategy employed by constituents of the New South is perhaps best revealed in the writing of Thomas Dixon, whose *Leopard's Spots* (1903) and *The Clansman* (1905) were great popular successes (a million copies of the former were printed, and over a million of the latter were sold).[19] Dixon's heroes were always Southern, and though he re-spectfully dissented from Yankee mores, his heroines were usually Northern—often culminating in a symbolic marriage between regions. The antagonists of his fiction were African Americans, depicted with a hostility barely balanced by his customary depiction of the faithful former slave who would just as soon remain in bondage. Even without his later career in film and theater, Dixon's celebration of the early Ku Klux Klan in *The Clansman* influenced the next generation of Southerners, most notably Margaret Mit-chell, whose depiction of the Klan in *Gone with the Wind* owed a great deal to Dixon.[20]

Outside the South, the major preoccupation in U.S. society was the accel-erating pace of industrialization and the corollary forces of immigration and urbanization. The causal relationship between the Civil War and these devel-opments can never be altogether fixed, though observers then and since have been struck by their seemingly inextricable character. Nowhere is their inter-face captured more vividly than in Stephen Crane's description of Henry Fleming at the Battle of Chancellorsville in *The Red Badge of Courage*: "He instantly saw that it would be impossible for him to escape from the regiment. It inclosed him. And there were iron laws of tradition and law on four sides. He was in a moving box."[21] Presumably, we are reading an ordinary soldier's account of one day in May of 1863; however, Crane also gives us a striking picture of industrial life in the late nineteenth century. The "regiment" here describes not only a military unit in the Union army, but also the life of millions of workers in Northern factories. And the moving box is an apt metaphor for the sense of seemingly inexorable social forces that fascinated and alarmed so many observers in the closing decades of the century. Crane, who was born after the Civil War ended, used the conflict to foreshadow— and symbolize—the new social order of his time.

For confident capitalists presiding over vast wealth and reaping the benefits of innovation, that time was an age of progress. For those displaced or struggling amid the sharpening polarities of class, the direction that U.S. society was taking revealed the impoverishment, if not the hypocrisy, of a Republican ideology predicated on equal opportunity and self-help. Either way, the pieties of organized religion or cosmic metaphors of Romantic intellectuals seemed increasingly inadequate to explain the world of the late nineteenth century. To imagine a better future, people needed new ways of thinking about the present—and the past.

The Civil War was becoming history at a time when history (the academic variety) was undergoing a transformation together with the development of the modern university and the growing prestige of science in a Darwinian age. Many practitioners of the new discipline hoped it would allow them to transcend the partisan passions and mutable perceptions so prevalent in popular culture or in history written by those who lacked the requisite training. It did not.

In the seventeenth century, the history of Anglo-Saxon settlement in the British colonies was a vehicle for imparting moral lessons. Written by clergy or laity, in the haste prompted by a need to secure basic survival, such works represented an effort to justify or reveal the colonial claim to the wilderness. Although the influence of the clergy on historical writing gradually diminished over time, religious institutions decisively influenced higher education until the Civil War.

Throughout the eighteenth and nineteenth centuries, however, the study of the past was increasingly assumed by patricians who considered history a branch of literature. These were men of leisure who saw themselves above the fray of religious fractiousness or the sordid distractions of commerce. Though they did not espouse objectivity in the way later professional historians did, these writers saw themselves as measuring the scales of posterity for a similarly leisured, cosmopolitan audience.[22]

By the mid-nineteenth century, there were exceptions to this rule, such as George Bancroft, who wrote with frank Jacksonian political loyalties from which true gentlemen were presumably detached. Like many of his New England contemporaries, Bancroft was deeply influenced by study at emerging German universities such as Göttingen, Heidelberg, and Leipzig. For Bancroft, as well as less Democratic[23] historians such as Francis Parkman, the purpose of historical writing "was to establish a meaningful relationship with the past, not to analyze it but to recreate it."[24] However, although historians such as Bancroft, Parkman, and John Lothrop Motley lived through the Civil War and were strong supporters of the Union effort, they did not write about it as scholars.

In the commercial press, by contrast, the war became history almost instantly, and authors were often anything but gentlemanly in fighting wars of words. A torrent of works were published beginning in 1861 representing a variety of views. While such writing could be considered a form of journalism, these works also explored the roots of the crisis through analyses of the Constitution and the long foreground to armed conflict. Orville J. Victor, who had worked with Erastus F. Beadle in establishing the latter's dime novel company, issued his history of the "Rebellion" monthly, periodically collecting these installments in volume form. The South lacked the North's publishing infrastructure, but in the early days of the war, histories were published there too—notably, by Edward A. Pollard, a Richmond journalist who was a strong supporter of the Confederate effort but a sharp critic of Jefferson Davis.[25]

The volume of popular histories dropped dramatically after Appomattox, perhaps reflecting a sense of cultural exhaustion that reflected the military and social exhaustion of a long and bitter struggle. In the ensuing years, most works on the war were memoirs or autobiographies penned by men and women who had actually participated in it. The first history of the war to be written by a nonparticipating academic was that of John W. Draper, an English-born chemist whose three-volume account was published between 1867 and 1870. His work was followed by that of Hermann Eduard Von Holst, a German historian who came to the United States after the war and included an account of the conflict in his seven-volume history published in the 1870s and 1880s.[26]

Most of these scholarly accounts continued the popular tradition of partisanship. For decades after the Civil War virtually all works—Northern or Southern, Republican or Democratic, prowar or antiwar—took a moralistic stance that identified villains, isolated causes, or both. Unionists tended to

stress the evil of slavery, whereas former Confederates usually took a constitutional view defending their legal right to leave the Union. To counter the
powerful influence of Northern accounts—and more complete Federal records of the war—the Southern Historical Society was organized by prominent
Confederates in 1869.[27]

Yet as the century drew to a close, a new tone in writing on the war became
apparent. This new tone is perhaps best represented in the work of James Ford
Rhodes. Rhodes, who was thirteen years old in 1860, came from an Ohio
family of committed Democrats; in 1893 he described his father as a Copperhead opposed to the war. Rhodes's own political loyalties varied over the
course of his life, but by the time he began writing history after a successful
career as a coal executive, he had developed a coherent view of the war whose
hallmark, in the eyes of his contemporaries, was balance. In seven volumes
that ran from the Compromise of 1850 to the end of Reconstruction in 1877
(published between 1893 and 1906), Rhodes depicted slavery as the fundamental cause of the war and saw it as a moral blight on the nation, but he
considered both sides blameworthy. Distinguishing between the institution of
slavery and generally "hospitable" slaveholders, he argued that the North had
once also been slaveholding and that broad impersonal forces—i.e., the
cotton economy—led the South to cling to the peculiar institution. If the
South made a mistake in fighting the war, Rhodes felt the North was mistaken in continuing to fight it through an awkward and unjust Reconstruction. With both the war and Reconstruction over, however, Rhodes thought
that the nation was on a firmer footing; all things considered, the outcome
had been positive.[28]

The writings of Rhodes immediately became the standard in the field,
garnering wide praise from both North and South. In synthesizing strands in
other writers' work of the time (the importance of slavery, the impracticality
of Reconstruction and its lasting negative impact) and in anticipating themes
that remained common for the next half-century (economic forces, a less
moralistic and more conciliatory outlook), Rhodes can be placed at the
center of what Thomas Pressly described as the Nationalist tradition in Civil
War historical writing.[29] Furthermore, though he was not a professionally
trained historian, Rhodes's broad national outlook and perceived judiciousness were perfectly suited to the emerging academic culture that was beginning to influence historical writing.

This new culture was part of a much larger reorientation in Western thinking that was taking place during the latter half of the nineteenth century. For
the previous 250 years, the primary intellectual force in U.S. colleges had

been Protestantism, especially the evangelical variety. At the close of the century, however, the accelerating prestige of science, bolstered by the tangible fruits of technology, created new pressures for reorganizing knowledge on more secular principles.

Seeking to replicate the techniques of science, a wide array of intellectuals in the United States, again inspired by German models, began to imagine ways of discovering fixed laws of human behavior. Drawing on the work of European thinkers such as Auguste Comte and Leopold von Ranke, scholars began to shape, under the general rubric of the social sciences, a variety of disciplines that rose to prominence in the twentieth century—sociology, economics, political science, psychology. By 1900, each of these fields had amassed enough specialized knowledge to become a discipline in its own right, complete with its own journals, professional organizations, and an often articulate sense of mission. But the federal government, still decentralized and inefficient, remained too weak to absorb this new breed of social scientists, some of whom lacked the social pedigrees of gentleman-scholars but belonged to a new middle class of white-collar workers. They turned to the universities not only for training, but also for employment and cultural authority.[30]

In at least one sense, history remained a special case. Whereas the social sciences (and philosophy, which at this point was also heavily influenced by science) sought universal laws governing behavior, history had always been about contingency: a belief that circumstance, individual choice, and random accident were the engines of change over time. Here too, however, the impact of science was felt in two ways. First, some historians began to believe that contingency itself was the product of imperfect knowledge—that careful empirical study of the past would yield the patterns so eagerly sought by anthropologists, for example. In a different but related way, the rise of realism in Western literature at this time can also be attributed to a desire to ground descriptions of reality in empirical observation. Although this idea never attained complete acceptance, it is a measure of its power that even so committed a skeptic as Henry Adams felt the pull of it. Perhaps a more cynical explanation of this movement within history is that a scientific model of history was more effective in the marketplace of ideas, where disciplinary jockeying for institutional funding was becoming increasingly competitive.[31]

The Johns Hopkins University opened the first graduate school, which came to include a history program, in 1876.[32] Graduate study brought with it a new historical form: the monograph, the key historiographic tool for the next century. Whereas Romantic historians such as Bancroft were apt to write evocative interpretations of the past, the monograph focused on highly specific, exhaustively researched topics that sought to define, explain, or categorize particular phenomena conclusively. The crucial underpinning for this cultural project was what historian Peter Novick calls "the myth of objectivity"—a belief that patient, professional work derived from scientific principles would yield incontestable understanding of the past. Compared to the works of previous historians, monographs were modest in scope, but each constituted an essential brick in the cathedral of truth that history was expected to build.[33] (Ironically, the work of the most interesting historian of the period, Frederick Jackson Turner, whose ideas about the frontier and sectionalism have fascinated and frustrated students for more than a century, has proved notoriously resistant to empirical verification.)

Many of these historians went about their work assuming an air of detachment, of letting the historiographic chips fall where they may and being unafraid to challenge hallowed myths. Yet a number of factors compromised this stance. One was the fact that unlike their predecessors, historians were employees of institutions that had the power to hire and fire them at the behest of wealthy donors or particularly active administrators. Another factor was the thirst for legitimacy and prestige, which led many to avoid conflicts when dealing with each other's work (in this regard, they greatly resembled their colleagues in law and medicine). Furthermore, there was a striking degree of homogeneity among these men, virtually all of whom were white Protestants blithely unaware of the inevitable biases of their position. Thus, although many saw themselves as safe from the distractions of the outside world in their academic laboratories, their shared conclusions sounded suspiciously like those of people who had a vested interest in the "scientific" outcome. At the heart of this interest was a continuing commitment to a longstanding tradition of exceptionalism—the idea that because of the unique circumstances of the nation's founding, the United States would escape the ills (read proletarian revolution) that loomed large over European societies.[34]

Nowhere was this sense of consensus more clear than in the Nationalist tradition of Civil War historiography, particularly as reflected in the writings of William Dodd, John Burgess, and Woodrow Wilson, all of whom built on the work of Rhodes to a greater or lesser degree. What is striking about the work of these early professionals is not the supposed objectivity of their findings but how well they reflected the culture at large, where secession was honorable, Union was necessary, and the Negro was the (Southern) white man's burden. Even Albert Bushnell Hart, a descendant of abolitionists and a mentor of W. E. B. Du Bois, ultimately concluded that "the Negro is inferior, and his past history in Africa and in America leads to the belief that he will remain inferior."[35] However different the tone or techniques applied to their work, their stance toward the Civil War was not fundamentally different from that expressed in Confederate memorial celebrations, minstrel shows, or popular fiction. In short, the *form* was new; the *content* less so. And that form could be adapted or combined with other forms (e.g., fiction and film) in the ongoing effort to define the meaning of the Civil War.

This point is well illustrated by the work of Thomas Dixon, who fused many strands of Civil War culture: the nineteenth and twentieth centuries; academic culture (he did a few months of graduate study in history at Johns Hopkins) and popular taste; and older cultural forms such as fiction and new ones such as film. For years, Dixon had been trying to produce a movie version of *The Clansman*. It had become a sensation as a play in both the North and the South in 1905–06, but Dixon had found no takers from established producers. Then he met D. W. Griffith, who more than any other man brought the Civil War into the twentieth century.

The motion picture industry in the United States began at the turn of the century as a working-class form of culture. In addition to providing an inexpensive form of entertainment that could cross language barriers—proliferating in the countless nickelodeons that sprang up along urban streets and in amusement parks—these brief, silent reels of celluloid also offered important employment and entrepreneurial opportunities to those immigrants, especially Jewish immigrants, who would have faced stiffer resistance in more established industries. The early industry was geared to working-class subjects and interests, arousing disdain and concern among self-appointed guardians of public morality and taste. Yet as the first decade of the twentieth century wore on, Progressive reformers also held out hope that movies could help correct societal deficiencies and promote what they considered proper behavior. Movies with strong patriotic themes were one means of promoting assimilation.[36]

With the ethnic and class appeal of film steadily widening, the Civil War became a viable cinematic subject. Edwin S. Porter, best known for his classic film *The Great Train Robbery* (1903), was one of a number of filmmakers who made a version of *Uncle Tom's Cabin*, which had thrived as a staged drama for a half-century following publication of the novel. Between 1908 and 1917, the war became a staple subject of motion pictures. As in the case of domestic novels, family themes predominated; fratricidal bitterness, intersectional romance, and border-state ambivalence were among the most common subjects in films such as *The Flag of His Country* (1910), *The Copperhead* (1911), and *A Question of Courage* (1912).[37]

Among those making movies with Civil War themes was Griffith, whose *In Old Kentucky* (1909), *His Trust,* and *His Trust Fulfilled* (1910) prefigured themes and techniques that later characterized his most famous work. A Kentuckian who was the son of a Confederate colonel, Griffith began his career in the theater as an actor and writer and began selling scenarios for one-reel films to Porter. Between 1908 and 1913, he worked as a director for the Biograph company, producing over four hundred movies that showed increasing innovation in his use of the close-up, the long shot, crosscutting, fade-ins and fade-outs, and other staples of what eventually became basic cinematic vocabulary. He also introduced many of the first movie stars to the screen, including Mary Pickford, Lillian Gish, and Lionel Barrymore.[38] In 1913, Griffith left Biograph to make pictures on his own for a company he called "The Epoch Producing Corporation"—a name that suggests the scope of his ambitions. Truly, Griffith's medium was his message.

Griffith was eager to make a movie based on Dixon's work, and the two spent several weeks in New York discussing the project before Griffith headed out to the film industry's new mecca, Hollywood, in early 1914. Over the course of the next year, Griffith expanded the scope of Dixon's novel, which dealt primarily with Reconstruction, to include the war itself and incorporated elements of *The Leopard's Spots* as well. The added war scenes gave the film added emotional power, dramatizing battles that could previously only be imagined and reenacting scenes—particularly the assassination of Lincoln—with a kind of documentary clarity that must have astonished 1915 audiences and makes viewers today feel as though they are watching archival records. With an almost messianic belief in the power of film to capture reality, Griffith had harnessed technology to long-standing hopes, fears, and prejudices. A dazzled Dixon suggested that *The Clansman* was too tame a title for such a work, which was subsequently renamed *Birth of a Nation.*[39]

As the first major motion picture to legitimate film as an art, create a vast national audience for the form, perpetrate damaging myths, and aid in the revival of the Ku Klux Klan, *Birth of a Nation* has received much comment, which needs little further elaboration here. But there are two points worth making. The first is to note the profoundly synthetic character of Griffith's enterprise. *Birth of a Nation* took elements of literature, drama, and history, forging them into something new that simultaneously inspired the reactionary conservative Thomas Dixon and the modernist revolutionary Sergei

Eisenstein (who studied Griffith's work before elaborating his own influential theories of film). That the former impulse dominated can be explained by history: The portrayal of blacks in *Birth of a Nation* tapped a racist iconography (e.g., ignorant blacks aping white behavior) that dates back to the origins of Jacksonian theater.

The second point reinforces my argument that the academy is hardly immune from the dangerous ideas that circulate through popular culture. *Birth of a Nation* caused controversy even before it was released, galvanizing the National Association for the Advancement of Colored People into action and provoking both censorship and race riots in a number of U.S. cities. Conspicuously absent from the group of people expressing concern about the derogatory stereotypes, inflammatory rhetoric, and less-than-measured representations of African Americans, however, were professional historians. Indeed, one former academic gave his unqualified approval. In an effort to blunt the growing criticism over the racial issue, Dixon made a visit to his old Johns Hopkins classmate Woodrow Wilson in February of 1915. Significantly, Dixon asked the president, who had presided over the governmental consolidation of Jim Crow throughout the South, to watch the movie "not as chief magistrate of the Republic, but as a former scholar and student of history and sociology." As a favor to his old friend, the author of *Division and Reunion* (1893) reputedly gave his famous description of *Birth of a Nation* as "history written with lightning," adding, "my only regret is that it is all so terribly true." Amid the furor the film caused during its subsequent theatrical release, Wilson was to regret this statement, and his adviser Joseph Tumulty later publicly repudiated it for the president. Wilson had touched a nerve that was proving politically dangerous.[40]

The complacent confidence in "progress" received a crippling blow from the First World War. Instead of bettering the human condition, progress had become, through weapons technology, a vehicle for savage barbarity. (It is worth noting, incidentally, that many of the new tools for modern combat— submarines, repeating rifles, trench warfare—had been introduced during the Civil War.) Moreover, the programmatic certitudes of Progressive reform encountered insuperable obstacles when confronted by irrational hatred as well as thoroughly rational resistance from masses unwilling to be subjected to social control. These lessons engendered a crisis of confidence among many Western intellectuals, especially social scientists. The moral they drew was that they should disavow the misty ambitions of Progressive reform and plunge deeper into empiricism. Science, the argument ran, offers no easy, quick solutions to social problems. It may not even hold any solutions at all. Nevertheless, it has an integrity, an immunity to political or moral corruption, that makes it a worthy enterprise in its own right. In short, science became a kind of existential religion.[41]

Many artists and literary critics drew a similar moral. Modernism, whose origins preceded the First World War, grew rapidly in the years following it by embracing a similar skepticism about progress.[42] In a world of rapid and often disorienting change, the problem of art was how to find meaning amid the lies and deceptions of commerce, politics, and religion. For the most part, this intellectual current circulated outside the university in the interwar years. But its tendency to isolate aesthetic values from moral or political considerations, to try to locate them outside history altogether, and to separate them from "mere" popular culture found an accommodating home in the academy after World War II, when the expansion of the university system offered the arts and humanities the institutional base that the sciences and social sciences had enjoyed since the turn of the century.

Meanwhile, academic history continued expanding its cultural presence. Professionally trained scholars did not eclipse popular historians such as James Truslow Adams in prestige until after the Second World War, though some, such as Charles Beard, enjoyed academic influence and popular success. *The Rise of American Civilization*, a two-volume history of the United States that Beard wrote with his wife, Mary, became a best-seller in 1927. (It was reissued in one volume in 1933.)

The Civil War continued to have a central place in popular and professional history alike, but the Nationalist model that had held sway since the beginning of the century was beginning to break down. The Beards, for example, depicted the war as an "irrepressible conflict" of feudal and capitalist cultures. Whereas the theme of opposing sectional economies was a familiar one in Civil War historiography from the very beginning, their foregrounding of material forces was relatively new. The Beards viewed the plutocratic aftermath of the war with disappointment and disapproval, in marked contrast to confident Nationalist interpretations of the war.[43]

Various white Southerners were also expressing disapproval of the war's outcome for very different reasons. In what might be considered a neo-Confederate effort to resist encroaching industrialization, poets, novelists, and essayists extolled the benefits of the antebellum South, most notably in *I'll Take My Stand* (1930), a cultural manifesto by twelve Southerners. This impulse was also apparent in academic history. A key figure in this movement was William A. Dunning, a Southerner born before the war who was best known for his *Reconstruction: Political and Economic, 1865–1877* (1907). However, it was as a professor at Columbia University, where he directed graduate work on Southern history for two decades, that he had his greatest influence. Many of Dunning's students wrote monographs exploring Reconstruction from a constitutional perspective generally sympathetic to the Southern point of view. Dunning's best-known student was Ulrich B. Phillips, whose writings in the 1920s and 1930s portrayed slavery less as a tragic mistake than as a positive good. Here, too, was a departure from the Nationalist perspective.[44]

Then there were the Revisionists. Many of these writers, horrified by the First World War, saw all war as a senseless crime that could be brought on only by misunderstanding or demagoguery on the part of blundering politicians. This had been the major criticism by antiwar leaders in the border states during the secession crisis of 1860–61 and was receiving its most sympathetic articulation in more than a half-century.[45] Revisionism reached its peak of influence in the late 1930s and early 1940s, particularly in the work of James G. Randall, whose work will be discussed in the chapter that follows.

The onset of the Great Depression, followed by the darkening international clouds of the 1930s, created new pressures for other perspectives on the Civil War. One of the most effective renderings came not from the academy but from popular culture—specifically, in a biography that epitomized the final flowering of popular history before the academy tightened its hold on the discipline.

In 1915 the young literary critic Van Wyck Brooks published *America's Coming-of-Age*, a work of cultural criticism that became an artistic manifesto for his generation of U.S. intellectuals. Decrying the "catchpenny realities" that gave the United States a soulless, materialistic culture, Brooks also considered the aestheticism of Modernists such as T. S. Eliot a "high ideal" detached from the rest of society, resulting in a huge gulf between highbrow and lowbrow. To bridge this gap, which had divided the classes in the United States since the seventeenth century, Brooks called for the creation of a "usable past" that would finally provide the United States with a tradition that would nurture native talent, enabling the nation to "emerge from our existing travesty of a civilization."[46]

The position Brooks was staking out later became known as middlebrow culture. Middlebrow enjoyed a relatively vital life in the interwar years by mediating between older notions of culture as a form of uplift and the new emphasis on consumer values. Generally rejecting the tenets of modernism, novelists such as John Erskine offered readers the promise of combining edification and entertainment. In a similar vein, historians such as H. G. Wells and Will Durant enjoyed successful careers synthesizing and summarizing large bodies of knowledge into outline form. At its best, middlebrow was genuinely democratic, for it made culture more widely accessible. At its worst, it exhibited a petit bourgeois elitism that packaged information into cocktail-party formats.[47]

One of the most successful middlebrow artists of the 1920s was Stephen Vincent Benét. A poet who enjoyed unusual popularity at a time when poetry had already begun a long descent out of popular favor, Benét was best known for *John Brown's Body* (1928), his epic poem of the Civil War. *John Brown's Body* represented perhaps the final flowering of Nationalist school ideology; the work begins with a love song to the nation and then proceeds to a depiction of a slave trader who, in the usual interests of balance, is a New Englander. Benét's Civil War is tragic but ends with an affirmation: From Brown's grave came a united nation and a powerful beacon of hope. Benét's work serves as a powerful reminder that Ernest Hemingway, F. Scott Fitzgerald, and the rest of the Lost Generation aside, alienation and despair did not necessarily dominate the national mood.

Meanwhile, Brooks was establishing himself as one of the premier intellectuals of his generation, though one who had great difficulty synthesizing the tensions he had delineated in his early work. In 1924, the still influential cultural critic was hired by the publishing firm of Harcourt, Brace and Company to evaluate a lengthy manuscript on Abraham Lincoln by the Chicago poet Carl Sandburg. Brooks pronounced Sandburg's material "great stuff" and even supplied the book's title—*Abraham Lincoln: The Prairie Years*.[48] How fitting it is that Brooks recognized what went on to become a touchstone for measuring usable pasts, not only for Carl Sandburg, but also for all those discussed in the chapters that follow.

Chapter 2

"A Tree Is Best Measured When It's Down"

Carl Sandburg,
James Randall,
and the
Usable Pasts of
Abraham Lincoln

Carl Sandburg is the worst thing to
happen to Lincoln since Booth shot him.

Edmund Wilson,
in a letter to John Dos Passos,
April 1953[1]

History has not been kind to Carl Sandburg. Although his monumental six-volume history of Abraham Lincoln won wide acclaim in the 1920s and 1930s, and still received occasional praise as late as the 1980s (one recent historian called his work "magnificent"),[2] it has rarely been cited in the Lincoln literature of the last fifty years. The reasons are apparent to any apprentice entering the field of academic history: Sandburg's sentimentalism, unabashed partisanship, and lack of historiographic scaffolding seem to offer a textbook case in how *not* to write history. This is true even for nonacademics such as Edmund Wilson and Gore Vidal, who, never one to mince words, called Sandburg "a biographer of awesome badness."[3]

As a poet, Sandburg has suffered an even worse fate than hostility: indifference. Practitioners of New Criticism, a literary version of modernism that came to dominate literature departments after the Second World War, rejected the parochialism and formlessness of his poetry, and his Whitman-esque celebrations of the national landscape and people would be anathema to postmodern critics, who would be appalled by what they would find if they ever bothered to deconstruct his work. For such people, Sandburg is a curio, an anachronism from an earlier time who lacks a necessary critical edge.

Sandburg's decline in stature among literary critics had begun even before his death in 1967. Although many praised his "loving, lofty spirit," such remarks were often tempered by assertions such as, "Sandburg was never a great and seldom even a very good poet. . . . His formal and spiritual indebtedness to Whitman, though far from slavish, is too obvious to permit us to think of him as a genuine innovator."[4] Not that he has lacked supporters. Much of his work remains in print; a stream of memoirs, previously unpublished work, and a few critical studies continued to appear throughout the 1980s; and a major biography was published in 1991—these publications suggest at least some interest in his work.[5]

Yet even Sandburg's fans usually recognize that they are in the minority. "Those who chronicle and interpret American letters are bound ultimately to

A 1961 portrait of poet and Lincoln biographer Carl Sandburg by William A. Smith. Upon his death six years later, President Lyndon Johnson was among the first to pay tribute, declaring that Sandburg "was more than the voice of America. He was America." Yet in the following decades, Sandburg's reputation underwent a serious decline—a decline that has obscured his achievement in fashioning a truly usable past. (Photo courtesy of the National Portrait Gallery, Smithsonian Institution, Washington, D.C.)

rediscover the excellence of Carl Sandburg," wrote one critic in the *Sewanee Review* in 1977. "When that happens the fine poet and masterful biographer will at last re-emerge from the dumps."[6]

How far the mighty have fallen! In his own day, Sandburg was considered not only a great writer, but also a great *presence*. Poet, biographer, novelist, folklorist, journalist, lecturer, and correspondent with everyone from Helen Keller to John Kennedy, Sandburg became a national icon as he made countless appearances to strum his guitar while singing a folk song or reciting one of his poems. He was the first private citizen to address both houses of Congress, on the 150th anniversary of Lincoln's birth in 1959, and by the end of his life, the good gray poet was warmly celebrated as an important link between the past and the present. At his death in July 1967, a front-page obituary in the *New York Times* called him "The American Bard." President Lyndon Johnson was among the first to pay tribute, declaring that Sandburg "was more than the voice of America. He was America."[7]

Not every day is a poet so eulogized by a president, particularly in the post-Camelot United States, and Johnson's statement offers more than the obligatory praise. It also raises some intriguing questions. Why was Sandburg such a commanding figure to millions of people who came of age before the Second World War? Why was Lincoln such a commanding figure to Sandburg? What functions did Sandburg's Lincoln serve, and how does his portrait illuminate our understanding of Lincoln today?

The answers to these questions lie in Sandburg's strikingly successful use of the sixteenth president in his two multivolume biographies—*Abraham Lincoln: The Prairie Years* and, especially for the purposes of this discussion, *Abraham Lincoln: The War Years*.[8] Sandburg was not the first person to draw on the Lincoln legend, and the particulars of his portrait were hardly unique. Nor was he the last to etch a Lincoln with strong contemporary elements. However, Sandburg's biographical character was the most fully defined and influential Lincoln to emerge from the era, and his work was a revealing document of its time.

Indeed, one senses just how distinctive Sandburg's Lincoln is by contrasting the character with that drawn by James Randall, a leading professional Civil War historian of the 1930s, 1940s, and 1950s. Randall's four-volume Lincoln biography is also a magisterial work, reflecting a different set of ideological commitments—among them, a belief that ideology itself is something that can and should be avoided through the methodological norms of professional scholarship. No less than Sandburg's, however, Randall's work also represents a particular use of the Civil War, which has become more clear in retrospect.

In tracing the rise and fall of Sandburg's and Randall's Lincolns, I wish to draw attention to the cultural and ideological forces that shape historical narratives. By cultural forces, I mean widespread perceptions that cut across an ideological spectrum (e.g., a sense of scarcity in the 1930s, or one of plenty in the 1950s, by which individuals or groups measured themselves). By ideological forces, I mean the responses that individuals or groups advocate to deal with those perceptions. There are limits to how far cultural and ideological forces can be stretched; by definition, a few irreducible facts are essential to the making of any history. (One could, through some rhetorical sleight of hand, argue that the South in effect won the Civil War, but one could not credibly deny that General Robert E. Lee surrendered to General Ulysses S. Grant at Appomattox Court House on April 9, 1865.) In drawing attention to the role of culture and ideology, I hope to encourage greater self-consciousness on the part of those who read history and more honesty—and artistry—on the part of those who write it.

Prairie Years, War Years

> It's a book about a man whose mother could not sign her
> name, written by a man whose father could not sign his.
> Perhaps that could only happen in America.
>
> Sandburg on *The Prairie Years*[9]

Carl August Sandburg was born on January 6, 1878, the second of seven children.[10] His parents had emigrated separately from Sweden seven years before and had married and settled in the small town of Galesburg, Illinois, known as a Swedish stronghold and the site of a Lincoln-Douglas debate in 1858. In his preface to *The Prairie Years*, Sandburg later wrote of listening to stories from those who had known Lincoln.

Sandburg's father was an illiterate blacksmith for the Chicago, Burlington, and Quincy Railroad. His mother was a maid without a formal education. Nevertheless, young Sandburg developed a passion for language at an early age, devouring newspapers, biographies of Revolutionary War heroes, and books on geography (fiction and poetry did not interest him much at first).

He attended public schools but received much of his education at the public library and in the streets and houses of Galesburg.

Like the itinerant Lincoln, young Sandburg held a variety of odd jobs, leaving home at age seventeen to wander the countryside. He made a living by painting houses, digging potatoes, washing windows, cooking at local lunch counters, or whatever else came up. Boxcars took him from Illinois to Kansas, out to the Rocky Mountains, and back again.

When the Spanish-American War broke out, Sandburg enlisted in the infantry. After training in Virginia he was shipped to Cuba but was soon moved to Puerto Rico because of a yellow fever epidemic. Sandburg spent eight months there; his letters home became his first published works when they appeared in the *Galesburg Evening Mail.*

After the war, Sandburg's veteran status allowed him to enroll at tiny Lombard College in Galesburg. He entered in 1898 without a high school diploma and left in the second semester of his senior year without a degree. After being rejected by West Point, Sandburg resumed his wanderings, this time in the East. He spent ten days in a Pittsburgh jail for riding the boxcars before settling in Milwaukee in 1907 as an organizer for the Social-Democratic party there and writing articles for a variety of Midwestern newspapers.

Sandburg immersed himself in the political ferment of leftist Milwaukee and was active at party headquarters, where he met his future wife, Lillian Steichen, sister of photographer Edward Steichen (they married in 1908). When the city elected a Socialist mayor in 1910, Sandburg was named his secretary, a post he held for a year before taking a job as an editor for the Social-Democratic newspaper in the city.

Sandburg did not remain a very committed Socialist, however. Although he supported Eugene Debs in 1908 and wrote for the *International Socialist Review,* he generally eschewed arcane debates over doctrine. He considered himself a pragmatist, a stance that later affected his politics and aesthetics. At its best, this point of view resulted in a humane sensibility that decried injustice even as it celebrated simple joys.

When a 1912 newspaper strike in Chicago left the Socialist organ the only paper functioning in the city, Sandburg took a reporting job there. The end of the strike caused the paper to collapse, leaving him without a job. Drifting around the city as a free-lance writer, he began showing editors the poetry he had been writing intermittently over the past ten years. He had published two books privately in 1904 and 1905, but he was beginning to attract editors who were willing to give his voice a wider audience. Sandburg's work began appearing in the well-known *Poetry* magazine edited by Harriet Monroe, and he won the prestigious Levinson Prize for his work in 1914. Two years later, his first major book, *Chicago Poems*, was published. *Chicago Poems* was an exuberant (and, for the times, slightly vulgar) celebration of the United States in the Whitmanesque tradition. Sandburg surveyed the urban landscape with bracing free verse, vernacular language, and an exciting vision of a maverick city emerging as a pillar of growing national might. He also displayed a deft touch and keen wit, as demonstrated in one of his most famous poems, "Fog," which transforms the pall hanging over Chicago into a playful cat. In 1918 *Corn Huskers*, a rural counterpart to *Chicago Poems*, was published, followed by *Smoke and Steel* (1920) and *Slabs of the Sunburnt West* (1922).[11]

Meanwhile, Sandburg wrote for the *Chicago Daily News*. When the First World War began, he supported the Socialists' pacifist platform, but he broke with the antiwar majority in the party when the United States officially entered the struggle in 1917. In 1918 he was sent to cover the Finnish Revolution for the Newspaper Enterprise Association, and he later published a book on the Chicago race riots of 1919, with an introduction written by Walter Lippmann.

Although Sandburg retained sympathy for many Socialist goals and remained publicly loyal to Debs after the imprisonment of the labor leader for his antiwar activities, Sandburg's vision of the war was strikingly close to that of President Wilson, of whom he had previously been skeptical. A letter to his wife at the end of the conflict suggests much about Sandburg's worldview:

> Every day action and action. The world turning over. A new thousand years
> beginning. For some weeks I felt the result in the balance, democracy
> defeated, checked, smothered, put off a long while. Now I can see a
> democratized earth on the way in about the same vague outlines that men a
> hundred years ago could see republican earth on the way—and by
> democracy I mean *industrial*. Always so far just as I am about to have doubts
> of Wilson he comes through. He certainly understands the impossibilists
> among the reds—and the frequent testimony from all sides that he is an
> "enigma" is a certificate of some good stuff in him. Terribly big days. . . .
> Always I have loved watching storms. And this world storm with all its
> shadows and pain and hunger has its points—I'm for it—just as I have no
> criticism of all the waste and afterbirth gore that go with a child born.[12]

A passage such as this suggests how Sandburg could become enchanted by the mythology surrounding the figure of Abraham Lincoln, whose view of the

Civil War as a purifying apocalypse is echoed in the quotation. In fact, Sandburg had for years been collecting anecdotes and information for a biography of Lincoln. The two-volume *Abraham Lincoln: The Prairie Years*, an account of Lincoln's life from birth to his election to the presidency, was published in 1926 to widespread acclaim.

This project, Sandburg's poetry, and his journalism (he spent thirteen years at the *Chicago Daily News* as a reporter and movie reviewer) were making his name familiar across the country. At the same time, the image of the literary Sandburg was augmented by Sandburg the folk figure. The children's books he wrote to entertain his daughters, *Rootabaga Stories* (1922) and *Rootabaga Pigeons* (1923), became favorites in many households, as did *The American Songbag* (1929, revised in 1950), a compilation of almost three hundred folk tunes and ballads. With his warm baritone voice and charismatic presence, he also became a fixture in town halls and college campuses (eventually, his persona reached mass audiences by means of television). He also continued to produce poetry. Sandburg followed *Slabs of the Sunburnt West* with *Good Morning, America* in 1928. The title piece was selected as the Phi Beta Kappa poem at Harvard in that year, suggesting the wide-ranging appeal of a figure who could both amuse children and move members of academic societies.

Like many of his contemporaries, Sandburg was dismayed by the disappointing aftermath of the First World War.[13] However, by the onset of the Great Depression, the drifting journeyman writer had focused his energies outward in an increasingly public life of journalism, poetry, and folklore. In 1928 he moved his family to a farm in Harbert, Michigan, where they remained until relocating to North Carolina in 1945. Sandburg largely escaped the ravages of the Depression; nevertheless, the severe strains caused by economic collapse affected his outlook and shaped his public voice throughout the 1930s.

Nominally, at least, Sandburg was politically independent. Though he supported Franklin Roosevelt through all four terms, he never formally joined the Democratic party. Nevertheless, his closing speech at a 1940 nationwide radio rally was said to have won millions of independent votes for the ticket. Shortly after the election, FDR wrote Sandburg to tell him how much "really and truly that broadcast of yours meant to me."[14]

Sandburg, for his part, held FDR in high esteem, at least as much for his style as for his program. In a letter to Raymond Moley in 1934, Sandburg praised the president for his adroitness "in political method, in decision amid chaos, in reading trends, in development of policy so as to gather momentum, in resilience and acknowledgement of hazards—and much else."[15]

Sandburg's heroic conception of history and politics is fully evident in his next major work of poetry, *The People, Yes* (1936). A long, rambling litany of folk wisdom and free verse, this three-hundred-page poem was considered a definitive statement of U.S. democracy by some, though others were skeptical. "Written with deceptive informality, packed with native phrases and examples of fresh, unstudied, lower-class humor, it succeeds in making 'the people' a hero worth a poet's tribute," said *Time.* Still, the magazine felt compelled to add that "the book narrowly misses a place with the best of U.S. poetry."[16] Many critics felt Sandburg's poetry lost its edge after *Smoke and Steel.*

In any case, the prolific Sandburg immersed himself in other projects. Publication of *The Prairie Years* had not exhausted his fascination with Lincoln, and he devoted the months of April through October throughout the 1930s to researching a sequel.[17] His one-million-word, four-volume history of Lincoln's presidency, *The War Years,* was unveiled in 1939 to almost unanimous praise and earned Sandburg the 1940 Pulitzer Prize for history. In the half-century since its publication the book has sold over a million copies in various editions, an extraordinary figure for a work of history, especially one on such a scale.[18]

The question is why. The answer, it seems, is Sandburg's unique synthesis of many strands of the Lincoln tradition, not only those that preceded his, but also those of the interwar years. It is to those Lincolns I will now turn.

Our Father (A Man of the People)

> Yes, a mountain of a book. And there was never a better
> time for it than this year of our Lord 1939.
>
> Stephen Vincent Benét
on The War Years[19]

Interest in Lincoln's life has been continuous since his nomination for the presidency in 1860, when the young William Dean Howells wrote his campaign biography (and was rewarded with an ambassadorship to Venice). In the decades following Lincoln's death, countless portraits were written. Many of these books are peppered with anecdotes and personal reminiscences, not all of which can be confirmed. At the same time, there arose a legendary Lincoln who inhabited novels such as Edward Eggleston's *Graysons* (1887), Mary Hartwell Catherwood's *Spanish Peggy: A Story of Young Illinois* (1899), and Winston Churchill's million-selling *Crisis* (1901). In stories like these, he is typically the good neighbor in Illinois, or friend in the White House, who makes an appearance at a key moment in the story to aid the main characters. In the overwhelming majority of cases, these Lincolns are positive characters, even to Southern writers such as Thomas Dixon, who gave Lincoln lofty portrayals in *The Clansman* (1905) and *The Southerner: A Romance of the Real Lincoln* (1913), and to Thomas Nelson Page, who rendered the charitable Lincoln of war's end in *The Red Riders* (1924). Certainly, there have been dissenting voices, ranging from Confederate dramas such as *The Royal Ape* and *King Linkum the First* to Edgar Lee Masters's portrait of Lincoln as an undersexed warmonger in his 1924 psychobiography *Lincoln the Man*. But these have been more the exception than the rule.[20]

In the half-century following his death, two major biographies, both written by contemporaries, exercised wide influence over Lincoln's image. The first was that of his Illinois law partner William Herndon (three volumes with Jesse Weik, 1889), who portrayed the president as a folksy Westerner. The other, by presidential secretaries John Nicolay and John Hay (ten volumes, 1890), depicted him as a towering political genius. In addition to drawing on the anecdotal and even legendary dimensions of Lincoln portraiture, Sandburg fused the Herndon and Nicolay/Hay viewpoints into a single coherent image. The key to this fusion can be found in the second volume of *The War Years:* "Around Lincoln gathered the hope that democracy can choose a man, set him up high with power and honor, and the very act does something to the man himself, raises up new gifts, modulations, controls, outlooks, wisdoms inside the man, so that he is something else again."[21]

Here is the central paradox in Sandburg's Lincoln: He is of the world but never quite in it. Time and time again, the poet renders panoramic descriptions of the United States in the early nineteenth century with a crisp sense of particularity and then punctuates them with prophecy or mysticism. Hence he traces Lincoln's genealogy and then proceeds to a line such as "The summer stars that year [1808, when Lincoln's mother was pregnant with him] shook out pain and warning, strange laughters, for Nancy Hanks."[22] Nancy is Mary, and Lincoln is an American Christ; the summer stars of his birth evoke the star heralding an earlier savior.

As the boy becomes a man, Sandburg goes to great lengths to portray his growing power, intellectual and spiritual, as well as his rootedness with ordinary people. Sandburg records that many observers noted "suthin' peculiarsome," in the assumed words of Lincoln's cousin Dennis Hanks, about the youth's development. "In the making of him as he was, the element of silence was immense," Sandburg explains. Yet this silence has a benevolent cast, and Lincoln always retains a common touch. Sandburg praises Lincoln's famous (and to some readers, rather ambiguous) "House Divided" speech because it is "so plain any two farmers fixing fences on a rainy morning could talk it over in all its ins and outs."[23]

There is a sense in which Sandburg sought to make his Lincoln transcend politics altogether. Sandburg portrayed the Lincoln-Douglas debates as less an ideological battle than a matter of personalities, and he tended to favor descriptions of people over analyses of issues. Instead of a discussion of the intricacies of popular sovereignty, the Kansas-Nebraska bill, or the contradictions of Douglas's politics in the 1850s, he seemed content to describe the Little Giant as a "strong, fearless, many-sided man, a Napoleon in politics, a performer of acrobatic and equilibristic marvels, this Stephen Douglas." Rather than exploring the deal Lincoln cut with fellow Whig party members to take turns running for Congress in their district, he chose to focus on Lincoln's facial expression (which "masked a thousand shades of meaning") or the way others describe him as he grows in stature.[24]

Similarly, Lincoln's enemies are dangerous less because of their politics than as a result of their seductive sway over the masses. Southern fire-eater "[William] Yancey of Alabama, tall, slender, with long black hair, spoke in a soft musical voice for the minority," Sandburg writes in *The Prairie Years*. In *The War Years*, which is somewhat sharper in its descriptions, he describes Yancey's "useless froth-mouthed spleen."[25] Sandburg also drew on a personal approach to discredit Unionist critics. General Benjamin Butler "could strut sitting down," and Ohio senator Benjamin Wade "could hit hard, if not always clean." Lincoln's "born sagacity" overcomes Secretary of the Treasury Salmon Chase's "cultivated intelligence."[26] But if Sandburg shared a widely prevalent perception of abolitionists as severe and unyielding, he did seem in broad sympathy with their goals. He ascribes Republican congressional losses in the midterm election of 1862 (which followed Lincoln's issuing the Emancipation Proclamation) not to "excess" but to the party's lack of "vigor" and describes Lincoln's differences with abolitionists in terms of means, not ends. "Now it was well that Lincoln had held to his genuine relationships among the Border State men," he says of the president's push to pass the Thirteenth Amendment. "Had he travelled with the radicals he could not now have made appeals and won results among certain House members."[27]

Yet to emphasize too heavily the degree to which Sandburg personalized the issues risks overlooking the degree of specificity and detail of his work. The first thing one notices upon encountering *The Prairie Years* or, more particularly, *The War Years* (which is a much more intensive and rigorous project) is the sheer bulk of the volumes. The latter is longer than the Bible or the complete works of Shakespeare.[28] By any standard, the Lincoln biography represents a herculean research effort—Sandburg went through a thousand source books over an eleven-year period to write *The War Years*.[29]

Sandburg's biography is a classic example of Depression-era documentary. The term *documentary* here does not mean an avowedly objective work that strives to present the facts as neutrally as possible but instead a cultural form that begins with human records and uses them to create a work that inspires not only thought, but also *feeling*, an essential component of truth. This definition allows us to see Sandburg's work as of a piece with the photographs of Dorothea Lange, the ballets of Martha Graham, and the films of Pare Lorentz.[30]

Both *The Prairie Years* and *The War Years* are too long, if only because Sandburg was able to combine them into an impressive one-volume edition in 1954. However, he had an interesting purpose for this huge compilation of facts: He used them to fashion myth. Take, for instance, this passage in *The Prairie Years* on the industrial explosion of the mid-nineteenth century:

> In the ten years between 1850 and 1860, the country grows; its 23,000,000 people become 31,000,000. The United States has 2,000,000 more people than Great Britain. The United States becomes one of the Powers of the World. And it is only beginning to grow. . . .
>
> In ten years the ships at the ports of the country unload 2,600,000 from overseas. In one year come 400,000. The East grows 21 percent, the South 28 percent, the Northwest 77 percent, in population. Little towns peep up on the prairies where there used to be only gophers and jack rabbits. . . .
>
> A territory of Kansas is organized, but there is civil war in this territory; riders from Missouri, a slave state, ride over into Kansas and battle with abolitionists from New England. . . .
>
> As his eyes sweep the years ahead of the nation, [Emerson] cries, "The hour is coming when the strongest will not be strong enough."
>
> On a late afternoon of an autumn day of the year 1850 Abraham Lincoln, sitting in his rattletrap buggy, might have been lost still deeper in his thoughts if he could have snatched the film of tissue off the Future and read events to operate in the ten years to come.[31]

It seems contrived and even a little silly to imagine Abraham Lincoln lost in thought while Emerson pontificates and Kansas bleeds. Nevertheless, there is real vision here, an expansive reach that seeks to translate broad impersonal processes into human terms.

What may be most objectionable to a professional historian, however, is Sandburg's implicit violation of "the pastness of the past": He made the future seem ordained (in this version of the story, Emerson "knows" a war is coming). Sandburg's point here was not to analyze choices or consider other outcomes but rather to re-create meanings for what *did* happen as dramatically as possible, and in so doing to allow the reader to participate in the past. History becomes a form of communion.

The man/hero and fact/myth dialectics form links in a chain that interlocks with another duality: the regional/national dialectic, expressed politically in the concept of federalism. This tension has been a recurring motif in the search for a national character—and a considerable cultural factor in the coming of the Civil War. The 1920s and 1930s saw one of the nation's great flowerings of regionalism in the arts, ranging from the poetry of Robert Frost to the paintings of Grant Wood, from the heroes and villains of Vernon Louis Parrington's *Main Currents in American Thought* to the Joads of John Steinbeck's *Grapes of Wrath*.

Carl Sandburg made his reputation as a regional writer of the "Chicago school" that included Edgar Lee Masters and Vachel Lindsay, and the specificity of his work is one of its great charms. But like Whitman—or, for that matter, Frederick Jackson Turner—Sandburg had a complex fascination with unity and multiplicity, the specific and the cosmic. The ultimate expression of these concepts is to compress the entire nation into a single figure, a man who would "carry in his breast Cape Cod, the Shenandoah, the Mississippi, the Gulf, the Rocky Mountains, the Sacramento, the Great Plains, the Great Lakes, their dialects and shibboleths. He must be instinct with regions of corn, textile mills, cotton, tobacco, gold, coal, zinc, iron."[32]

Even before Sandburg reimagined him, Abraham Lincoln was an ideal choice to embody this archetype. For one thing, he was, like Sandburg himself, Midwestern, which gave him an identity that was literally and figuratively the center of the nation. This is particularly true of half-Northern/half-Southern Illinois and the Midwest in general, as noted by a number of regionalists. Then there is the strange paradox that has haunted Lincoln historians for the past century, namely, that for all the material collected about him, Lincoln remains an enigma. He is probably the most plastic figure in U.S. history—grave and comic, eloquent and awkward, magnanimous and shrewd.

Sandburg reveled in this malleability, compiling examples (and even chapters) to illustrate facets of Lincoln's character. Once again, fact creates myth. It is not that Sandburg rejected the idea of a human Lincoln—after all, heroes get their vitality from a belief that in some basic ways they are just like you and me—but that he used each little anecdote to build a whole that transcends the sum of its parts. Facts are merely a starting point in the making of truth.

Whatever the specific components of his portrait, Carl Sandburg was only one of many people writing about Abraham Lincoln in the 1920s and 1930s. It is a period that might well be considered the golden age of Lincoln culture, with portraits as varied as those by one-time Indiana senator Albert Beveridge (two volumes, 1928), journalist Ida Tarbell (she published eight books on Lincoln, including several for children), and Katherine Holland Brown, whose Lincoln-as-friend novel *The Father* won a $25,000 literary prize in 1928.[33]

Why this outpouring? I would like to begin answering this question by exploring an obscure controversy in Lincoln mythology and the way in which it suggests, albeit indirectly, the cultural impulses underlying the creation of a heroic Lincoln as the 1920s gave way to the challenges of the 1930s.

One of the most curious aspects of Lincoln literature as far back as the 1890s was a widespread fascination with Ann Rutledge, a woman Lincoln reportedly loved but who died before they could marry. Rutledge's life is shrouded in mystery, with our knowledge of her largely resting on reminiscences collected by Herndon after Lincoln's death. According to Herndon, Rutledge was a gentle, beautiful young woman in New Salem, Illinois, in the early 1830s, when Lincoln lived there. She was engaged to a man who went home to New York to straighten out some affairs before marrying her. In the interim, during which her fiancé failed to return her letters, she and Lincoln fell in love, and after agonizing over the ethics of breaking the engagement to her betrothed, the two decided to marry. Ann suddenly fell ill and died in 1835. Lincoln was shattered and plunged into a deep depression (indeed, that he was depressed has been widely corroborated by a number of people who knew him at the time). Rutledge remained the only woman Lincoln ever really loved, and his later marriage to the needy, demanding, and oppressive Mary Todd Lincoln was portrayed as an act of duty that prepared him for the burden of dealing with the Civil War in the White House.[34] (It should be noted that Herndon and Mary Todd Lincoln had a notoriously poor relationship that itself has become legendary.) In any case, *Herndon's Lincoln: The True Story of a Great Life* remained a standard source of raw material on Lincoln for the next century. Although Herndon's version of the story has been questioned—indeed, there is a whole subgenre of Lincoln literature on it[35]—the Rutledge myth has never been conclusively proved or disproved.

Sandburg believed the story, though he was relatively kind to Mary Todd Lincoln. Nevertheless, in *The Prairie Years*, he took the Rutledge myth and embellished it considerably:

> After the first evening in which Lincoln had sat next to her and found that bashful words tumbling from his tongue's end really spelled themselves out into sensible talk, her face, as he went away, kept coming back. So often all else would fade out of his mind and there would be only this riddle of a pink-fair face, a mouth and eyes in a frame of light corn-silk hair. He could ask himself what it meant and search his heart for an answer and no answer would come. A trembling took his body and dark waves ran through him sometimes when she spoke so simple a thing as, "The Corn is getting high, isn't it?"[36]

"The corn is getting high indeed!" Edmund Wilson observed a generation later. (Wilson's own Lincoln, unsurprisingly, is an ambitious, unsentimental intellectual.)[37]

Two years later, interest in the Rutledge myth reached fever pitch after a California woman named Wilma Francis Minor came forward claiming to have letters authenticating the Lincoln-Rutledge romance. Despite doubt by some Lincoln scholars, the august *Atlantic Monthly*, in a rare moment of descent into the valleys of popular taste, published the letters to capitalize on the curiosity of the public. "You need a wife that will be a help to you, not a drag-bak like sum ar," reads one letter from the "Lincoln the Lover" articles run in the December 1928 and January and February 1929 issues.[38] Sandburg not only believed the letters were authentic, but also wrote an article for the *New York World* to promote their acceptance: "While this is a case where no one can prove the documents to be absolutely authentic any one who tries to impeach them will have difficulties and end in disaster. They have come to stay in the Lincoln record."[39]

The letters, it was soon verified, were forged. Sandburg had retreated even before this disclosure, however, convinced by the skepticism of friends and Lincoln experts Oliver Barret and Paul Angle. "When I scrutinize the original source material of this kind I let my emotions have full play," he wrote for the *World* the next day. "I try to do my hard-boiled analyzing later."[40] A chastened Sandburg cut much of the Rutledge material from the 1954 edition of the biography, though he did not let go of it completely. Perhaps his embarrassment was a factor in making *The War Years* somewhat less hyperbolic.

Despite the revelation that the letters were counterfeit, the Rutledge myth continued to have broad currency straight through the 1930s. "I reckon I ort to try and live th' way she'd want me to," says a grieving Lincoln, beginning his journey from backwoods bumpkin to polished politician in E. P. Conkle's *Prologue to Glory*, a play produced by the Works Progress Administration's Federal Theatre Project in 1937–38.[41] Rutledge also figures prominently in Robert Sherwood's Pulitzer Prize–winning play *Abe Lincoln in Illinois*—inspired, according to the author, by *The Prairie Years*—which was produced for the stage in 1939 and released in a film version in 1940.[42] Sherwood's play portrays Mary Todd Lincoln particularly harshly: Whereas Ann gently urges Lincoln, Mary relentlessly drives him. The good woman dies, and the other one—who is notably smart, ambitious, and quick to know who her enemies are in virtually all accounts, fiction and nonfiction—is bad because she acts like a man.[43]

A woman acting like a man was a particularly big problem for men during the Great Depression. Besides the lingering anxieties raised by the advent of modern feminism, there was an ongoing fear of competing with women in a time of economic scarcity. Few men could imagine wanting a wife like Mary Todd Lincoln—and few men imagined Lincoln's wanting one either. To paraphrase William Faulkner's *Sound and the Fury*, he endured.[44]

Saddling Lincoln with a "difficult" wife was one way—a deeply personal way, a way to which we could presumably all relate—to give him a tragic air suitable to the Great Man. Thus, Sandburg's use of the Rutledge myth was one component in the construction of his heroic Lincoln. The Great Man is one of the people (he falls in love, he helps his neighbors, he comes to see that slavery is a real problem), but there is also that intangible sense of transcendence about him (he is often quiet, he would rather read than wrestle, and there is a sadness about him that makes him noble). But the Great Man so effectively embodied by Lincoln is ultimately a public figure, and his private sorrows are important because they prepare him to handle collective crises.

Rarely in U.S. history has there been a collective crisis as pressing as the Great Depression. With corporate capitalism completely discredited in the eyes of millions of people, the time seemed ripe for a major overhaul of the nation's political, social, and cultural institutions. The 1930s, especially the early 1930s, were the high-water mark for communism in U.S. history, and many intellectuals were fascinated—and even moved—by the dramatic changes in the postrevolutionary Soviet Union. If ever there was a time for "it" to happen here, this was it.

However, as many observers then and since have noted, popular thought was Januslike: People were oriented toward the past as well as the future. Change, if it was to take place, had to be justified in terms of tradition, which is one reason why the Popular Front of the late 1930s embraced folk culture with such alacrity.[45] Though there was in the United States, as in most nations at most times in human history, a desire for a strong leader to fuse past ideals and future hopes, this desire coexisted with a longstanding practice, originating in the Jacksonian era, for that leader to be well versed in the rhetoric and iconography of the common man. Abraham Lincoln won the election of 1860 because he was able to achieve this fusion for most of the Northern electorate, and he has remained the supreme embodiment of it ever since. During the Great Depression, a time of enormous social and psychological instability, Lincoln could simultaneously represent ideals of freedom and equality, order and democracy, ordeal and victory.

Nowhere are these dialectical tensions more vividly depicted than in *Young Mr. Lincoln* (1939), a film directed by the auteur of Monument Valley, John Ford. The main story line of *Young Mr. Lincoln* (which includes a Sandburg-esque rendition of the Rutledge affair) concerns Lincoln's defense of two brothers who have been wrongly accused of murder. At one point in the trial the prosecuting attorney, a small-minded man less astute than his partner Stephen A. Douglas, finishes questioning a witness. He turns the floor over to Lincoln (played by Henry Fonda), wondering aloud how the bookish young greenhorn is going to make his case. "I may not know much about the law," Lincoln replies, "but I know what's right and what's wrong."

Now that is a line of poetry, a line that speaks volumes about the yearnings of the 1930s and why Lincoln embodied so many of those dreams. Imagine: a good, decent man of the people, determined but gentle, cutting through the Gordian knot of law (i.e., special interests, ideology, and everything else that makes the world so complicated) to do what he—and everybody else—knows to be right. In a world of chaos and impending doom, that is what democracy is all about, is it not?

Well, not exactly. Not letting the law get in the way of justice is a short step from saying the end justifies the means, and another short step to electing a Hitler or a Mussolini. In Germany, where economic problems had pressed the nation long and hard, economic recovery ("what is right") overrode any other considerations (such as "the law"). Indeed, the crisis of the 1930s was sufficiently severe in the United States that some embraced domestic forms of fascism. Demagogues such as Huey Long and Father Charles Coughlin gained huge followings through promising "simple" solutions to complicated problems. We will never know what would have happened to the assassinated Long, but Coughlin's anti-Semitic stridency did eventually alienate most of his followers.

The reason, one suspects, is sufficient hostility to the kind of centralized control these men represented.[46] At the same time, there has always been an opposing tendency toward centralization in U.S. history, not all of it salutary, that has coexisted with that hostility. But centralization has often required a sense of virtue—even if false—to make it palatable during and after the fact. The greatest drive for centralized governmental power the nation experienced was during the Civil War (followed by that of the New Deal), and correspondingly, that call was made more compelling by a Sandburg-styled Lincoln.

The mind that imagines—or simply accepts—this Lincoln often wants to have its cake and eat it too. Ford's Lincoln may not know much about the law, but he still helps the good guys win using conventional, albeit brilliant, legal tactics. Sandburg's Lincoln takes on responsibility for untold death and misery and when it is all over fatalistically resigns himself to becoming the final casualty. Such a figure needs no logic or consistency. It is precisely such nonrational tensions (between bending the rules and breaking them; between controlling others' destinies and surrendering to one's own) that give myths their vitality.[47]

This mythic hero is not a static figure carved in stone, however. He is wrought from a forge of urgency, even necessity. Positing a strong but humane Lincoln creates a usable precedent that paves the way for another leader to assume his mantle during another crisis. The Great Depression becomes less menacing when juxtaposed with the Civil War, and the need for a strong leader becomes less menacing when the nation feels it survived one previously. This was the "cultural work" Sandburg sought to perform in his Lincoln biography.[48]

Franklin Roosevelt was smart enough to both recognize this use of Lincoln and employ it to his advantage. At first glance, one might not think that the patrician FDR could inherit the throne of the earthy Lincoln, though Lincoln, a wealthy railroad lawyer, was less plebeian than the popular imagination would allow. But FDR's overwhelming charisma—symbolized by the fireside chat—appropriated the kind of closeness to the people that was associated with the Lincoln legend. This intimacy was vitally important. As one historian explained, "In a moment of crisis so severe that crumbling institutional structures seemed capable of carrying social and moral values with them, a leadership based on respect, even admiration, was insufficient. What was needed was a leader whose love of the masses he led was so clear that it could generate love as a response, and along with love, a confidence that did not depend on rational judgements of programs or on technical and complex economic analyses."[49]

Roosevelt was also shrewd enough to use history with amazing effectiveness, and one might say that FDR's signal cultural achievement was his successful transformation of Abraham Lincoln into a Democrat. The process began as early as 1929, shortly after he was inaugurated governor of New York. "I think it is time for us Democrats to claim Lincoln as one of our own," he wrote to Jefferson biographer Claude Bowers. "The Republican party has certainly repudiated, first and last, everything he stood for."[50] The recruitment of Lincoln did not begin in earnest until FDR became president, however. In 1934 FDR took a cue from Republican New York mayor Fiorello LaGuardia and began quoting Lincoln's assertion that the legitimate object of government is to do for a community of people whatever they cannot do for themselves. Roosevelt visited Lincoln's birthplace in the spring of 1936, breaking a tacit policy of leaving such rites to Republicans. During the furor over the court-packing scheme of 1937, FDR tried to defuse criticism by pointing out that Lincoln, too, had increased the number of U.S. Supreme Court justices. Such tactics exasperated Republicans, who found a potent political symbol stolen from them and given new meaning. In 1939 a frustrated ex-president Herbert Hoover felt compelled to say, "Whatever this New Deal system is, it is certain that it did not come from Abraham Lincoln."[51] The fact that he said so, however, indicates a common perception to the contrary.

In addition to his own rhetoric, Roosevelt employed that of others, including Sandburg. Robert Sherwood, whose Lincoln says "Thank God we live under a system by which men have the right to strike!" in *Abe Lincoln in Illinois*,[52] was hired by the Roosevelt campaign to write speeches in 1940. Stephen Vincent Benét, whose best-selling epic poem *John Brown's Body* (1928) also cast Lincoln in a heroic light, wrote an election-day poem, "Tuesday, November 5, 1940," in honor of Roosevelt. By this point, Sandburg had been an FDR convert for years, having written the president in 1935, "You are the best light of democracy that has occupied the White House since Lincoln." On election eve, he took to the radio and described Lincoln's struggle to get himself reelected in 1864. Quoting a minister who described Lincoln as "not a perfect man and yet more precious than fine gold," Sandburg concluded his speech by saying, "And for some of us, that goes, in the main, in the present hour of national fate, for Franklin Delano Roosevelt."[53]

But Lincoln's work was not yet done. The depression was ending, but war was coming. For Roosevelt and his history brokers, the sixteenth president would prove even more useful to the thirty-second for the coming conflict. In June 1940, Roosevelt hosted the American Youth Congress at the White House and was asked why preparedness was getting more attention than the New Deal. FDR answered with a question: "Have you read Carl Sandburg's *Lincoln?*" He continued, "I think the impression was that Lincoln was a pretty sad man, because he could not do all he wanted to at one time, and I think you will find examples where Lincoln had to compromise to gain a little something. He had to compromise to make gains. Lincoln was one of those unfortunate people called a 'politician' but he was a politician who was practical enough to get a great many things for his country. He was a sad man because he couldn't get it all at once. And nobody can."[54] A translation: I, like Lincoln, am a mere mortal. But I know what our priorities should be and can make difficult choices. Follow me.

Just as Roosevelt was not the only one using Lincoln to get through the depression, he was not the only one using Lincoln in the struggle against fascism. One of the most notable examples of this is the three thousand volunteers who went off to fight in the Spanish civil war, calling themselves the Abraham Lincoln Battalion.[55] One can get a glimpse of why they went by considering (Republican) William Allen White's contention that in a shrinking globe, the world cannot live "half slave and half free."[56] The notion that Axis governments were enslaving minorities is perhaps the most direct—and most powerful—analogy that one could make between World War II and the Civil War. As in the case of Northerners in the Civil War, some would fight a world war to end that slavery, others simply to stop its spread.

The Great Emancipator notwithstanding, there were also those who would not fight at all, the most famous of whom was Charles Lindbergh. For this adversary, FDR drew a parallel with Clement Vallandigham, the Democratic congressman from Ohio who attacked Lincoln over the war and led Copperhead efforts to end it. When Vallandigham was arrested by a Union general, Lincoln decided against trial or incarceration in favor of having him escorted behind Confederate lines. He later returned and lost an electoral bid for governor before leading the peace wing of the Democratic party in the presidential race of 1864. When asked about Lindbergh, FDR replied, "If you go back to the roster of the Army in the Civil War . . . there were—what shall I call them?—there were Vallandighams. Well, Vallandigham, as you know, was an appeaser. [Note the employment of a 1930s term in an 1860s context.] He wanted to make peace from 1863 because the North 'couldn't win.'"[57]

Sandburg, characteristically, reacted less mildly to the "famous flyer who has quit flying and taken to talking." Noting that Lindbergh was "calling interventionists like me hysterical," Sandburg told a national unity meeting in Chicago in June 1940, "Very well, then we are hysterical. Very well, then the Declaration of Independence is hysterical, the Constitution of the United States is hysterical, the Bill of Rights is hysterical, the Gettysburg Speech and the Second Inaugural of Abraham Lincoln are hysterical—and the men who fought and died to establish those documents and give them meaning, they were all hysterical."[58]

Maybe Lindbergh was right—Sandburg is a little hysterical here. In a larger sense, however, Sandburg was surely right in his belief that these documents made a difference (even if they amounted to less than he thought they did) and that some battles were worth fighting. In any case, he need not have worried—the United States entered the war and the Axis powers were defeated, with Abraham Lincoln successfully enlisted in the struggle to make the world safe for democracy.

Sandburg continued to be an active participant in the "good fight." When the war broke out, he supported the Allied effort with radio broadcasts for the Office of War Information and by writing commentary for the government film *Bomber* and captions for his brother-in-law Edward Steichen's 1942 mural show *Road to Victory*. He also wrote a political column for the *Chicago Times* syndicate from 1941 to 1945.

In the years that followed, however, Sandburg's appeal began to wane. The hard-nosed, text-centered approach of the New Criticism made his poetry seem dated if not simply banal, and a new generation of historians began questioning his view of Lincoln. Sandburg's decline was also more broadly cultural. A new generation of artists, more decisively Modernist, was arriving on the scene. The rage for Thomas Hart Benton gave way to the cool appeal of his student Jackson Pollock.[59]

Indeed, even in Sandburg's glory days, a broad effort was being mounted that ultimately challenged the form as well as the content of his Lincoln. This challenge came from professional historians, most notably a friend of Sandburg's whose own multivolume biography ultimately supplanted the poet's as the definitive work on the subject. To understand how and why, it would be helpful to take a closer look at the texts in question.

Great Are the Myths

> If history is to be attempted, the standards of historical craftsmanship must not be neglected. Statements must be tied to reality, and this not merely by way of something to quote or cite, but in terms of tested and competent evidence. There is nothing cryptic about this.
>
>   James G. Randall,
>   *Lincoln the President*[60]

"Has the Lincoln Theme Been Exhausted?" asked one scholar in the title of a January 1936 article in the *American Historical Review*. The author, James Garfield Randall, had been steadily making a name for himself as a professional Lincoln scholar. As he noted, however, much of the work on Lincoln had been done by amateurs, whereas professionals had been generally limiting themselves to monographs. This diffidence, Randall argued, was not good for history. The professor noted French premier Georges Clemenceau's famous quip that the United States had passed from barbarism to decadence without ever passing though civilization, and he wondered if "Lincoln authorship shall pass from its present imperfect state to decadence without undergoing further critical development by historically trained scholars." Despite the huge volume of writing (including, for example, articles such as "Dogs Were Ever a Joy to Lincoln"), Randall felt that some key questions about Lincoln remained unanswered and that *the* Lincoln biography was "still awaited."[61] In retrospect, "Has the Lincoln Theme Been Exhausted?" seems to have been Randall's bid to clear himself some space in the Lincoln thicket for his own work.

Randall's career pattern resembles that of professional historians to this day. Born in Indianapolis in 1881, he graduated from Butler College in 1903 and entered the University of Chicago, where he received his Ph.D. in 1911. In keeping with the new emphasis on "scientific" monographs, his dissertation, *The Confiscation of Property during the Civil War*, analyzed data from court records and outlined the legal problems of the Lincoln administration in dealing with property rights. Portions of it were published in the *American Historical Review* in 1912 and 1913.

After holding brief appointments at Roanoke College, the University of Pennsylvania, and Richmond College, Randall won a coveted tenured post at the University of Illinois at Urbana, where he remained until his retirement. His second book, *Constitutional Problems under Lincoln*, was published in

1926, expanding on the themes of his dissertation. Not until 1937 did Randall's full treatment of the war, *The Civil War and Reconstruction*, appear. It remained the standard text until 1961, when it received another lease on life as revised by David Donald (more on this below). The book exhibits many of the themes that have since been identified as quintessential Randall: a relatively pro-Southern cast, a belief that a "blundering generation" of inept politicians had brought on the war, and the premise (in contrast to the "irrepressible conflict" theme so prominent in the writings of Nationalist historians) that the Civil War was—indeed, all war is—avoidable.

Randall, more than his successors, held Sandburg in high regard, commenting in 1942 that Sandburg's Lincoln made all other biographies "dull or stupid by comparison." He dedicated a collection of essays, *Lincoln the Liberal Statesman* (1947), to Sandburg, and the poet was one of Randall's last visitors before he died of leukemia in 1953. Nevertheless, Randall, in his own four-volume opus, *Lincoln the President* (1945–55),[62] eschews Sandburg's tactics even as he compliments the poet in each of the volumes. (He also gently criticizes the length of *The War Years* and devotes about half of his review of the biography in the *American Historical Review* to listing factual errors.)[63]

Meanwhile, Lincoln remained in the forefront of Randall's work, and Randall's work was in the vanguard of an emerging generation of Civil War scholars that included Avery Craven and Charles Ramsdell. In 1929 Randall was commissioned to write an essay on Lincoln for the *Dictionary of American Biography*, published in 1933. He was particularly troubled by what he considered the inadequately objective nature of most Lincoln literature, and he lamented "the party influence, if not indeed the party label" (a distaste for party politics marks much of his work). "If every man is 'his own historian,'" Randall concluded, alluding to—and subtly subverting—an essay by Carl Becker, "then every historian can contribute something new, provided he does not make the uniqueness of a preconceived point of view an end in itself."[64]

The first two volumes of Randall's magnum opus, *Lincoln the President: From Springfield to Gettysburg*, were published in 1945 to wide praise and have been highly regarded ever since. Indeed, although Sandburg may still get occasional compliments, Randall still gets *cited*, which in the historical guild is the highest compliment of all. Though he had reservations about it, James McPherson called Randall's biography "a scholarly *tour de force*" in *Battle Cry of Freedom*, now the standard work on the Civil War.[65]

Randall lays out his agenda at the start of *Lincoln the President*. In his preface to the first two volumes, Randall again asserts the need for a clear-eyed biography and presents the reader with his attempt to produce one.

"The muse is strict and exacting," Randall explains. "Without submitting to these requirements one can dabble in history, but it is a field where the tyro falls short and the amateur betrays himself. This is not said with the least assumption of professionalism. It is simply a recognition of the realities within which the author has had to work."[66]

Randall insists on a role of sober detachment where the historical chips fall where they may, even if they do not flatter the subject. "The historian searches; he presents his findings; if he works validly he destroys nothing except misconception and unfounded tradition. It is only so that scholarship can be constructive." The goal, he explains, is restoration. "The historian seeks out original records, excavates, so to speak, clears away unhistorical debris, and endeavors, if he can, to restore events and essential situations of the past."[67]

Randall did not presume to actually accomplish this restoration. In the third volume of the biography, *Midstream*, published in 1952, he writes that "a new delineation may have value without aspiring to finality." He is even a little apologetic about the presence of footnotes, which "should be held guilty until proven innocent." And he praises Sandburg as "that eloquent voice, eminent Lincoln writer, and beloved interpreter of the American spirit."[68] Yet virtually everything about his text resists Sandburg's means (and many of his ends), and it is clear that Randall put great stock in the opening of the Robert Todd Lincoln Collection of the Papers of Abraham Lincoln in 1947, which, he seems to have believed, would open new vistas of Lincoln scholarship and the opportunity to finally get the facts straight. In the appendix to the third volume, in which Randall discusses the opening of the papers, he barely restrained that most ahistorical of states: excitement. "If this [his description of the papers] suggests enthusiasm, the researcher must plead guilty to the charge, but it was an enthusiasm that came with that accent on reality that arises from being at the very source of things."

It is even more illuminating to compare the way the two writers handled the same material. One of the best examples is the Bixby episode. In November 1864, the president wrote a widely published letter to a Mrs. Lydia Bixby, who had reportedly lost five sons in battle (as it turned out, only two had died, but that does not substantially affect the meaning of the letter). Since it is brief, it can be quoted in full, as indeed both Sandburg and Randall did:

> Dear Madam:
> I have been shown in the files of the War Department a statement of the Adjutant General of Massachusetts that you are the mother of five sons who have died gloriously on the field of battle. I feel how weak and fruitless must

be any words of mine which should attempt to beguile you from the grief of a loss so overwhelming. But I cannot refrain from tendering to you the consolation that may be found in the thanks of the Republic they died to save. I pray that our heavenly father may assuage the anguish of your bereavement, and leave you only the cherished memory of the loved and lost, and the solemn pride that must be yours to have laid so costly a sacrifice upon the altar of freedom.

> Yours very sincerely and respectfully,
> Abraham Lincoln. [69]

"It is futile to try to paint the lily and it is a question of how far one needs to comment on a literary classic," writes Randall in *Last Full Measure,* the last volume of *Lincoln the President* (which was completed upon Randall's death in 1953 by Richard Current, about whom more will be said below). [70] Ironically, he could not leave well enough alone, spending the next five pages analyzing the origins of the letter before concluding that a theory he always thought was suspect—namely, that Lincoln's private secretary John Hay wrote the letter—was indeed as ridiculous as he had originally thought. For Randall, truth meant verification, and he seems to have thought that verification was more important than exploring what even he considered "a masterpiece in the English language." [71]

Sandburg was not willing to let the letter speak for itself, either. To heighten the pathos, he goes on to quote hostile newspaper articles that attacked Lincoln for his "cheap sympathy," and he concludes by arguing that it was one more step in the evolution of a great leader:

> As the months passed after Lincoln's first inaugural address, his sense of the comic, his occasional role of comedian stayed with him, while significantly on the other hand he came to know more keenly and fittingly what could be done with the authoritative mantle of the President. He learned how better to wear it publicly, to adjust it as the garment of solemn spokesman. He believed the majesty of the office backed him in telling Congress that "the fiery ordeal" through which they all were passing would be written as history and the players weighed and the balances cast up. At Gettysburg, he stood in the ceremonial role. Across many months of '64 his authority hung by such threads that he knew his cue was silence; no statements could be wrung from him. Again in the Bixby letter he performed a rite, managing language as though he might be a ship captain at midnight by lantern light dropping black roses into the immemorial sea for mystic remembrance and consecration. [72]

The language is a little excessive, but Sandburg here helps us understand the larger significance of the Bixby letter, namely, the way it illustrates Lincoln's mastery of public and private roles and their function in effective leadership.

The most obvious difference between the two studies is the authors' treatment of the assassination. Randall and Current gave the assassination a paragraph; Sandburg over 150 pages. (I have used the title of Sandburg's chapter on the aftermath of the assassination as the title of this chapter.) The former account was brief to keep the focus on Lincoln the man; Sandburg's version was written with an eye for the ages. Although never a writer of great restraint, here he made an unabashed pitch for our emotions: The previously rambling narrative focuses and moves into the present tense, while the antagonist of the story becomes not simply John Wilkes Booth but the Outsider (Lincoln is the Friend of Man). For Sandburg, Lincoln's death was not merely an unfortunate event with significant political ramifications; it was a personal tragedy to be viscerally reexperienced. History is something to be felt in the present tense. It is also played in the key of providential history; experiencing the assassination (along with thousands of other readers) becomes a confirmation of sorts, a rite that reinforces one's membership in the national community. Despite all this—or perhaps because of it—the effect is quite moving, which is exactly what Sandburg intended.

Then there is the question of politics. At first glance, it would seem that Sandburg's Lincoln is simply the Great White Hope, loved by children and slaves, admired by men, magnetic to women. (In one passage in the biography Sandburg described an encounter between Lincoln and the widow of the governor of Wisconsin in phrases having strikingly, even shockingly, sexual overtones.)[73] Yet a more textured picture of where Sandburg stood politically and historiographically emerges when he is juxtaposed with the more explicit Randall.

Randall's Lincoln is the Great Conservative. Indeed, the term *conservative* crops up in regard to Lincoln five times in the first volume alone.[74] In part, what Randall seems to mean by this is that Lincoln was the voice of moderation between the hotheaded fire-eaters on his right and mean-spirited Republican radicals on his left. Actually, it often seems that the radicals, not the Confederates, were the president's biggest problem. Randall saw people on both sides as "ideologues." To him, ideologues were people with axes to grind, zealots who foment unreal issues and in so doing blunder into war. And if ideologues write bad history, they are even worse politicians because they disrupt the peace, and to Randall disrupting the peace was the biggest problem of all. Hence the opening of *Lincoln the President:* "In the year of Our

Lord 1860 the United States was at peace. In all that was sound and fundamental, in every instinct that was normal and sane, the people of America,
and their genuine friends abroad, wanted that peace to endure."[75] By contrast, "vicious forces" would tear that peace apart, and in Randall's mind,
Lincoln's greatness resided in his heroic attempts to keep those forces from
getting out of hand. "There was in Lincoln more of Euclid than Demosthenes," he explains.[76]

The choice of metaphor is revealing. Demosthenes means "voice of the
people," and there is a tendency in the "blundering generation" school to
distrust the judgment of the people. Masses are easily swayed; unscrupulous
"vicious forces" (such as, say, abolitionists) may lead unwitting people to fight
for more than they expected. It is not hard to understand the source of this
point of view; Randall and other "blundering generation" historians had
witnessed the overheated nationalism of World War I, and by the 1930s they
were watching European democracies swept into the vortex of nazism and
Stalinism.

But Carl Sandburg was also writing in the 1930s, and he did not come to
the same conclusion. Unlike Randall, Sandburg was not as afraid of conflict
("Always I have loved . . . storms"), seeing in struggle the possibility of
renewal, even if at great cost. And the amount of attention he gives to
Lincoln's elections, particularly Lincoln's reelection, implies an affirmation
of the possibility that left to their own devices, the people of the United
States can make good choices, even if they also make mistakes.

Nor was Sandburg quite as wary of ideology as the "blundering generation"
scholars (or, for that matter, consensus historians such as Daniel Boorstin and
Arthur Schlesinger, Jr., who dominated the postwar years).[77] Although also
portraying Lincoln as navigating between the Scylla of the right and the
Charybdis of the left, he was less disgusted by the grittiness of the political
arena. Nor was explicit ideology necessarily anathema. Sandburg seemed to
take great pride in Lincoln's encouraging address to the workingmen of Man-
chester and London in 1863. Karl Marx, who reported on the war from
London, is altogether absent from *Lincoln the President*. However, he makes a
number of cameo appearances in *The War Years*, serving as a kind of cheer-
leader urging Lincoln on, most notably when Sandburg includes Marx's telegram to the reelected president congratulating the people of the United
States on their choice to continue fighting a war on slavery.[78]

Randall regarded ideology as a fatally subjective point of view that some
(leftist) writers made the mistake of espousing. A half-century later, however,
his views seem no less subjective. One is amazed at the glaring omissions

implicit in a view of antebellum society as "sound and fundamental, in every instinct that was normal and sane," or his regard for the "emphasis on human worth" in the slaveholding South. And if one regards a view of radical Republicans as "vindictives" who had less interest in ending slavery than in consolidating power as an "objective" interpretation, is the description of Congressman Thaddeus Stevens as a man of "dour countenance, protruding lower lip, limping clubfoot" a paragon of fair-minded description?[79]

Of course, Carl Sandburg was hardly a model of judiciousness either. But then, he never claimed to be. The argument here is not that Sandburg's biography is better than Randall's—Randall, after all, fashioned a coherent expression of his own position and cultural milieu—or that Sandburg's weaknesses are less problematic. It is that there are aspects of Sandburg's vision— his commitment to democracy, his desire to reach out to a large community of readers, his feel for the emotional and even spiritual dimensions of history—that have been overlooked in the decades since Randall's ascendancy.

Governing Perceptions

> The legitimate object of government, is to do for a
> community of people, whatever they need to have done, but
> can not do, *at all,* or can not, *so well do,* for themselves—in
> their separate and individual capacities. . . . Making and
> maintaining roads, bridges and the like; providing for the
> helpless young and afflicted; common schools; and disposing
> of deceased men's property, are instances.
>
> Abraham Lincoln,
> "Fragments on Government," 1854?[80]

In the years following the publication of Sandburg's biography, history was on James Randall's side. By this I mean not simply that his Lincoln seemed more durable than Sandburg's, but also that Randall's style proved consonant with the temper of a postwar profession that came to dominate historical discourse.

At the end of the previous chapter, I outlined the way the influence of the Nationalist school of Civil War historiography had begun to wane in the years following the First World War. To some degree, the erosion of this consensus reflected a weakening in a profession predicated on a scientific mission of objective reconstruction. That so many learned, carefully trained people could disagree—and disagree emphatically—on as fundamental an issue as the cause of the Civil War suggested that at the very least, establishing an empirical foundation for the discipline was going to take longer, and prove more difficult, than some early practitioners had hoped.[81]

Not all historians looked upon this situation with dismay. Charles Beard, whose relationship to the academy had long been uneasy (he had resigned from Columbia University in 1917 over the firing of faculty for exhibiting insufficiently patriotic wartime views), entitled his 1933 address as president of the American Historical Association "History as an Act of Faith." Two years before, Beard's friend and colleague Carl Becker had entitled his democratically minded AHA address "Everyman His Own Historian."[82] James Harvey Robinson, restless with the strictures of professional historical practice, sought a New History that essentially laid the foundations for the contemporary subdiscipline of cultural and intellectual history.[83]

To varying degrees, these and other people questioned the empiricist assumptions that girded the creation of the profession, and they were willing to accept a measure of relativism in their understanding of the past. In doing so, however, they were at least implicitly conceding that the authority of disciplinary interpretation was provisional, subject not only to change over time, but also to competing claims of truth from other kinds of history (such as the essentially poetic approach of Sandburg, who was ritually complimented even by those who did not share his sensibility).

The rise of fascism, Stalin's purges, and the events of the Second World War made these premises less appealing. The claim that there could be many interpretations of the past smacked of a dangerous relativism all too easily manipulated by totalitarian regimes. So did the explicit invocation of ideology, which could pit partisans of right and left against a reinvigorated capitalist middle. This was the kind of criticism Randall had leveled against the leaders of the "blundering generation" of the Civil War, and this criticism gave the first volume of Lincoln the President pointed relevance when it was published in 1945. Although Randall was faulted for failing to make important moral distinctions—surely, historians such as Oscar Handlin and Arthur Schlesinger, Jr., argued, there was a difference between being a fanatic for slavery and a fanatic for freedom[84]—his conservatism was widely equated with judiciousness.

This presumed evenhandedness, which Schlesinger himself called "the vital center,"[85] seemed best served by a renewed commitment to objective history. Indeed, one of the striking characteristics of postwar intellectual life was the way in which a moralistic embrace of U.S. policy on the cold war was funneled into a social science mission. To some extent, this effort stemmed from a sincere belief that U.S. civilization in the 1950s really did represent the most effective model for governing societies at home and abroad. At the heart of that model was a glorification of expertise, which won the war with the atomic bomb, overtook the Soviet Union in the space race, and graced consumers with a democracy of goods. In such a climate, historians—enjoying economic security from the defense dollars engorging universities—renewed their commitment to the social sciences, which were themselves making even more intensified efforts to pursue "hard" research with "realistic" or "responsible" applications.

One can detect such currents in Civil War historiography. David Donald's *Lincoln Reconsidered*, a widely read collection of essays published in 1960, ended with "An Excess of Democracy"—a piece implying that the absence of rational political professionals had allowed the antebellum political situation to get out of hand. In his 1959 study *Slavery*, Stanley Elkins depicted slaves as hapless victims of all-powerful social technicians, and abolitionists as impractical idealists ignorant of the Southern social system they sought to criticize. Other writers deplored any kind of partisanship and considered quantification and value neutrality as the most effective means for studying the conflict.[86]

Randall's work was well suited for this historiographic disposition, and Donald's revision of Randall's 1937 textbook twenty-five years later seems especially apropos. Along with the Lincoln biography, completed by Richard Current in 1955, it consolidated Randall's reputation as one of the nation's preeminent Civil War historians well into the postwar era.

Ironically, however, Randall's success in fashioning the dominant view of Lincoln soon had unintended consequences. The conservative Lincoln he envisioned began to seem less impressive with the rise of the Civil Rights movement. As the movement gained momentum, the very quality Randall cherished about Lincoln—his moderation—was increasingly suspect to those outside the academic establishment. The sixteenth president became, in the words of the acerbic I. F. Stone, "the Great Equivocator." Lerone Bennett, Jr., a senior editor for *Ebony*, summed up the view of many on the left in 1968 when he described Lincoln as "the very essence of the white supremacist with good intentions," citing the work of a number of historians, including Randall, to make his argument. Such writers emphasized the reluctance with which Lincoln emancipated slaves and his evasiveness in initially freeing them precisely where he had no effective power to do so. Meanwhile, the abolitionists received their first major reevaluation in a century. Similarly, radical Republicans such as Thaddeus Stevens also received reappraisal and were compared positively with Lincoln.[87]

Of course, the drop in Lincoln's stock cannot be blamed solely on Randall, whose view of Lincoln as relatively unconcerned with the fate of slaves—seen as a positive good by some nonacademic writers—is part of a century-old tradition, and one that was carried forward in Benjamin Thomas's 1952 biography of Lincoln, which also downplayed racial questions.[88] Randall did, however, fashion an influential "moderate" Lincoln every bit as suitable to his own sensibilities as those portrayed by his predecessors, and his scrupulous use of the facts hardly left his interpretations less vulnerable to challenge by those outside the historical profession.

In any case, some efforts were made to wrest Lincoln from Randall's grip. The best example is Stephen B. Oates, whose With Malice toward None (1977) has achieved wide circulation. Oates rescued Lincoln from attacks on the left by calling radical Republicans "liberals" and describing Lincoln as a good party man fundamentally in sympathy with them. Oates was criticized for this strategy and for other reasons, but his work achieved wide circulation and suggests one facet of the New Left's impact on the historical profession in the 1970s.[89]

The other major cultural current in this period was the effect of psychology on Lincoln historiography. A series of biographies published in the late 1970s and early 1980s sought to explain Lincoln's behavior in office by drawing on his early experiences and the ways they affected his later life.[90] To greater or lesser degrees, all these works picked up a strand of inquiry first pursued by Edmund Wilson in Patriotic Gore, his classic study of Civil War literature written in the late 1950s. In that work, Wilson analyzed an 1838 speech Lincoln had given to the Young Men's Lyceum of Springfield, Illinois, in which he had warned of the risks of tyranny that would result from ambitious men seeking to bask in the glory of the Founding Fathers.[91] "The experiment is successful: and thousands have won their deathless names in making it so," Lincoln said of the American Revolution. "But the game is caught; and I believe that it is true that, with the catching, end the pleasures of the chase. This field of glory is harvested, and the crop is already appropriated." The danger, as Lincoln saw it, was that ambition would lead ensuing generations astray. "It thirsts and burns for distinction; and if possible, it will have it, whether at the expense of slaves or enslaving freemen," he said.[92] These remarks have a strangely sad—and prophetic—dimension, and in them some observers have noted an oedipal subtext of a man trying to come to terms with his forefathers.

Though we can grant the legitimacy of much of this work, it is hard not to feel that the psychological approach is a little deflating, suggesting an impoverishment of politics in which any public act can ultimately be reduced to private neurosis. Given the presidential behavior of the 1960s and 1970s, it is easy to see why this approach was compelling. Nevertheless, although such psychobiographical visions of Lincoln represent a real alternative to that of Randall, they do not offer a foundation for the building of a usable past.

Actually, the most compelling recent Lincolns have come not from the academy but from popular culture: Gore Vidal's Lincoln: A Novel (1984) and William Safire's Freedom: A Novel of Abraham Lincoln and the Civil War (1987), both of which topped the New York Times best-seller list. Of course, the novel is an altogether different cultural form than the biography, though both of these books were composed with an attention to factual detail rare in popular fiction (in addition to a lengthy bibliography, Freedom includes a 150-page "Underbook" where Safire cites the sources he used as the basis for the actions of his characters, distinguishes fact from fiction, and places himself historiographically in the context of Civil War literature). Even though novels and histories are apples and oranges on the structural level, they can function very similarly on an ideological one.

Safire's case is particularly notable in this regard. He is now best known as a New York Times political columnist and linguist, but he also worked as a speech writer in the Nixon White House and has carried the intellectual banner of conservatism for the Republican party through the 1970s and 1980s and into the 1990s. If Ronald Reagan presided over the collapse of the New Deal coalition Franklin Roosevelt had forged, Safire's Lincoln is a perfect foil for the one Sandburg fashioned a half-century before.

One of the most noticeable aspects of this turn to the right is the novel's racial politics. Although Safire is certainly aware of the importance of race— the book's title refers, in part, to Lincoln's steady path toward emancipation —race in Freedom is generally a scaffolding on which white men (and a handful of women) conduct politics. In something of a return to Randall's vision, much of the drama in the novel comes from the way Lincoln holds off "vindictive humanist" radical Republicans and expertly manages the art of the politically possible.[93] It is symptomatic of Freedom that in a novel of nine parts, eight are given titles referring to specific people from whose points of view the narration unfolds, while one part is generically entitled "The Ne-gro," and even that is cluttered with the points of view of whites.

Safire also reveals his politics in other ways. Though the novelistic form gave him the opportunity to take another stance, *Freedom* is a book that looks at the war from the top down; politicians, journalists, and generals do most of the talking. He does assign important roles to women such as Anna Ella Carroll (whom Safire credits with a plan generally given to General Winfield Scott for choking the Confederacy with a blockade) and Rose Greenhow (whose spying was instrumental in Confederate victory at the first battle of Bull Run). However, he has an annoying predilection for imposing romantic liaisons on these people to drive the plot along, as if they cannot be credible or interesting without strong sexual drives. Of course, many men in *Freedom* have sex on their minds, too. But for at least some men—notably Lincoln himself—it is not so central a concern. Whatever his politics, Safire rendered his interpretation with considerable coherence and cogency.

Unlike the ultimate Beltway insider Safire, Vidal has made a career as an intellectual gadfly and political iconoclast. The grandson of Oklahoma sena-tor Thomas Gore, he began his writing career overseas as a GI in World War II and wrote novels such as the international best-seller *The City and the Pillar* (1948) and wrote for Broadway and Hollywood during the 1950s and 1960s. He made unsuccessful bids for Congress in 1961 and the U.S. Senate in 1982, and from 1970 to 1972 he was cochairman of an alternative political organi-zation, the People's Party. However, it has been as the author of celebrated novels constituting his American Chronicle—which besides *Lincoln* includes *Washington, D.C.* (1967), *Burr* (1973), *1876* (1976), *Empire* (1987), and *Hollywood* (1990)—that he has won his greatest fame. Vidal's chronicle represents an alternative U.S. history that animates old monuments—the George Washington of *Burr*, for example, is an overweight Virginia planter whose primary political gift is the ability to look presidential.

But Vidal's characters are not simply stick figures that invert the conven-tional wisdom, or cynical hacks in the dusky light of the imperial presidency. In some cases, his renderings take on a complexity that eludes the best historians. Take, for example, this passage on Mary Todd Lincoln enduring a White House visit from her nemesis, William Herndon:

On the one hand, Mary resented Herndon's presence, no matter how brief, in their splendid new life; but on the other, she had to be grateful for anyone who would distract her husband, even for a moment, from what she was only just beginning to realize was a burden beyond any one man to bear, much less the high-strung melancholic, Richard the Second sort of man she had married, a fragile creature who seemed to be living off some inner source of energy unknown to her even as it, literally, consumed him before her eyes. Mary somewhat softened . . . producing a smile [for Herndon]. There was no sacrifice she would not make for her husband, who had made—and would be obliged to keep making, she thought, glumly—so many for her.[94]

Here is the traditional "difficult" Mary Todd Lincoln, but a remarkably textured one—loving, wise, jealous, aware of her limitations as well as those of her husband. This passage also offers a fascinating glimpse of the enigmatic Lincoln from a different perspective than that in which he is commonly seen. In fact, one of Vidal's signal—and best—strategies in this novel is to show Lincoln from a number of points of view (the rival-turned-ally William Seward; the continually rivalrous Salmon P. Chase and his daughter Kate; the bloodthirsty John Wilkes Booth) without ever presuming to enter the president's own mind. The resulting composite portrait is revealing but elusive, informative but contradictory, just like Lincoln himself. Sandburg himself used precisely the same strategy, albeit in a much more windy style.

In other ways, Vidal's approach resembles Safire's. It is striking that in the cynical aftermath of Watergate, the Great White Father of Sandburg has been replaced by consummate political insiders on the left and the right. Vidal also generally has a top-down approach like that of Safire, but his canvas is a little broader. His cast of characters includes assassination conspirator David Herold, with all the resentment and indifference a working-class white youth would have toward Northern elites contemptibly ignorant of the daily mechanics of slavery. And though there are few black characters, the pictures Vidal does give are nuanced. The novel opens, for example, with an irritated congressman who issues a brusque command to a black coachman. "I hear you sir," the driver replies, as "white teeth were quickly bared and unbared in the black, cold-puckered face."[95] Accommodation, resistance, and inscrutability are conveyed in a phrase.

Vidal's Lincoln is racist. Many of the usual qualifications are there—the relative mildness of Lincoln's belief in white supremacy, his fundamental compassion toward all people—but Vidal's Lincoln appears foolish in his efforts to persuade African Americans to adopt his scheme for blacks to colonize Africa or South America. "If intelligent educated men such as yourselves won't go, then how will the former slaves manage to organize themselves?" he asks a delegation at the White House. "Well, Mr. President," comes the reply, "for three centuries they have done a fine job of supporting themselves and their masters, so I think we can assume that if they are not obligated to sustain a white population in luxury, they will be able to look after themselves nicely."[96] Vidal has Lincoln clinging to the belief that colonization was possible as late as 1865, an unproved, but not disproved, assertion.

On the whole, however, Vidal's Lincoln gets a positive assessment, even in race relations. As the author explained four years later, "Since the race war goes on as fiercely as ever in this country, I think candor about blacks and whites and racism is necessary. It was part of Lincoln's greatness that, unlike those absolute abolitionists, the Radical Republicans, he foresaw a long and ugly confrontation, and tried to spare future generations by geographically separating the races. The fact that his plan was not only impractical but inadvertently cruel is beside the point. He wanted to do something; and he never let go of the subject."[97] Compared to his renditions of Thomas Jefferson or Theodore Roosevelt, Vidal's portrayal of Lincoln is downright charitable. However, the air of caustic amusement that marks so much of his writing, amusement that shades into condescension and even contempt for U.S. politics, makes one wonder how much confidence he actually has in democracy. Nonetheless, his and Safire's fluid writing style and the seriousness and self-consciousness with which they interpret Lincoln pose an impressive challenge to the academy's generally unquestioned hold on the mantle of interpretive legitimacy. In that regard, they provide a model for those who wish to fashion credible history in the domain of popular culture.

Meanwhile, in academe, no full-scale Lincoln biography has been published for about twenty years. The influential writings to emerge in this period—James McPherson's "Abraham Lincoln and the Second American Revolution" (1986/90)[98] and Garry Wills's widely acclaimed *Lincoln at Gettysburg: Words That Remade America* (1992)—have stressed the revolutionary character of his presidential thought, specifically, the prominent role of the Declaration of Independence in shaping Lincoln's rhetoric and behavior. This amounts to an emphatic rejection of Randall's view. Wills in particular notes the powerful egalitarian ramifications of the Gettysburg Address and its ongoing impact in the United States.[99] In his brief one-volume biography *The Last Best Hope on Earth* (1993), Mark Neely offers an implicit dissent to this view, emphasizing the degree to which the sixteenth president was an "arch-capitalist" who reluctantly expanded the power of the federal government. But this is a quantitative disagreement, not a qualitative one.[100]

With the closing of the twentieth century it seems appropriate to speculate on who the next Lincoln might be. Without denying the value of these recent views, I think of Lincoln as the apostle of government, a man who passionately believed in the collective democratic enterprise as the best means for securing the common good. From his very first campaign, a successful bid for election in the Illinois General Assembly in 1832, he advocated government investment in internal improvements, and for the rest of his career—which included support for public works, land grants to homesteaders, the chartering of state universities, and an unprecedented expansion of the federal government to fight the Civil War—he remained committed to the proposition that good government could make a difference in people's lives.

This was not a naive belief, and Lincoln was well aware of its costs, financial and otherwise. "The best framed and best administered governments are necessarily expensive; while by errors in frame and maladministration most of them are more onerous than they need be, and some of them are very oppressive," he once noted. Nevertheless, he concluded, majoritarian rule, with judicious applications of state power, did more good than harm.[101]

This was, of course, the starting point for Carl Sandburg's ideological conception of Lincoln, a conception that had to cut through the lassitude of Republican rule in the 1920s and the panic of a collapsed economy in the 1930s. There are important parallels between that situation and ours, parallels that can and should be drawn. There are differences, too—our resources are narrower, and a string of failures have engendered an understandable skepticism on the part of voters (or, more pointedly, nonvoters). However, unless we have *some* faith in the ability of democratic government to solve problems, the Great Depression will ultimately seem mild indeed.

Carl Sandburg's Lincoln is dead now. But his example furnishes us with the lineaments of a used past that can be used again.

Chapter 3

Screening the Book

The Civil War of Margaret Mitchell's *Gone with the Wind*

> It is my understanding, and that of my A.P. class at Sacred Heart academy that you feel there are no great female characters in American literature. I feel, however, that Scarlett O'Hara of Margaret Mitchell's *Gone With the Wind*, should be considered for the following reasons. . . .
>
> a letter to literary critic
> Leslie Fiedler[1]

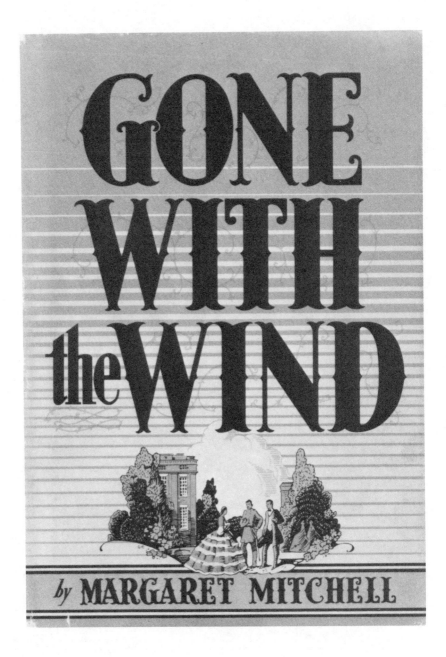

It is possible to imagine a time when *Gone with the Wind*[2] ceases to be a fixture in the firmament of U.S. popular culture. At the end of the twentieth century, however, such a fate does not appear imminent. *Uncle Tom's Cabin*, the most widely read novel of the nineteenth century, remained the supreme work of popular culture in the United States before becoming a relic over the course of the last hundred years, albeit one finding new life in the academy in recent decades. By contrast, *GWTW* (as it is commonly abbreviated) seems to be growing more ubiquitous. The rise of the paperback and the advent of home video have made it possible to pick up the book or movie along with a loaf of bread at the supermarket, and the 1991 publication of Alexandra Ripley's *Scarlett: The Sequel to Margaret Mitchell's Gone with the Wind*—followed by a paperback edition and a television miniseries—virtually ensured an ongoing interest in the original saga. If a shared national culture can be said to exist, *GWTW* would have to be at the heart of it.

Some numbers alone tell a vivid story. An instant best-seller upon publication in June 1936, the novel sold 50,000 copies in one day, a million—at $3 a copy during the middle of the Great Depression—within six months, and an average of 3,700 copies a day for the rest of the year. At least 28 million have been sold since then. The novel has continued to sell roughly 40,000 copies a year, except in years such as 1986 (the book's fiftieth anniversary) and 1991 (the year of the sequel), when it returned to the *New York Times* hardcover best-seller lists. It has been estimated that 90 percent of the U.S. population have seen the movie at least once, and countless people have seen it worldwide.[3]

Indeed, *GWTW* has become an icon of U.S. culture. During the Second World War, the book was banned by the Nazis and was prized by the French Resistance as a symbol of resilience amid occupation. During the trial of China's Gang of Four, it was charged that the book was held up as an example of "people's literature" to be studied instead of Western classics during the Cultural Revolution. The movie was one of two films (the other was *King Kong*) requested by the Hanoi government as part of a friendship-building

A facsimile of the original 1936 cover of Gone with the Wind, *which returned to hardcover best-seller lists for the book's fiftieth anniversary in 1986 and again upon publication of* Scarlett: The Sequel to Margaret Mitchell's Gone with the Wind *in 1991. In its book and film versions, GWTW finally supplanted* Uncle Tom's Cabin *as the defining work of popular culture about the Civil War. (Reproduced with the permission of Macmillan Publishing Company. All rights reserved)*

cultural exchange after the Vietnam War. In Japan, GWTW has been adapted into a long-running all-female musical. In 1990, the movie made its
premiere, after fifty-one years, in Moscow. Media magnate Ted Turner, who
had bought the rights to the movie, told the economically ravaged audience,
"I know the Soviet Union and the Soviet people can do like Scarlett O'Hara
did after the war and build everything better than before."[4]

It seems that in the decades following its appearance, about the only
people besides the Soviets unfamiliar with GWTW were U.S. literary critics.
The novel was not mentioned in standard histories such as *Modern American
Fiction: Essays in Criticism* or even a book such as *American Historical Fiction*.
Other books, such as Edmund Wilson's *Patriotic Gore*, mention it only in
passing and disparagingly.[5]

To be fair, record-breaking sales do not a classic make, though they indi-
cate the presence of *something* worth studying other than accounting records.
In any case, literary interest in the novel has grown considerably since the
1970s (earning an entry, for example, in *The Dictionary of Cultural Literacy*).[6]
This interest resurfaces as the New Criticism canon erodes and the influence
of disciplines such as feminist theory and criticism grows.

Nonetheless, if GWTW has received more attention in literature of late, it
continues, as I have suggested in the introduction to this book, to be overlooked as a work of history. Yet even those who have trouble accepting the
novel on this basis would agree that it is a document of its time. To examine
why this is so, however, an important distinction must be made about a
matter that has been thus far glossed over: GWTW exists in two different
versions.

For most people, GWTW is a movie starring Clark Gable and Vivien
Leigh. Many of those who have seen the movie are aware that GWTW was
first a novel by Margaret Mitchell; relatively few (when one considers that
the television premiere of the movie alone drew 110 million viewers) have
actually read the book. In many ways, the novel and the movie are in accord.
At the same time, however, the technical and cultural demands of the cinematic form required much of the novel to be compressed or omitted. These
changes are highly revealing in what they show about both Mitchell and the
Hollywood culture that interpreted her work for a cinematic audience.

In this chapter I am trying to accomplish three separate, but interrelated,
tasks. The first is to explore Margaret Mitchell's interpretation of the Civil
War in her novel and how it reflected her highly specific milieu as a Southern, white, upper-middle-class woman in the 1920s, when most of the book
was written. For Mitchell, *Gone with the Wind* was a romance of the South.

Certainly, this is an important way of understanding her novel, and it will be central in the biographical sketch that follows. However, there are other ways of looking at the book as well, ways that illustrate how intimately Mitchell's understanding of the war was connected with the cultural currents of the South in the interwar years. I have picked three themes that were important in her time as well as ours: race, class, and gender. The ensuing sections of this chapter will examine the text of the novel more closely to see how Mitchell handles them in her depiction of the days before the Civil War, what happened during it, and the events in the years that followed.

My second objective is to compare Mitchell's vision of the war with that of the movie, using the same three themes. If Mitchell's *GWTW* has an avowedly particular view of the war, producer David Selznick and his collaborators sought a more accessible, general *GWTW* that would appeal to a broad national (and even international) audience. In one sense, the powerful, lasting appeal of the film suggests that Selznick succeeded. But in another sense, the film version of *GWTW* is no less a document of *its* time, reflecting cultural tendencies of the late 1930s and long afterward.

Third, I conclude the chapter with a brief look at the recently published sequel. The popularity of this sequel despite criticism of it leaves room for speculation on the reason for the saga's ongoing popularity and relevance.

A Little Woman Who Wrote a Big Book

> It makes me very happy to know that *Gone with the Wind* is
> helping refute the impression of the South which people
> abroad gained from Mrs. Stowe's book. Here in America
> *Uncle Tom's Cabin* has been long forgotten and there are few
> people today who have read it. They only know it as the
> name of a book which had a good deal to do with the
> bitterness of the Abolition movement.
>
> Margaret Mitchell
> to a fan in Berlin, 1938[7]

As I have discussed, *Uncle Tom's Cabin* was the major work of popular culture in the nineteenth century, disseminating a critical depiction of Southern culture that continued to haunt the region in the decades following the Civil War. No work came close to dislodging Harriet Beecher Stowe's hold on the popular imagination until the turn of the century, when Thomas Dixon's *Leopard's Spots* (1903) and *The Clansman* (1905) became best-sellers, later to burst into lasting notoriety as the basis for D. W. Griffith's *Birth of a Nation* (1915).

It took another "damned female scribbler," in the words of Nathaniel Hawthorne, to replace Stowe's moral indictment with a new master narrative of the Civil War.[8] In some ways, that novel distilled the cultural project Dixon had come to symbolize. His effect on a developing mind can be vividly illustrated in a letter written to Dixon after he had written an admiring note to the new novelist. "I was practically raised on your books, and love them very much," Mitchell wrote, noting that a neighborhood enactment of Dixon's play *The Traitor: A Story of the Fall of the Invisible Empire* (1907) had provided her with a lasting childhood memory:

> The clansmen were recruited from the small-fry of the neighborhood, their ages ranging from five to eight. They were dressed in the shirts of their fathers, with the shirt tails bobbed off. I had my troubles with the clansmen, as, after Act 2, they went on strike, demanding a ten cent wage instead of a five cent one. Then, too, just as I was about to be hanged, two of the clansmen had to go to the bathroom, necessitating a dreadful stage wait which made the audience scream with delight, but which mortified me intensely. My mother was out of town at the time.[9]

Despite—or because of—Mitchell's humor, it is instructive to read about a group of young children staging a lynching. Although there can be no doubt that children today engage in equally macabre forms of play when their mothers are not around, it is unlikely that lynching is the chosen format, for it belongs to another time and place, part of the long foreground of *GWTW*.

If *GWTW* were nothing more than a distillation of the anti-Tom tradition,[10] it would have long since passed into a twilight zone that Dixon—and, for that matter, D. W. Griffith—inhabits, a zone scholars enter for background to write essays on the origins of forms, themes, and ideas we now find familiar when expressed by more well-known people. Though much of the novel *is* a familiar distillation of old ideas, particularly in terms of racial politics that may change form if not content, there must be something else at work that keeps *GWTW* the kind of story that people without undergraduate degrees or postdoctoral fellowships (and some that have college degrees, as well) read or watch in their leisure time. Generally speaking, popular culture is a complex mixture of confirmed and challenged beliefs, familiar and subverted formulas; GWTW is no exception. We can begin to understand this mix by looking at the life of the diminutive woman (she was less than five feet tall) who wrote this very big book.

Debutante, journalist, housewife, novelist, Margaret Munnerlyn Mitchell was born on November 8, 1900, in Atlanta, Georgia.[11] Her family's roots in the South date back to the seventeenth century. Her maternal grandparents refused to leave the city when Union general William Tecumseh Sherman's troops entered Atlanta, and their home was used as an army hospital. Images of the war were vividly transmitted to Mitchell as a child when family and friends—many of them veterans—recalled their experiences. Later, she wryly described those memories: "I heard about the fighting and the wounds and the primitive way they were treated—how ladies nursed in hospitals—the way gangrene smelled—what substitutes were used for food and clothing when the blockade got too tight for these necessities to be brought from abroad. I heard about the burning and looting of Atlanta and the way the refugees crowded the roads and trains to Macon. I heard about everything in the world except that the Confederates lost the war."[12]

Mitchell's father, Eugene, was an attorney who lost a great deal of money in the depression of 1893, and he henceforth regarded maintaining the family's upper-middle-class standard of living as a struggle. According to his son Stephens Mitchell, the depression took from his father "all daring and put in its place a desire to have a competence assured to him."[13]

Mitchell's mother, May Belle, seems to have been a pivotal figure in her daughter's life; an ambivalence toward mothers and motherhood suffuses GWTW. A convent-educated Irish Catholic, May Belle Mitchell was also president of Atlanta's most militant suffrage group. Her political commitments were matched by a sense of social and familial duty, which she sought to transmit to her daughter. The duality between feminist self-assertion and traditional self-abnegation became a crucial tension in the novelist's life and work.[14]

After attending a private school for girls in Atlanta, Mitchell was accepted at Smith College for the fall of 1918. That summer, as the United States sent soldiers to fight in the First World War, she socialized with young men based at nearby Fort McPherson, and she became engaged to a Connecticut poet-soldier before he went overseas. His death in France was the first shock she had to endure in Northampton; the second was the death of her mother, a victim of the worldwide influenza epidemic. Mitchell left Smith in the spring of 1919 a popular and vivacious though not intellectually distinguished student, never to resume her studies.

Eugene Mitchell was shattered by the death of his wife, and his daughter's return to Atlanta represented her ascension to adult responsibility for her father and the family household. At the same time, however, she submitted to pressure from him and her maternal grandmother to make a formal debut in Atlanta society so as not to ruin her marital chances. She was approved for membership in the city's elite Debutante Club for the 1920–21 season and was poised to enter proper Atlanta society.

But not quite. Although Mitchell quickly made friends with other debutantes and attended a whirl of parties at country clubs, she showed signs of rebelling against the role into which she was being cast. Some of these signs suggest a lingering tomboy style. Others, such as Mitchell's smoking and occasional drinking, reflect an adoption of a flapper persona. She also attended a ball with a Valentino-styled escort, wore a suggestive Apache costume, and danced with shrieks of simulated passion. In response, Mitchell was pointedly overlooked when it came time to invite debutantes to join the Junior League, the symbol of social distinction of Atlanta society. (She later exacted revenge when she pointedly declined to attend the Junior League ball held to celebrate the world premiere of the movie *Gone with the Wind*.)

The conflicting tensions in Mitchell's life coalesced in her relationship with a man who haunted her the rest of her life: Berrien "Red" Upshaw. Upshaw came from a respectable Georgia family, but there was an air of scandal about him. He twice "voluntarily resigned" from the U.S. Naval Academy in Annapolis, and after his parents cut him off financially, he was apparently able to support himself at the University of Georgia by bootlegging. Despite vigorous opposition from her family and friends, the two married in 1922.

Upshaw's best man was his roommate John Marsh, a quiet, retiring, World War I veteran who stood in sharp contrast to his rakish friend. Marsh had also made an unassuming bid for Mitchell's affections, but after her engagement to Upshaw, he accepted a role as trusted friend to bride and groom. When the marriage got off to a rocky start on the honeymoon and remained tense after the couple decided to live in her father's house, Marsh served as a middleman arranging for conciliation. After fights over money, Upshaw's drinking, and his lack of a steady job, the two agreed to a divorce, and Upshaw abruptly left Mitchell. Occasionally he returned: most notably a few months later, when he found Mitchell alone in her house and assaulted her so brutally that she required weeks to recover. Upshaw died after leaping from a fifth-story window of a Texas hotel in 1949, seven months before Mitchell's own death.

In the months following the failure of her marriage, Mitchell and Marsh grew increasingly close. Lacking financial support from Upshaw, and reluctant to depend on her father, Mitchell landed a job, possibly through family connections, at the *Atlanta Journal* as a feature writer for the paper's Sunday magazine.[15] Between 1922 and 1926 she wrote 129 signed articles, ranging from an interview with Rudolph Valentino to a series on Georgia's Confederate generals. In 1925 she married Marsh and left her father's home for an apartment in downtown Atlanta.

It was around this time, at Marsh's urging, that she began focusing on fiction writing. Injuries and ailments of the kind that plagued her and Marsh for the rest of their lives led her to quit the paper, and Marsh's job as a publicist for the Georgia Power Company provided some financial stability. Mitchell had long been a short-story writer, but during the mid-1920s she wrote her first major work, a novella about a decaying Southern family (it has since been lost). She also began *Gone with the Wind.*

Many observers of Margaret Mitchell's development note her Southern background, flapper youth, and journalistic experience. Fewer have noted that Mitchell began writing *GWTW* at the very moment that the Southern literary renaissance burst into full flower. In the late 1920s and early 1930s, a brilliant array of writers gained national attention—and judging from Mitchell's later correspondence, Mitchell's attention as well. Robert Penn Warren, Alan Tate, Stark Young, and, of course, William Faulkner all arrived on the scene, crisscrossing poetry, fiction, criticism, and history. Nor were all these literary lights men. Evelyn Scott's book *The Wave* (1929) brought modernist experimentation to the Civil War novel, and Frances Newman gained attention with witty, epigrammatic novels such as *The Hard-Boiled Virgin* (1926) and *Dead Lovers Are Faithful Lovers* (1928). At the same time, slightly older figures such as James Branch Cabell and Ellen Glasgow served as intellectual godparents for these new arrivals, and other mavericks such as W. J. Cash and Lillian Smith were not far behind.[16]

Mitchell held her own ambitions firmly in check for quite some time. She had essentially written a draft of *GWTW* by 1929, and although family and friends were aware she was doing *something* at home, no one was aware of the scope of her work (she kept her typewriter and manuscript covered with a bath towel and called her writing "therapy for my leg").[17] In 1935 a friend in publishing told Macmillan editor Harold Latham, who was going South to scout for talent, about Mitchell's novel; he sought her out but was persistently refused a look at the manuscript. It was only when an acquaintance expressed surprise that she was "the type who would write a novel" and suggested she "lacked the seriousness necessary to be a novelist"[18] that an indignant Mitchell chased down Latham and gave him a copy of the manuscript just as he was about to leave the city.

This, of course, set off a chain of events that made Mitchell a literary giant, even though she never wrote another book. She also became sickly, defensive, and fanatical about protecting her foreign rights until she was hit by a car and killed in 1949. GWTW became the best-selling novel in U.S. history and set off a scramble for the rights and roles for a movie. David Selznick of Selznick International emerged the master of this melee, paying $50,000 to Mitchell for movie rights—the highest sum paid any novelist, and one of the best investments in film history—and spending the next three years choreographing the project in his inimitable (if overbearing) style. When he finished, the parochial vision of one Southern woman completed its transformation from an impressively popular work of regionalism to a massively popular, worldwide symbol of U.S. culture.

Color Lines

> Freedom became a never-ending picnic, a barbecue every
> day of the week, a carnival of idleness and theft and
> insolence. Country negroes flocked into the cities, leaving
> the rural districts without labor to make the crops. Atlanta
> was crowded with them and still they came by the hundreds,
> lazy and dangerous as a result of the new doctrines being
> taught them. Packed into squalid cabins, smallpox, typhoid
> and tuberculosis broke out among them. . . . Relying upon
> their masters in the old days to care for their aged and their
> babies, they now had no sense of responsibility for their
> helpless. And the [Freedmen's] Bureau was far too interested
> in political matters to provide the care plantation owners
> had once given.
>
> Gone with the Wind, p. 655

The question of audience confronts every writer, and generally speaking, the most successful ones have a clear sense for whom they are writing. Margaret Mitchell was no exception. Although she often expressed gratitude for her global audience, she wrote first and foremost for white Southerners: not all white Southerners, but those she considered everyday, ordinary Southerners, the kind who wrote her letters telling her how much they liked the book and to whom she wrote back replies by the thousands. Though Mitchell was flattered by the seriousness with which *GWTW* was regarded by reviewers (to whom she also wrote grateful letters), she seemed neither surprised nor troubled by those intellectuals, particularly leftists, who challenged her portrait of the Old South.[19] "I would be hurt and mortified if the Left Wingers liked the book," she wrote in a 1936 letter to Stark Young, whose novel *So Red the Rose* (1934) she greatly admired. "I'd have to do so much explaining to family and friends if the aesthetes and radicals liked it."[20]

Mitchell was modest, even self-deprecating, about her work, but she had very clear standards by which to measure herself. She sought to write a book "with precious little obscenity in it, no adultery, and not a single degenerate."[21] She saw herself as lacking literary style but liked to consider that an asset; indeed, there is a clarity to her prose that suggests careful pruning.

Above all, Mitchell wanted her book to be accurate. Like Carl Sandburg, who was at this time toiling away at *Abraham Lincoln: The War Years*, Mitchell was a prodigious researcher who carefully confirmed her facts as she revised the novel in the 1930s. "I knew the history in my tale was as watertight and air proof as ten years of study and a lifetime of listening to participants would make it," she wrote to Henry Steele Commager after the historian's positive review in the *New York Herald Tribune*.[22] From the slightest of variations of dialect between her African American characters to the actual weather during the siege of Atlanta, she painstakingly strove to recreate the past by means of total immersion in her sources. The irony is that like Sandburg, she took the facts and used them to make myth. She was writing fiction and Sandburg was writing nonfiction; she was a Southerner and he was a Northerner; he was in many ways progressive while she was in many ways reactionary. Still, the two provide case studies not only of the documentary impulse of the 1930s in action, but also the way in which that presumably "objective" sensibility could be used in highly charged ways.

The most charged aspect of Mitchell's vision concerned race. "I do not need to tell you how I and all my folks feel about Negroes," she wrote in a 1939 letter to a friend in Hollywood who had been hired as a historical consultant for the movie. "I had and have no intention of insulting the race." She went on to explain what presumably needed no explaining: "We've always fought for colored education, and, even when John and I were at our worst financially, we were helping keep colored children in schools, furnishing clothes and carfare, and oh, the terrible hours when I had to help with homework which dealt in fractions. I have paid for medical care and done the nursing myself on many occasions; all of us have fought in the law courts and paid fines. Well, you know what I mean, you and your people have done the same thing."[23]

In the context of the white Southern intellectual community, Mitchell was more liberal than many of her peers and said she found "Professional Southerners" as irritating as "Professional Negroes."[24] On one level, she was undoubtedly sincere when she claimed her relations with the African American community were good. And why not? The able assistance of her various cooks, housekeepers, and laundresses hired over the course of the 1920s and 1930s gave her the free time necessary to write *GWTW*. Fundamentally, however, her novel betrays not only a strong streak of paternalistic condescension, but also an overt sense of hostility that at times became visceral.

One glimpses this hostility in the offhand descriptions of Mitchell's African American characters, even those she considers "good." In many cases, she engages in an inverted anthropomorphism, whereby human beings are described as animals. Although she does this with white characters, too (see the description of the Wilkeses as horses in the next section, as one of a number of such examples), there is a more malignant resonance in her descriptions of blacks. Hence lines such as "Jeems was their [the Tarleton Twins'] body servant, and, like the dogs, accompanied them everywhere" (p. 10). When Scarlett runs into Big Sam, the former overseer at Tara, his "huge black paws" embrace his mistress, and he and his comrades "caper . . . with delight" at being able to show off their master (p. 307). And when Scarlett ventures into Shantytown, her attacker is "a squat black negro with shoulders and chest like a gorilla" (p. 787).

Nor is this creation of a biological hierarchy limited to men. Mammy, presumably one of the most positive characters in the novel, is described as having "the uncomprehending sadness of a monkey's face" (p. 415), and at the end of the book, her face is puckered "in the sad devilment of an old ape" (p. 991). The most dignified slave in the book is Dilcey, whose "Indian blood was plain in her features, overbalancing the negroid characteristics" (p. 62). Mammy, by contrast, is "pure African" (p. 23)—a detail that also informs the reader that there is no messy miscegenation involved here.

Within the structure of Mitchell's fictional world, Mammy's blackness is more important than her gender. Although her very name and "broad bosom" (p. 1037) signify motherhood, her African fallibility takes over at crucial moments in the text, such as her ineffectuality at Tara after the fall of Atlanta or her departure from Scarlett at the end of the book. Perhaps the best example of this weakness is revealed a little earlier, when she tearfully confesses to Rhett that she is responsible for his daughter Bonnie's fear of the dark. "Ah tells her dar's ghos'es an' buggerboos in de dahk," she explains (p. 996). One imagines we are to believe that the "natural" superstitiousness of African

Americans makes Mammy's ghost story all the more compelling to a young child. Even Mammy's otherwise considerable maternal wisdom is explained more in terms of race than gender. The reader is told that unlike Scarlett's biological mother, Ellen, Mammy is "under no illusions" about her calculating "chile" (p. 59); the reason for this seems to be the same "unerring African instinct" that allows the field hands to accurately measure the warmth behind Gerald O'Hara's bluster and thus take "shameless advantage of him" (p. 51).

Similarly, Mammy's race seems to disqualify her from any kind of sexuality. She mothers without giving birth, runs a household without being married. The only person remotely able to see her as a woman is Rhett, who brings her back a stiff red petticoat after his honeymoon with Scarlett—and playfully demands to see it when her skepticism of him finally breaks down and she wears it. Indeed, Rhett's respect for her seems to transcend both race and gender (though it is hard to imagine him interacting with her as a potential marriage partner or even as a social equal). Such exceptions remind one that the racial order of *Gone with the Wind* is not completely airtight. It also reminds one that this order is complicated: Mammy is clearly in a class by herself, and Mitchell went to great pains to allude to the subtle gradations between house slaves and field hands; coastal slaves from large plantations and up-country slaves with slightly different accents; country slaves such as Mammy and city ones such as Miss Pittypat's Uncle Peter.

Nevertheless, these details are drawn on a canvas that includes plenty of broad, condescending strokes. "Negroes were provoking sometimes and stupid and lazy," thinks Scarlett, "but there was loyalty in them that money couldn't buy" (p. 472). Mitchell also drew on the moral authority of Melanie, the epitome of virtue in the novel, to assert the benevolence of the slave order. "All this talk about the militia staying here to keep the darkies from rising," Melanie says during the Confederate high tide of 1862. "Why, it's the silliest thing I ever heard of. Why should our people rise?" (p. 177).

There is a striking duality in the commonly used Southern phrase "our people," which here implies a familial sense of closeness—and a sense of property ownership. The Civil War wrought the destruction of at least the literal "our," and there is a rich vein of writings, notably those of Mary Boykin Chesnut, that vividly evoke the responses that result from this revolution in the social order.[25]

Mitchell's protagonist Scarlett O'Hara becomes a compendium of responses to this revolution during and after the war. One response was exasperation. Amid the lies and failures of her slave Prissy during Melanie's childbirth and the siege of Atlanta, Scarlett declares, "And the Yankees wanted to free the negroes! Well, the Yankees were welcome to them" (p. 371). Another response to the new order was denial: "It did not enter Scarlett's mind that he [Sam] was free. He still belonged to her, like Pork and Mammy and Peter and Cookie and Prissy. He was still 'one of our family' and, as such, must be protected" (pp. 782–83). Nor is Scarlett the only one indulging in such fantasies. The only time Mammy mentions she is free is when she insists on accompanying Scarlett on her schemes to marry Frank Kennedy or is speaking her mind regarding Scarlett's marriage to Rhett—in effect, asserting her freedom to keep on serving her "former" mistress.

In addition to frustration and denial was another response: fury. Walking the streets of Atlanta after the war, Scarlett fumes that she would like to have all the "insolent" negroes "whipped until the blood ran down their backs. What devils the Yankees were to set them free, free to jeer at white people!" (p. 589). At times, such thoughts lead to action. During the siege of the city, for example, Scarlett slaps Prissy, striking a slave for the first time in her life. In this case, at least, the identification between author and character is clear. "When Scarlett slapped her, it was really Margaret Mitchell yielding to an overwhelming urge," Mitchell wrote to an Alabama reader in 1936.[26] Indeed, one could argue that the very creation of Prissy was an assault on African Americans—so powerfully humiliating a character was she that the young Malcolm X, viewing the movie in small-town Michigan, "felt like crawling under the rug" as he was watching her.[27]

Violence is the particular province of the Ku Klux Klan. As the narrator explains in a chapter that outlines the outrages of Reconstruction, "The negroes were on top and behind them were the Yankee bayonets. She could be killed, she could be raped and, very probably, nothing would ever be done about it" (p. 648). Under such circumstances, Scarlett, who has generally been indifferent or irritated by the war and its consequences, "fell to trembling and, for the first time in her life, . . . saw clearly that Scarlett O'Hara, frightened and helpless, was not all that mattered. There were thousands of women like her, all over the South, who were frightened and helpless. And thousands of men, who had laid down their arms at Appomattox, had taken them up again and stood ready to risk their necks on a minute's notice to protect those women" (p. 648).

Scarlett's itch for money and control of her lumber mill ultimately overrides this fear and sisterhood, and she makes an unaccompanied ride through Shantytown. She pays for this transgression by being stopped by a white man, who orders a black man to attack her—a perfect allegory of the white Southern belief that Northerners controlled new freedmen. Only the arrival of the faithful Big Sam on the scene a moment later saves her. Unhurt but shaken, she is appalled when her husband Frank leaves her to go to "a political meeting." When Scarlett later learns that the "political meeting" is really a Klan ride, she is fearful:

> "The Klan!" she almost screamed it. "Ashley isn't in the Klan! Frank can't be! Oh, he promised me!"
> "Of course, Mr. Kennedy is in the Klan and Ashley, too, and all the men we know," cried [Ashley's sister] India. "They are men, aren't they? And white men and Southerners. You should have been proud of him instead of making him sneak out as though it were something shameful." (p. 798)

Even Rhett, who is hardly India's idea of a gentleman, performs violence in the name of white womanhood. After being released from jail on murder and other charges, he confirms a widely held suspicion: "I did kill [a] nigger. He was uppity to a lady, and what else could a Southern gentleman do?" (p. 623).

In the final analysis, however, neither Scarlett nor Rhett approves of the Klan, although the reason for this has nothing to do with morality. Scarlett sees the Klan as bad for business and likely to harden Yankee occupation, and Rhett agrees. At the end of the book, he tells Scarlett that he and Ashley joined forces to disband it. He explains, "We decided that it did more harm than good because it just kept the Yankees stirred up and furnished more grist for the slander mill of his excellency, [Occupation] Governor Bullock. He knows he can stay in power just so long as he can convince the Federal government and the Yankee newspapers that Georgia is seething with rebellion and there's a Klansman hiding behind every bush. . . . But he's shooting at a nonexistent target and he knows it" (p. 981).

Whatever may have become of the Klan in the 1870s and 1880s, it was very much on the rise during World War I and the 1920s, sparked at least to some extent by the phenomenal popularity of *Birth of a Nation*. Atlanta at this time was "the imperial city of the Invisible Empire," which ran a national office literally down the road from where Mitchell lived. In 1923, Georgia's governor, one of its senators, and a state supreme court judge had Klan ties; so did Atlanta's mayor. In addition to espousing antiblack views, the Klan by this point was also strongly antiethnic and anti-Catholic. Mitchell had rejected her mother's religion, but like Judaism—which the Klan also attacked—Catholicism tended to be an identity to which one was born, an ineradicable stain.[28]

Nevertheless, Mitchell's opinion of the organization remained positive. As she explained to a Minnesota reader of her novel:

> One of the earliest purposes of the Klan was to protect women and children. Later it was used to keep the Negroes from voting eight or ten times at every election. But it was used equally against the Carpetbaggers who had the same bad habit where voting was concerned. Members of the Klan knew that if unscrupulous or ignorant people were permitted to hold office in the South the lives and property would not be safe . . . practically any history of South Carolina or biography of General Wade Hampton will give you an excellent idea as to why the Klan did not want Negroes on Judges' benches or in the governor's chair.[29]

In one sense, Mitchell was right: As I have suggested at the end of Chapter 1, practically any history of Reconstruction at the time, inside the academy or outside it, *did* describe Reconstruction as a never-ending picnic for African Americans. Some dissident voices, notably W. E. B. Du Bois, whose *Black Reconstruction*[30] is now considered a classic in the field, were beginning to speak. However, they were not widely heard for another twenty-five years. Mitchell professed not to hear them. "As I had not written anything on the Klan which is not common knowledge to every Southerner, I had done no research upon it," she wrote.[31]

In short, Mitchell made slaveholding whites the true victims of the Civil War. In her rendition, the South was hounded by fanatics, cornered into defending a way of life, overrun by alien invaders, and forced to endure a harsh (and ridiculous) occupation. Some strong individuals did survive these outrages, occasionally relying on less-than-genteel means to achieve this end. If African Americans were not exactly the cause of war, and if some really meant well, they nevertheless aggravated the problems facing people such as the O'Haras—and, one infers, their heirs. Mitchell was not the only person to make this case in the 1920s and 1930s.[32] However, she made it very compellingly at a time when racial questions were beginning their long ascent to the top of the national agenda, culminating in the Civil Rights movement.

The making of the film version of *Gone with the Wind* is an epic in itself, and by any Hollywood conventional wisdom then or since it should have been a colossal failure. The three tortured years it took to bring the novel to the screen; fights over casting and the byzantine complexity of deals with other studios to contract the stars; the number of directors who handled the project (three, two of whom worked simultaneously); conflicts between actors and directors, directors and the producer: All augured disaster.

Above all, there was the script—or, more accurately, the lack of one. Paring the novel down to a workable size proved extremely difficult, particularly for the demanding Selznick, and despite a number of attempts to entice her, Mitchell categorically refused to have anything to do with it. As she explained to screenwriter Sidney Howard:

> If I even so much as looked over the script, without passing judgement on it, and there was some small item in the finished production that incensed or annoyed the people of this section, then I'd get the blame for it. Southerners have been wonderful to my book and I am grateful indeed that they like it and are interested in the forthcoming picture. Not for worlds or for money would I put myself in the position where if there was something they didn't like in the picture, they could say, "Well, you worked on the script. Why did you let this that or the other get by?" I would never live it down. [33]

Such an attitude exasperated Selznick, but it also gave him opportunities. Mitchell's abdication gave him a freer rein than he might otherwise have had, and although he thought it important to remain faithful to the original text, internal and external pressures led him to make many subtle but significant changes.

To a great extent, Howard shaped the final product. His first draft of the screenplay compressed Mitchell's novel into four hundred pages, and although he did not finish the project (having other work and, one suspects, enough of David O. Selznick), his version became the slab at which subsequent writers chipped away to sculpt the final draft. Howard ultimately received the sole screenwriting credit, in part for sentimental reasons: He died shortly before the film's premiere. [34]

But in January 1939, with filming under way, there was still no final text from which actors could work. Seventeen writers had tried their hand at it (including F. Scott Fitzgerald, in the gray twilight of his career), all failing to satisfy Selznick. [35] In desperation, he called in playwright Ben Hecht for the second time on *GWTW*. Hecht had never read the book, so Selznick and (second) director Victor Fleming acted out the whole story while Hecht typed away, trying to forge the rewrites, revisions, and notes into a coherent script. Although proponents of the auteur theory could plausibly argue that Selznick remained the artistic locus of the movie, imagining this scene be-

tween the three men suggests how collaborative a process moviemaking is
even on the most fundamental level. Similarly, imagining the secret Sunday
afternoon sessions between fired director George Cukor and the female
leads—Cukor had a reputation as a "woman's director"—suggests how much
unofficial collaboration takes place as well.[36]

Although some of the changes that were made in this group effort from
1937 to 1939 simply reflect the process of adapting the novel for the screen,
others were part of a conscious effort to rework the ideology of Mitchell's
novel. Nowhere was this more true than on the subject of race: "Common
knowledge to every Southerner" was not common knowledge everywhere
else. Clearly, Mitchell's Minnesota reader and many others were taught—
and believed—a Confederate view of the war. The filmmakers of GWTW
feared that this angle would get in the way of the romance they sought to
produce for mass consumption at a time of less-than-complete national
homogenization.

They had reason to be concerned. The lingering controversy over Birth of a
Nation—though widely hailed across the country, the film had also drawn
protest from the African American community and a segment of the white
audience—offered an object lesson in racial politics. The liberal climate
surrounding Franklin Delano Roosevelt's reelection in 1936 was also a factor.
"In our picture I think we have to be awfully careful that the negroes come
out decidedly on the right side of the ledger," Selznick wrote to Howard.[37]

At times, this effort dovetailed with the demands of the medium. Movies
generally do not have omniscient narrators, so there could be no descriptions
comparing slaves to dogs, bears, or monkeys. Similarly, movies are not particularly well adapted to the kind of exposition Mitchell used to explain the
intricacies of postwar Reconstruction and the rise of a "Redeemer" government in Georgia. The movie's version of this chapter of history is compressed
into the speech of an unnamed carpetbagger:

ORATOR: Do you know what we're going to do?
AD LIB: What?
ORATOR: We're going to give every one of you forty acres and a mule.
NEGRO: An' a mule?
ORATOR: Forty acres and a mule . . .
NEGRO: Gee-ee!
ORATOR: . . . Because we're your friends and you're going to become
     voters—and you're going to vote like your friends do.[38]

In this exchange, Reconstruction emerges as the cynical exploitation of ignorant African Americans by unscrupulous schemers—a story echoing the dominant view of the period. But the stridency of fanatical abolitionists or the monstrousness of African Americans in power, staples of the dominant view, are not depicted. Clearly, this is not the most benevolent picture of Reconstruction, but just as clearly, it is more muted than Mitchell's.

The script softens the novel's racial politics in a number of other ways, too. The Klan is not mentioned as such, and "the political meeting" Frank, Ashley, and others attend is never described as anything but an isolated act of retribution for the wrong done to one woman. No mention is made of Rhett's killing of a black man. And the attack on Scarlett is not made by an African American—rather, the roles get reversed and it is the white man who attacks her while the black man observes it. Mammy never makes the mistake of making Bonnie afraid of the dark; instead, she expresses reservations about the way Bonnie rides her horse—a statement that suggests prescience, as the child later dies from her recklessness in riding it.

In addition to changes in the script, there were also revisions made in the film after the shooting was finished. Scarlett's tongue-lashing of her sisters in the cotton patch at Tara originally included Mammy and Prissy; they were edited out. So was a shot of Prissy eating watermelon (though one where she cuts it was left in).[39]

None of this is meant to suggest that the filmmakers' version of GWTW represents the triumph of enlightenment over the novel. Indeed, without outside intervention the movie might have been more racist than it was. Howard's version of the screenplay, for example, retained the term nigger, and Selznick resisted removing it until pressure from the Production Code Administration and the African American press led him to yield in the winter of 1939 (a decision he later regretted).[40] Indeed, too much attention on changes that were made can obscure the extent to which Mitchell's vision prevailed.

For the changes that were made, the role of African Americans was crucial. Selznick conferred with Walter White and Roy Wilkins of the National Association for the Advancement of Colored People (NAACP) during production of the movie, though he did not, as they suggested, hire an African American consultant. Leon Washington, publisher of the Los Angeles Sentinel, wrote an editorial—"Hollywood Goes Hitler One Better"—that helped Selznick change his mind on the "nigger" issue. Selznick, who was Jewish, often pointed out that he, too, was a member of an oppressed people, and it seems that appeals to his conscience worked in some cases if not others (he apparently submitted to pressure, for example, to keep the black stars from attending the Atlanta premiere).[41] On the set, Hattie McDaniel (Mammy) and Butterfly McQueen (Prissy) emphatically stated their displeasure with some scenes, but although they felt uneasiness with their respective roles, their presence in the movie represented important economic and cultural gains for African American actors; McDaniel became the first African American to win an Academy Award. Blacks hardly spoke with one voice—the NAACP tacitly endorsed the final product, whereas William Patterson of the *Chicago Defender* led a picket line over it—but on the whole, they forged a coalition that shifted the terrain of the movie slightly toward a better view of African Americans.[42]

Indeed, the term *coalition* is crucial. In terms of race it is possible to speak symbolically of the film *Gone with the Wind* as a New Deal document. By this I do not mean that anything in the movie explicitly endorses specific elements of that political program; nor did it, as Carl Sandburg's work did, function as an ideological justification for the New Deal. But the film does reflect a larger pattern of interest-group cultural politics that emerged in the 1930s, where disparate collections of people and perspectives forged a working consensus.[43] As such, *GWTW* represents a middle ground between Mitchellesque and (Eleanor) Rooseveltian[44] views of race relations during and since the Civil War. By whites, that is. Although African Americans were able to moderate the movie's views, they had little power in creating it. To be sure, there was plenty of ground on either side of the Roosevelt/Mitchell boundaries, and what constituted a middle ground changed in the future. If nothing else, however, the movie suggests what became an enduring Hollywood ability to repackage particularistic cultural visions for national—and even international—consumption.

Class Acts

In them [the Wilkeses] there was no such conflict as frequently raged in Scarlett's bosom where the blood of a soft-voiced, overbred Coast aristocrat mingled with the shrewd, earthy blood of an Irish peasant.

Gone with the Wind, p. 87

In the world of Scarlett O'Hara—and in the world of Margaret Mitchell—the term *class* connoted not simply one's occupation and income, but also a cluster of attributes that included ethnicity and religion and one's social position in the country or city. As with race relations, the Civil War marked a watershed in class structure in the United States, North and South. Margaret Mitchell paid considerable attention to Southern class dynamics in *GWTW*, but her careful shadings did not transfer to celluloid: To usefully oversimplify, a colorful book became a black and white movie.

Primarily, what is missing from the movie is the sense of a middle class within Southern society. At the beginning of the novel, this class is embodied in the figure of Scarlett's father, Gerald O'Hara. "Gerald had come to America from Ireland when he was twenty-one," the narrator explains (p. 42). "He had come hastily, as many a better and worse Irishman before and since, with the clothes he had on his back, two shillings above his passage money and a price on his head that he felt was larger than his misdeed warranted." (He had killed a rent agent in a quarrel.) After working for his brothers, who had emigrated previously to Savannah to start a business as merchants, he won his first slave and a run-down plantation, to be called Tara, in a poker game. With a loan from his brothers, the goodwill of his neighbors, and a growing work force of slaves, he became a "self-made" man. In Gerald O'Hara one finds a working model of the mythic American Dream that unites the South with the rest of the nation.[45]

Still, despite his mobility, Gerald stands out for his accent, his religion, and his general coarseness. One of the primary reasons for his success is that he settles in the red clay hills of northern Georgia, away from the coastal aristocracy. His adopted home also has an elite, symbolized by Twelve Oaks and the Wilkes family, but it is a more forgiving one. Thus, the small farmer Able Wynder can be elected second lieutenant of the troop that forms near Tara when war breaks out. Gerald also can be accepted for who he is: "When Mrs. Wilkes, 'a great lady with a rare gift for silence,' as Gerald characterized her, told her husband one evening, after Gerald's horse had pounded down the driveway, 'He has a rough tongue, but he is a gentleman,' Gerald had definitely arrived" (p. 50).

Well, almost. For Gerald has not yet married, and "no family wanted a daughter to wed a man about whose grandfather nothing was known" (p. 52). But he once again enjoys good fortune in asking for the hand of the elegant Savannah resident Ellen Robillard immediately after her failed romance. She agrees to marry a man she does not really love (foreshadowing the fate of her daughter) and serves him dutifully without his ever really knowing the difference.

Scarlett O'Hara, then, is a hybrid of Huguenot nobility and Celtic energy. However, as Mitchell made abundantly clear, although Scarlett strives to be like her mother, she is very much her father's daughter. And this, as the course of the story demonstrates, is her principal asset in life. Charlestonian Rhett Butler, who retains many of the prejudices from the background he rejects, later dismisses her father as "a smart Mick on the make" (p. 902), but it is also clear that his love for Scarlett stems from her Irish inheritance.

Like many an assimilated American before and since, Gerald prizes his ethnicity. Confident in his own identity, "he entertained the liveliest respect for those who had more book learning than he [but] he never felt his own lack" (p. 44). Thus, when trying to counsel the heartbroken Scarlett—who, in zenlike fashion, longs for Ashley, whose burnished character is so unlike her own—Gerald explains that although he likes the Wilkeses, a match between the two families would be a poor one: "I tell you they're born queer. Look at the way they go tearing up to New York and Boston to hear operas and see oil paintings. And ordering French and German books by the crate from the Yankees! And there they sit reading and dreaming the dear God knows what, when they'd be better spending their time hunting and playing poker as proper men should" (p. 35). The evisceration of the elite is put even more succinctly (and prophetically) by the vigorous Beatrice Tarleton, whose economic station in life is similar to Gerald's: "Now, don't misunderstand me. The Wilkes are fine folks in their way, and you know I'm fond of them all, but be frank! They are overbred and inbred too, aren't they? They'll do fine on a dry track, a fast track, but mark my words, I don't believe the Wilkes can run on a mud track. I believe the stamina has been bred out of them, and when the emergency arises I don't believe they can run against the odds. Dry-weather stock. Give me a big horse who can run in any weather!" (p. 89).

If the richest landowners are unsatisfactory in this vision of the class order, so too are those below the O'Haras and Tarletons. Indeed, the most common epithet in the novel is "white trash"; trash is so rich a term, in fact, that even slaves such as Mammy use it to describe fellow African Americans they dislike (such as those who run away). The key figures here are the Slatterys, "a rabbity-looking brood" who, although they own land, fail to improve their holdings the way Gerald does. Over the course of the novel, the Slatterys create many of Scarlett's problems. At the beginning of the story, the birth of Emmy Slattery's illegitimate daughter calls Scarlett's mother Ellen away from Tara, and later, the family passes on the fatal case of typhoid Ellen contracts while nursing them. After the war Emmy Slattery marries Tara's former overseer, the Yankee Jonas Wilkerson (Yankees are aliens in a way Gerald never is). They seek to exploit Scarlett's difficulty in paying taxes to acquire Tara for themselves. Envy of the uppity Slatterys finally leads Scarlett's sister Suellen to agree to the humiliation of the senile Gerald by having him swear loyalty to the Union in exchange for government compensation.

The class order of Mitchell's *GWTW* undergoes an important shift as a result of the Civil War. This shift is symbolized by Scarlett's move from rural Tara to urban Atlanta and, more importantly, in her return to the city after the war. In the aftermath of the region's destruction, Atlanta becomes an island of vitality as the commercial values of a conquering North become a pillar of the New South's prosperity. This is seen most obviously in the success of Scarlett's general store and lumber mills, though her gender and her rapaciousness in leasing convicts make her something less than an ideal model for the new order. But Mitchell provides plenty of others:

> Tommy Wellburn, in spite of his crippled back, was the busiest contractor in town and coining money, so people said. Mrs. Merriwether and René [Picard] were prospering and now had opened a bakery downtown. René was managing it with true French thrift and Grandpa Merriwether, glad to escape from his chimney corner, was driving René's pie wagon. The Simmons boys were so busy they were operating their brick kiln with three shifts of labor a day. And Kells Whiting was cleaning up money with his hair straightener, because he told the negroes they wouldn't ever be permitted to vote the Republican ticket if they had kinky hair. (p. 744)

These urbanites also occupy a middle landscape in the South's white class structure. Above them economically, if not socially, are the grasping carpet-baggers and scalawags, who use military occupation to cement ill-gotten gains. (To this class one might add Rhett Butler—"a mule in a hawse harness," according to Mammy—though he redeems himself over the course of the story.) Below them economically, though not socially, are those such as Ashley and Melanie Wilkes, who maintain a genteel poverty rather than compromise their values. For them, Scarlett has little patience. "To her mind, there were few, if any, qualities that outweighed gumption," she realizes at one point (p. 666). Gumption—or what might have been called crass Yankee materialism before the war—is precisely what people such as Ashley lack, as Scarlett herself occasionally admits: "The ones who were not busy were the men of Hugh [Elsing's] type—or Ashley's" (p. 744).

There is also another layer in the class structure of the city, represented by Scarlett's wage-earning driver, Archie: the redneck. A former convict from the mountains, he is not without his dignity, "a fierce silent pride that permitted no liberties and tolerated no foolishness" (p. 748). His sense of honor leads him to refuse to drive Scarlett after learning she leases convicts. Still, he is ugly, unkempt, and rude. Most importantly, Archie hates blacks and women (he went to jail for killing his wife). "It was them niggers that started the war. I hates them for that," he tells Scarlett. "But you fought in the war," she points out to him. "I reckon that's a man's privilege," he replies. "I hates Yankees too, more'n I hates niggers. Most as much as I hates talkative women" (p. 750). The comic stridency of Archie's opinions make those of Scarlett seem more moderate. Mitchell's strategy in this exchange suggests one that remained popular throughout the twentieth century: self-styled moderates holding reformers at bay by pointing out the irrational hatreds of a working class prone to backlash.[46]

Scarlett's move to Atlanta hardly curbs her interest in Tara, nor does Mitchell's delineation of class structure in the city curb her interest in the postwar farming sector. Here, too, the war wrought decisive changes. Twelve Oaks was burned, whereas Tara remains standing—an important symbolic comment on the Wilkes and O'Hara families. Nevertheless, the suffering brought on by Sherman's march cuts across class lines. And race lines, too: Gerald's house servant Pork is forced to become a field hand who steals chickens, while Scarlett, her sisters, Mammy, and Prissy toil away together in the cotton fields, a humbling experience even for the slave women.

Into this milieu enters Will Benteen. A South Georgia cracker who lost his leg in combat, he stays at Tara after convalescing from an illness and, lacking family ties, sets down roots there. With native gifts far exceeding anything Scarlett—or Ashley—could do, he turns Tara into a successful farm with the financial support she sends him from her lumber profits. Eventually, he saves Suellen O'Hara from spinsterhood and ostracism over her father's death by marrying her—hardly a match of passion, but one that gives both a stake in the land and a stable future. In his own quiet way, Benteen is perhaps the most attractive character in GWTW—a responsible, grateful, and clear-eyed man who is rewarded with upward mobility. In this he is also a middle figure, the happy medium between hapless plantation owners and heartless white trash. Finally, he represents continuity between the aspirations of the more colorful Gerald O'Hara and the opportunities that await the ambitious man in the years following the war, even one who does not move to the big city.[47] It is an agrarian vision of America on which many a white Southerner could take his stand.

Still, for all her obvious affection for the new rural and urban middle classes, one senses—as in so many other aspects of the book—an ambivalence about the system Mitchell criticized. Melanie, an important representative of the old aristocratic order, embodies its best ideals after the war and becomes an important moral and social resource for the entire community, from insiders such as Miss Pittypat to outsiders such as Belle Watling. Rhett's epitaph for her, "a very great lady" (p. 1025), speaks for all. Rhett himself, for all his rebellions, in the end decides to go back to Charleston to recover his own past. Depending on temperament, some readers will see this as the final capitulation on Rhett's part, the ratification of an increasingly apparent ennui; but others (like Mitchell herself?) see it as the mature realization of what old ways have to offer.

Mitchell's depiction of the Southern class order can be placed squarely within the Southern literary awakening. Like Faulkner, she portrayed the prewar plantation elites as desiccated; like W. J. Cash in *The Mind of the South* (1941), she focused her antebellum attention on the grasping regional immigrants who made fast bucks from growing cotton. Like Erskine Caldwell (another writer sometimes excluded from the list of academically respectable Southern voices), she strove for sociological realism, and although Mitchell might have expressed distaste for the sordid world of *Tobacco Road* (1932), the presumably Victorian *GWTW* includes scenes or discussions of rape, abortion, alcoholism, murder, and a host of other deadly sins. Mitchell has been traditionally excluded from such company, among other reasons for lacking a saving Modernist irony that made writers such as Faulkner suitable for canonization. This may underestimate the degree of sly commentary that does inhabit the novel's pages. In any case, these writers shared Mitchell's ambivalence about the class order they criticized; witness in Faulkner's work Quentin Compson's attraction/repulsion toward his origins.[48]

In terms of class, then, Mitchell was part of an intra-Southern generational movement that questioned assumptions about the old order. It was an ambiguous effort, marked by a complexity that might escape an outsider unfamiliar with subtle gradations within white Southern society. It is not surprising, then, that the filmmakers rewired some ideological circuits.

The movie version of *Gone with the Wind* lacks the complexity of the novel's class dynamics. To be sure, for example, Gerald O'Hara is the same windy Irish charmer on screen as on the page. But besides his telling Scarlett, "'Tis proud I am that I'm Irish, and don't you be forgettin', Missy, that you're part Irish too," the presentation of his character is matter-of-fact, as if finding an Irish plantation owner outside Atlanta was every bit as unremarkable as

finding an Irish fireman on a New York street. Gerald is clearly more vigorous
than the elegant John Wilkes, but only a viewer steeped in Southern history
and culture would be likely to surmise that Wilkes elegance is rooted in
Virginia Tidewater blood. When trying to console the heartsick Scarlett,
Gerald tells her, "If Ashley wanted to marry you, t'would be with misgivings
that I'd say 'yes.' I want my girl to be happy . . . and you'd not be happy with
him." *Why* she would not be happy—which Gerald explains in a fair amount
of detail in the novel—is not mentioned. Income, religion, ethnicity, accent, or any other social factor seems to be irrelevant: Ashley is just *different*.

Certainly, the O'Hara patrimony makes little economic difference. The
key symbol of this is Tara itself. Mitchell describes the house as "built by slave
labor, a clumsy sprawling building" (p. 48). By contrast, in the movie, although perhaps not as palatial as Twelve Oaks (we cannot be sure, since we
do not see perfectly parallel shots of the two houses' interiors), Tara is no
modest abode. One index of this is the presence of columns at the front
entrance. In a 1942 letter to Southern writer Virginius Dabney, Mitchell
described a tug-of-war between the filmmakers and consultants over them:

> Many of us were hard put not to burst into laugher at the sight of "Twelve
> Oaks." We agreed afterwards that the only comparison we could bring to
> mind was with the State Capitol at Montgomery, Alabama. In the pages of
> unwritten history, no fiercer fight was ever fought than the one centering
> around columns on the motion picture "Tara." The Georgians present at the
> making of the film, Susan Myrick and Mr. and Mrs. Wilbur Kurtz, of
> Atlanta, weren't able to keep the columns off "Tara" entirely, but they
> managed a compromise by having the pillars square, as were those of our
> Upcountry houses in that day, if they had columns at all.[49]

Other departures from Mitchell's sensibility were more obvious. Perhaps the
best example is the very first title card in the movie, written by Hecht:

> There was a land of
> Cavaliers and Cotton Fields
> called the Old South . . .
> Here in this pretty world
> Gallantry took its last bow . . .
> Here was the last ever to
> be seen of Knights and their
> Ladies Fair, of Master and of

Slave . . .
Look for it only in books,
for it is no more than a
dream remembered,

A Civilization gone with
the wind . . .

Look for it in books, but do not start with *Gone with the Wind*. Although Mitchell did romanticize the antebellum South, the fantasy can be found in its most unalloyed form in the work of Thomas Nelson Page and other late nineteenth-century writers. For writers of Mitchell's generation, this vision had become a joke. "Some of us organized a club, The Association of Southerners Whose Grandpappies Did Not Live in Houses with White Columns," Mitchell told Dabney. "May I extend an invitation to join? Its membership would be enormous if all the eligibles came in."[50]

The act of compressing the novel into a screenplay also simplified class dynamics. This is most apparent in the absence of Will Benteen from the movie. It is more subtle but perhaps even more important in the cast of urban characters. The absence of the Hugh Elsings, the reduced role for the René Picards, the lack of description of Atlanta's economic revival effectively rooted out the middle ground Mitchell so carefully tended. What we are left with, essentially, is a world in which some people make it and some do not.

This does not necessarily violate the spirit of the novel. "I still say feebly," Mitchell said amid the learned exegesis of historians, psychiatrists, and literary critics who commented on the book, "that it's just a simple story of some people who went up and some who went down, those who could take it and those who couldn't."[51] Perhaps. The irony of the movie, then, is that it did a better job than Mitchell herself in telling the story.

Regardless of Mitchell's intent, if it is possible to detect a difference between the class dynamics of the book and movie, it is harder to explain that difference. One could say that unlike the racial issues, there was no broadly based, coherent effort to comment or protest on what the filmmakers were doing. It is also possible that the film's focus on romance made all other issues secondary. Romanticizing the Old South to emphasize the extent to which it was gone with the wind enhances the movie's escapist value. One spends a few hours in another time and place.

In an odd way, though, the film version of *GWTW* also anticipated the coming of the postwar middle-class myth of consensus. Retaining Mitchell's

view of the city as the economic lifeline of its characters, and continuing to
celebrate a home in the country as more natural than the city, the film offers
an almost suburban view of society whereby focusing on a class order seems
less important than a privatized world where one's religion, ethnicity, or any
other factor (except race) is ultimately less decisive than what Scarlett—and
Margaret Mitchell—calls "gumption."

Mother Knows Best, Right?

> Ellen's life was not easy, nor was it happy, but she did not
> expect life to be easy, and, if it was not happy, that was
> woman's lot. It was a man's world, and she accepted it as
> such. The man owned the property, and the woman
> managed it. The man took the credit for the management,
> and the woman praised his cleverness. The man roared like
> a bull when a splinter was in his finger, and the woman
> muffled the moans of childbirth, lest she disturb him. Men
> were rough of speech and often drunk. Women ignored the
> lapses of speech and put the drunkards to bed without bitter
> words. Men were rude and outspoken, women were always
> kind, gracious and forgiving.
>
> Gone with the Wind, p. 58

Pat West did not really wish to become a nurse. But with London struggling
to hang on in the wake of German bombings in World War II and pressure
from both sides of her family to continue her aunts' tradition, she entered the
city's Hospital for Sick Children for training. Then she went to see Gone with
the Wind. "I saw Scarlett O'Hara enter that barn [Atlanta's "hospital" during
the siege of Atlanta], take one look at the wounded men—and walk out!
That was a real turning point in my life," she said. "I realised in an instant
that you could walk away from illness and what people expected of you. I
guess it was my first real anarchist moment. I promptly threw in the towel and
left after two and a half years of misery."[52]

It is impossible to know how many Pat Wests there were—are—in the
world whose lives were changed by GWTW. For at least one woman at the
time, the movie had the opposite effect it had on West: Mrs. Edith D. Taylor
of Newcastle claimed GWTW strengthened "[my] grim determination to

obtain my nursing examinations and 'get somewhere.'"[53] Though not explicitly stated, both responses to the movie seem strongly affected by gender
considerations.[54] Nursing is widely considered "women's work"—which, in
the United States, it became as a result of the Civil War. It is also a classic
case of work where traditional "women's" values such as caring and healing
are paramount. Thus, Pat West's abandonment of nursing is a violation of not
only family tradition, but also gender convention. At the same time, however, nursing is a profession, one requiring training—and, for Taylor, offering
an opportunity "to get somewhere." It may still be largely "women's" work,
but it is work in the "men's" sense of the term: something one does for pay.
Even now, it has an ambiguous status.

Of all the dimensions of GWTW, perhaps the issues of gender have sustained its popularity longest and most widely. In other lands—or parts of this
one—people may miss (or ignore) the racial dynamics of the Civil War and
Reconstruction, as well as the class gradations of antebellum Georgia. In both
book and movie, however, it is the relationship between men and women
that seems most direct—and, at the same time, the most ambiguous. As has
been previously suggested, Margaret Mitchell was a woman of great ambivalence on the subject of being a woman. This ambivalence permeates her
novel, survives its dilution in the movie, and may provide the most satisfying
explanation of the lasting appeal of Gone with the Wind.

In setting down her own account of the war and its aftermath, Margaret
Mitchell inherited a body of beliefs that constituted the Southern lady. She
also, like many writers who have struggled to come to terms with that body of
beliefs, revised it. Generally speaking, the Southern variety of Victorian
womanhood—a term that also has (white) race and (upper-to-middle) class
implications—resembled that of the North in its creation of a "woman's
sphere" and the attendant cluster of attributes associated with it: purity,
piety, domesticity, and submissiveness. But the Southern strain tended to
exalt the aristocratic dimension of ladyhood and to de-emphasize the utilitar-
ian elements that distinguished the Northern variety.[55]

As we have seen from the above sketch of her biography, however, Mitchell also had another model that came into prominence at the same time she
came of age: the flapper—some of the most famous of whom, such as Frances
Newman and Zelda Sayre (later Fitzgerald), were from the South (Southern
flappers were a staple of F. Scott Fitzgerald's early fiction).[56] For many young
women in the 1920s, the flapper offered a vision of social and sexual freedom
without the joyless moralizing critics found characteristic of Southern ladies
and feminists alike. Yet if Mitchell found the Southern lady oppressive, she

also seemed to consider the flapper decadent. Her novel projects these arche-
types back in time and uses the Civil War as a means for exploring the
tension between them. Mitchell's difficulty in finally choosing between the
lady and the flapper (a conflict embodied in the important female characters
Ellen O'Hara, Melanie Wilkes, and Scarlett) is the key dynamic tension in
her novel.

The supreme example of the Southern lady in GWTW is Scarlett's mother
Ellen O'Hara. Beautiful and remote, generous and moralistic, she cures the
sick, soothes the anxious, and resolves the complex. At the same time, her
velvet glove hides a will of steel that guides the household without Gerald's
ever realizing it. "It had never occurred to him that only one voice was
obeyed on the plantation—the soft voice of his wife Ellen," the narrator
reports. "It was a secret he would never learn, for everyone from Ellen down
to the stupidest field hand was in a tacit and kindly conspiracy to keep him
believing that his word was law" (p. 30).

Scarlett reveres her mother but, alas, is her father's daughter—and a kind
of son, as the three sons born to him died in infancy. She is also a girl who
wants to have fun. "Scarlett wanted very much to be like her mother. The
only difficulty was that by being just and truthful and tender and unselfish,
one missed most of the joys of life, and certainly many beaux. And life was
too short to miss such pleasant things" (p. 60). Ellen, by contrast, thinks
about another life altogether. The scene where the O'Haras pray after dinner
encapsulates the difference between mother and daughter: At a moment
when Ellen is unambiguously pure, pious, domestic, and submissive, Scarlett
is thinking of another woman's fiancé, only pretending to pray, imagining a
barbecue, and planning to make Ashley follow her wishes.

Scarlett does not know what the reader does: that Ellen, too, once was a
girl who wanted to have fun but whose true love, her dashing cousin Philippe,
died in a barroom brawl. She has come to recognize "that it's a man's world,
and she accepted it as such" (p. 58). Ellen's tone in this passage is one of
resignation, but Mitchell's—this is one point where one can really hear the
author talking through her character—is one of anger. Yet this anger never
leads to a complete rejection of the order Ellen accepts.

Indeed, although Scarlett in some ways rejects this order, she still longs for
her mother and strives to be like her. War and death later take Ellen from her
physically, but emotionally Ellen lingers to haunt Scarlett. The power of
Ellen's expectations are vividly apparent the day after the Confederate ball
where, still officially in mourning for her husband Charles, Scarlett dances
with Rhett. "She would rather die than face her mother," Scarlett thinks,

reflecting on the city's opinion of her. "She wished she were dead, this very minute, then everyone would be sorry they had been so hateful" (p. 203). Presumably, Scarlett is referring to herself here, but grammatically, at least, she could also be referring to Ellen. Scarlett would never admit to wanting her mother dead—indeed, her Catholic conscience would be genuinely mortified at the thought—but the sentence suggests how oppressive it can be to live in the shadow of an ideal that cannot be realized.

One of the most interesting aspects of the novel is that it really offers other models for Scarlett. There is Beatrice Tarleton, a vigorous woman (before the war, anyway) who cares far more for her horses than she does her four sons. There is also Grandma Fontaine, a salty-tongued old woman who admires Scarlett's grit, if not her judgment. But not right away. "Well isn't this generation soft and ladylike!" she tells Scarlett, who is horrified at the thought of having to pick cotton. "Let me tell you, Miss, when I was a girl my father lost all his money and I wasn't above doing honest work with my hands and in the fields too, till Pa got enough money to buy some more darkies" (p. 448). Grandma Fontaine is nothing if not a survivor, even if she would rather survive with other people doing the work, and one of Mitchell's points in the book is to demonstrate how resilient many Southern women were before, during, and after the war. A 1936 letter to Julia Collier Harris (daughter-in-law to the Joel Chandler Harris of "Uncle Remus" fame) demonstrates Mitchell's regard for them:

> My central woman character does every thing that a lady of the old school should not do. *And so do many of the characters.* . . . The old ladies were certainly not lavender and lace ladies. They had more drive at eighty than their children and grandchildren and when they had nothing better to do they went to meetings of patriotic societies and rended those societies apart. And while they scorned votes for women, they could go to the Mayor and the City Council and reduce them to jelly by a few well chosen words concerning male shilly-shallying and inefficiency—and they got civic improvements in a way that voting women never did. [57]

There are plenty of weak and ineffectual women in this world as well, the Aunt Pittypats, the India Wilkeses, the Suellen and Carreen O'Haras. They fare less well, but many of them get by, too.

Ellen does not survive the Civil War, so we never know exactly how she would have handled its aftermath, but the ideal she embodies is carried forward by her symbolic daughter, Melanie, a woman whom Mitchell called on a number of occasions the character who was really her heroine. [58] "What

Melanie did," the narrator explains, "was no more than all Southern girls were taught to do—to make those about them feel at ease and pleased with themselves. It was this happy feminine conspiracy which made Southern society so pleasant" (p. 156). Like Ellen, Melanie acts on what she is taught and is a party to the "conspiracy" to conceal the function of women in Southern life. And like Ellen, she is loving, gentle, and firm when it comes to her principles. But unlike Ellen, Melanie survives the war. In the end, she dies, like all people (and ideals) must, but one of the substories in GWTW is Scarlett's gradual realization that Melly has a kind of gumption, too. From her willingness to help Scarlett kill her would-be rapist, to her unwillingness to bar Rhett from her home, Melanie shows in ways large and small her ability to transgress the boundaries of gender convention.

As in so many other ways in Mitchell's work—and that of other historians—the Civil War forced those boundaries to move.[59] As Scarlett notes, "The ever-present war in the background lent a pleasant informality in social relations, an informality which older people viewed with alarm" (p. 218). As a result, certain actions that had been unthinkable for Melanie— donating her wedding band to the army; giving Dr. Meade her "permission" for ladies to be "auctioned" for dances at the Confederate ball; helping Scarlett bury the dead Yankee who invaded Tara—become imperative. However, such actions do not constitute an abrogation of Southern ladyhood; rather, they fall under the dicta of a new ladyhood whereby duty and sacrifice are enlisted in the service of the Confederate war effort.

But boundaries are boundaries, even if they move. Scarlett's behavior aside, a woman's sphere continues to exist, and at the heart of that sphere is motherhood. In this model, Melanie is motherhood par excellence. Motherhood is nonsexual and imbued with ideals of duty and even suffering. By contrast, not only is Scarlett's seventeen-inch waist important to her in a way children never are, but her delivery of her son is so easy as to be "scandalous—just like one of the darkies," in the words of Mammy (p. 354). Scarlett considers children "useless, crying nuisances . . . always demanding care, always in the way" (p. 403). Moreover, pregnancy is a major irritation. For Melanie, by contrast, childbirth is agony. Her first pregnancy mirrors the remorseless struggle going on in Atlanta, and her second kills her.

Significantly, Melanie's ultimate act of womanhood takes place in wartime, that ultimate moment of manhood. Before the war, "raising good cotton, riding well, shooting straight, dancing lightly, squiring the ladies with elegance and carrying one's liquor" (p. 4) were the only things that mattered. But during the war, battle becomes the measure of manhood, and one can rank the male characters of GWTW by how they react to the crisis. Scarlett's first husband, Charles, dies of measles before the fighting ever gets under way, underlining his weakness. Her second husband, "old ginger whiskers" Frank Kennedy, measures up, though just barely, as a quartermaster. For Gerald O'Hara, the war marks his transformation into a childish old man. Ashley, however, like his better half, makes the grade. For all his dabbling in literature and distaste for poker, he courageously leads his men in the cavalry and is honored for his contributions. His actions are all the more honorable in light of his reservations about "the cause" and his fatalistic sense of its prospects. As Melly explains, "He thinks the war is all wrong but he's willing to fight and die anyway, and that takes lots more courage than fighting for something you think is right" (p. 234). (Melanie's idea was echoed during and after the lost cause of the next century, Vietnam.)

Rhett Butler provides an interesting case in this regard. For most of the war, the West Point dropout scoffs at the Confederacy and runs blockades only because it is in his economic interest to do so. Yet, depending on one's point of view, he either comes to his senses or loses them by joining the artillery unit that later fights the Battle of Franklin. Here is duty and sacrifice indeed. It is hard to imagine a more futile exercise than this battle, a hopeless attempt to lure Sherman out of Atlanta that resulted in the decimation of an entire army and marked the collapse of Confederate resistance in the West.[60]

Although Rhett may soften under the rhetoric of "the cause," which brings other white men and women together, Scarlett does not give a damn. Early in the war, she realizes that she is not like other women, women who blaze with "the white heat of devotion to the Cause that was still shining on every face." To her, "the war didn't seem to be a holy affair, but a nuisance that killed men senselessly and cost money and made luxuries hard to get" (p. 172). Indeed, while exactly what constituted "the cause" brought about much bickering in the Confederacy, Scarlett has unfailingly pragmatic instincts about what her own cause is: herself and her family (in that order). During the war, the Yankees are monsters for what they did to Tara and all it represents to her. However, she is quick to accept the new order after the war and sees noncooperationists in general and the Democratic party and the Klan in particular as counterproductive. Mitchell "punishes" her for these views with her assault in Shantytown, and Rhett's later reconciliation with the Democrats suggests that he is the one who is ultimately the most pragmatic. Still, romance, tact, and party politics aside, Scarlett is generally good at recognizing her opportunities and exploiting them (indeed, as far as many of the men are concerned, that is precisely the problem with her).

Her biggest opportunity is the war itself. It allows her to do things that would have otherwise been unimaginable: live without male supervision in Atlanta; enjoy the attentions of Rhett and other men at the beginning of the war; buy and run two sawmills; marry three times (and ignore her children by three different husbands); establish a luxurious home in the city and keep her base in the country. Whereas other women, most notably Melly, continue to dwell in the domestic sphere, Scarlett wanders far beyond it and beats men at their own game, ruthlessly undercutting competition and maximizing profits.

In all of this she stands alone. The women have their sewing circles, musical societies, and grave-decoration activities; the men have the saloon, the whorehouse, and the Klan, presumably to protect the women and hence give manhood some purpose. The only woman remotely like Scarlett is the equally enterprising Belle Watling, who also runs her own business. The belle of the county has nothing on Belle the prostitute: Scarlett "wanted to feel superior and virtuous about Belle but she could not" (p. 557). Indeed, Belle can be as successful as Scarlett and still have the proverbial heart of gold. She donates money for Confederate hospitals, establishes a relationship with Melly based on mutual respect, and is even a devoted mother to a son the reader strongly suspects was fathered by Rhett.

Scarlett has Rhett, too; he is about the only person who understands and appreciates her. Nevertheless, having mastered the mechanics of controlling most men, she is frustrated by his unconventional behavior, repeatedly telling him he is not a gentleman (much to his amusement). Most readers regard Scarlett's resistance to his charms a foolish, irritating, or tragic mistake on her part, and in this they may be right. However, it is also possible to argue that here, too, pragmatism reigns. When Rhett suggests she become his mistress, for example, she quickly exclaims, "Mistress! What would I get out of that except a passel of brats?" (p. 341). By some standards, a man who repeatedly calls his lover "my pet" makes for a less-than-ideal husband. In fact, the very intensity of Rhett's passion for Scarlett results in his rape of her, an assertion of power that in this story seems to result in the first sexual satisfaction in Scarlett's life.

Of all the aspects of gender in GWTW, Scarlett's sexuality is one of the most striking and is yet one more example of the ambivalent contradictions in Mitchell's heroine. Clearly, sex is one of the great weapons in Scarlett's arsenal. Although the very first sentence of the novel states flatly that "Scarlett O'Hara was not beautiful," her "arresting face" and "magnolia-white skin" captivate men such as the Tarleton twins. Scarlett is aware of her power over men and uses it to great effect yet is completely oblivious of her own sexual desires. "Of course, she knew that married people occupied the same bed but she had never given the matter a thought before," and she blanches at the thought of sex with her first husband (p. 130). Rhett finally awakens her sexuality when he kisses her for the first time:

> Something vital, electric leaped from him to her at the touch of his warm mouth, something that caressed her whole body thrillingly. . . . She had not bargained on this—this treacherous warm tide of feeling that made her want to run her hands through his hair, to feel his lips upon her mouth.
> She wasn't in love with him, she told herself confusedly. She was in love with Ashley. But how to explain this feeling that made her hands shake and the pit of her stomach grow cold? (p. 339)

Ashley also arouses Scarlett when he kisses her, but her arousal is more ethereal, romantic, and, ironically, maternal: "Her body seemed to melt into his and, for a timeless time, they stood fused together as his lips took hers hungrily as if he could never have enough" (p. 533). For the only time in the book, Ashley shows some real ardor here, though the honor he so prizes leads him to regain his distant composure.

Literally and figuratively, Mitchell allies sexuality with the forces of darkness. "Good" characters such as fair-haired Ashley or Melly seem almost completely sexless; "bad" ones such as dark-haired Rhett and Scarlett are fascinating in their sensuality. Sexuality also seems keyed to class and race: The very name *Slattery* is evocative with sexual imagery (slattern), and Rhett is repeatedly described as "dark" and "swarthy." "He looked huge, larger than she had ever seen him, a terrifying faceless black bulk that swayed slightly on its feet," Mitchell wrote, just before he rapes Scarlett (p. 933). The rape itself is filled with images of blackness and death.[61]

In this dark portrayal of sex—and her fascination with it—Mitchell reflected the social tensions of her milieu. The Victorian lady in her was something of a prude, but the New Woman was an avid collector of pornography and erotica, particularly the work of Havelock Ellis.[62] Her relationships with men also suggest this duality. She indignantly asserted that her relationship with Clifford Henry, who was killed in World War I, was completely chaste. Yet she later claimed that "there's nothing in the world to boost a girl's morale like the knowledge that there's a gempmum fren' all ready to seduce her if she gives him one half a chance."[63] (Note the use of black dialect, which evokes the sensuality people like Mitchell so often attributed to African Americans.) Her marriage with Red Upshaw seemed to conflate sexuality and violence; but the pendulum appears to have swung back to abstinence with John Marsh, a distinctly less sexual character who nurtured her talent as well as her health (when the sickly husband was not being nursed by his wife).

The gender contradictions extend to men as well. For all his virile masculinity, Rhett has a distinctly feminine sense of intuition in reading Scarlett's mind—and, for that matter, the minds of other women as well. He also shows a real flair for costume, not only for himself, but also in picking out clothes for Scarlett. In addition, his love of children, not only his own, but even those from Scarlett's previous marriages, might very well be described as maternal. Ironically, Mitchell was able to appealingly synthesize the gender tensions for a male character in a way she never quite could for herself.[64]

In terms of the historiography of Southern women, Gone with the Wind represents an important, if partial, revisionism. In the years following the Civil War, and particularly at the end of the nineteenth century, men and women ritualistically celebrated the achievements of Southern womanhood in the face of wartime privations.[65] But that heroism was predicated on a vision of purity, chastity, and other elements of the Southern lady. In Scarlett O'Hara, however, Mitchell offered a woman whose achievements rest precisely in a rejection of those elements. If she is not exactly a hero, she is certainly a woman worth watching.

Certainly David Selznick thought so. Still, he felt compelled to contain her.

Of all the excitement surrounding the film version of Gone with the Wind, few matters aroused as much speculation and excitement as the casting of Scarlett O'Hara. From the first, it seemed a consensus had formed that Clark Gable had to play Rhett, but little agreement existed as to the perfect Scarlett. Bette Davis, Katharine Hepburn, and Joan Fontaine were among those most often named as in the running, but all were rejected. Selznick made highly publicized announcements that he was looking for an unknown, raising the prospect that a lucky Everywoman could be plucked from obscurity. His ultimate choice, British actress Vivien Leigh, was hardly Everywoman in her acting talent, and her widely remarked upon beauty was not exactly in keeping with the spirit of Mitchell's description of Scarlett at the start of the novel. If Leigh brought depth and intelligence to the role, she also suggested Selznick's different cultural priorities.

In general, the changes made to bring GWTW to the screen amount to an effort to limit Scarlett's threat to patriarchy. As in the case of race, reducing the novel's sheer bulk to manageable proportions resulted in cutting many thoughts or statements that might shock viewers. The rape scene, of course, would have been censored if it had been portrayed with anything other than a symbolic staircase, and even if depicted, the interior thoughts of the charac- ters would probably still be more vivid than anything actually shown on screen.

Nevertheless, some very basic omissions suggest a systematic taming of Scarlett's character. In the movie, she only has one child, not three. Abor- tion, which becomes an issue in the novel when Scarlett considers not having Bonnie—Rhett categorically refuses to consider termination, fearing it will kill Scarlett—is not mentioned in the film. Scarlett owns one lumber mill, not two, and her decision to get Ashley involved is unrelated to the physical complications of her second pregnancy.

Even scenes that remain in the movie have subtle changes that soften Scarlett's edges. Take, for example, her shooting of the would-be rapist at Tara. In the book, Scarlett's reaction is horror. Then another feeling takes over: "Murder! she thought dully. I've done murder. Oh, this can't be hap- pening to me! Her eyes went to the stubby hairy hand on the floor so close to the sewing box and suddenly she was vitally alive again, vitally glad with a cool tigerish joy. She could have ground her heel into the gaping wound which had been his nose and taken sweet pleasure in the feel of his warm blood on her bare feet. She had struck a blow of revenge for Tara—and for Ellen" (p. 440–41). It seems unlikely that Ellen would have been altogether pleased. But that is beside the point by now. If giving birth is women's work, killing is man's work, and Scarlett takes a visceral, almost sexual pleasure in this act of violence. In the movie, the shooting is hardly gentle domestic drama, but there is definitely a softer tone: "SCARLETT (*looking down at him*) Well, I guess I've done murder. (*she draws back the back of her hand across her eyes, throws out her chin*) Oh, I won't think about that now. I'll think about that tomorrow."[66]

In the novel, Scarlett also concludes the episode with her customary eva- sion of thinking about unpleasant things tomorrow. However, that is not the last word on the matter, for the narrator continues, "She did not think of it consciously but in the back of her mind, whenever she was confronted by an unpleasant and difficult task, the idea lurked giving her strength: 'I've done murder and so I can surely do this'" (p. 445). Scarlett's "shell of hardness" is thickening, and if it is insulating her further from Ellen, it is also giving her a crucial sense of self-sufficiency.

Indeed, in the movie, as in the book, Scarlett stands alone. However, although there are alternatives to Scarlett in the latter, there is no Beatrice Tarleton or Grandma Fontaine in the movie. Belle Watling remains in the picture, but her occupation is even less socially acceptable than Scarlett's exploitation of convict labor. And ultimately, Belle is less dashing than Scarlett. So viewers who admire Scarlett's imagination, assertiveness, and charm are stuck with the rest of the package: her thick-headedness, bossiness, and crudity. Melanie, meanwhile, carries her subtle strength from the novel to the film. The cards seem stacked in her favor. Yet Scarlett still seems the clear winner—as Selznick must have realized, for without at least a somewhat appealing protagonist, he would not have a movie.

Nor could Margaret Mitchell resist the appeal of Scarlett O'Hara. She had meant for Melanie to be her heroine, but somehow, Scarlett had simply taken over.[67] Three years after her novel was published, attending the premiere of a movie in which she refused any involvement, she expressed her appreciation to a capacity crowd at Atlanta's Loew's Grand Theater "for everything people have done for me, to be kind to me and my Scarlett."[68]

The fundamental ambiguity of GWTW has served to prolong its vitality for over half a century. Appalled by Scarlett's actions, women may still identify with her strengths. Such identification tends to be private, not public.[69] Scarlett herself disdains collective action. "Of course, there were unfortunate women who drank, to the eternal disgrace of their families," she thinks, reaching for brandy, "just as there were women who were insane or divorced or who believed, with Miss Susan B. Anthony, that women should have the vote" (pp. 685–86). For Scarlett—and for Margaret Mitchell and, I believe, for millions of readers—the political is personal.

For the filmmakers, the goal was to avoid the political altogether. Even today, the idea that "politics" and "entertainment" can and should be kept separate is widely prevalent. The producers of this movie sought to tell a story set during a highly contested period of U.S. history, and to do this, they forged a consensus about what kind of assumptions they thought the public would take for granted and thus would not get in the way of their romance. They were guessing, of course, and in their guesses they revealed their own assumptions about race, class, and gender. Such assumptions, by virtue of their massive dissemination, did not necessarily become majority views but did become so powerful that even those who disagreed would take them into account. For those who shared the moviemakers' assumptions, such views became what was then considered "normal."

GWTW is often dismissed as a story filled with stock characters and romantic conventions; in this chapter I have tried to suggest that such a view overlooks the variations and even subversions of those conventions, and I have noted how striking those that were observed seem today. At the same

time, in looking at what was considered common sense to the Margaret
Mitchells of the 1920s and the David Selznicks of the 1930s—and the differences between them—one can discern a book that was at once more racist,
more classist, and more feminist than the movie.[70] Whatever the variations,
in serving as the source for the movie—and in making the Civil War the
crucial turning point on which her own interpretations rested—Margaret
Mitchell can be said to be the most influential historian of the twentieth
century, and her work a point of departure for countless million understandings of the Civil War.

Scarlett O'Hara and the American Dream

> Ooooh, I love it. I got it the day it came out. It's still the
> best book and movie ever, and I can't wait to read the new
> one. It's a book everyone in Atlanta can relate to. Look at
> me. I started with nothing, and now I own this pawn shop.
> I'll never be hungry again.
>
> Sandra Tucker, owner of the Tara I Pawn Shop
> in Jonesboro, Georgia[71]

A million copies of Alexandra Ripley's *Scarlett: The Sequel to Margaret
Mitchell's Gone with the Wind* arrived in bookstores in the fall of 1991, and
Warner Books printed 50,000 more a day at one point to keep up with
demand. In its first week, the book sold ten times as fast as the number two
novel on the *New York Times* best-seller list (Tom Clancy's *Sum of All Fears*)
and produced the most one-day sales of any book sold by the nation's largest
book retailer, Barnes and Noble. It also propelled the original novel upon
which it was based, which has never gone out of print, back onto the best-
seller list, prompting Macmillan to print an extra 155,000 copies.[72] Although there may come a time when Scarlett O'Hara ceases to become a
fixture in the firmament of U.S. popular culture, such a fate appears even less
imminent now.

Despite the ambiguity of its ending, Margaret Mitchell had always stead-
fastly refused to write a sequel for *GWTW*. She also refused to say definitively
whether she thought Rhett and Scarlett would get back together. Her brother's children, claiming to fear that anyone could write a sequel after the
book's copyright expires in 2011, have shown less diffidence. In the late

1970s, they allowed Mitchell's future biographer, Anne Edwards, to write a sequel, *Tara: The Continuation of Gone with the Wind*, which was to be turned into a motion picture. When the movie deal collapsed, Edwards was left with an unpublishable manuscript, since the book's release was contingent on the film. Then, in the 1980s, the Mitchell estate hired a committee of lawyers to find another writer for the sequel. They appointed Ripley, a commercially successful Southern historical romance novelist, with the admonition not to include any obscenities or miscegenation. The family was paid $4.9 million for the book (Ripley received $160,000, plus royalties, which will push that figure far higher).[73]

   Scarlett opens in 1873 with the funeral of Melanie Wilkes, followed quickly by the death of Mammy. Scarlett hopes Rhett will return to her, but he makes it clear that he wants no part of the relationship. Scarlett goes to Charleston, where she spends time with Rhett's family, much to his dismay. The two strike a deal that they will appear to be happily married for the social season before Scarlett leaves for good—with a half-million dollars of Rhett's gold. After an unexpected tryst, Rhett strengthens his resolve to stay away from Scarlett, who, unknown to him, is pregnant. A hurt Scarlett flees, first to Savannah and then to Ireland, where she spends time with her father's family. There she learns that Rhett has divorced her and remarried, leading her to resolve to stay abroad and develop her extensive landholdings (which includes the site of the original Tara, site of Irish kings). Political unrest in Ireland and the amorous attentions of English aristocracy do not stand in the way of true love, and Rhett arrives on the scene at a climactic moment to save the day, discover his daughter, and finally find peace with Scarlett (conveniently, his wife dies just in time for this to happen).

   One would expect a fair amount of disdain, even condescension, in the critical reception of the book, and Ripley received plenty of both. "Chewing, shopping, and changing clothes do not a novel make," observed M. G. Lord of *Newsday*, aptly summarizing much of what goes on in the book and much of the critical opinion about it.[74] At the same time, however, such a dismissive view overlooks how effectively Ripley targeted the book to the middle-aged white female readers for whom clothes, shopping, and travel are relevant matters—as indeed they were for Scarlett herself in the original book.[75]

   That said, criticism of the book was not limited to intellectuals. "To tamper with Peggy Mitchell's tragic ending is to ruin the world's most wonderful, bittersweet story ever," said one male Atlantan who saw the movie fifty-five times. Ripley herself heard about an "I Won't Read the Sequel Club" and after rereading her manuscript asked to join it (she received a member-ship plaque).[76]

Scarlett is indeed a far less interesting book than GWTW, and one sees why by looking at the elements that have been analyzed in this chapter. In the matter of race, for example, Ripley retains Mitchell's harsh view of Reconstruction—the Yankees are habitually damned throughout the narra-tive, particularly in South Carolina, which is still under Federal occupation—but she told interviewers she wished to avoid racial stereo-types.[77] To that end, she eschewed dialect. Hence, Mammy says things such as, "Tell old Mammy what's troubling her lamb," which amounts to the worst of both worlds: the same old patriarchy without any of the care (or even flair) Mitchell brought to her phonetically correct dialogue.[78] Yet Ripley's most fundamental strategy regarding race seemed to be avoiding it as much as possible. Killing off Mammy in the first twenty-five pages, sending Prissy off to join Pork and Dilcey (who, newly enriched by Rhett, seem to be laying the foundation for the black middle class), and carting Scarlett off to Ireland for hundreds of pages effectively eliminated the need to engage with black char-acters at all. We are left with a late twentieth-century white fantasy of race: a world where it just goes away. Here, truly, is a literature of the suburbs.

Actually, one could argue that Scarlett symbolizes the realization of a 140-year-old Southern quest to bury Uncle Tom's Cabin. Harriet Beecher Stowe broke the bonds of the domestic novel by making race an explicit political issue in literature for women. Ripley effectively eliminates that political issue, making the romance novel a seemingly safe form of literature for women.

Ripley engages more with class, but the result remains problematic. Like Mitchell, she ties it to religion and occupation, but unlike Mitchell, she indulges in a kind of garish shorthand. The Irish love good music, dancing, and each other (they become surrogate blacks, except that they are upwardly mobile), while Scarlett's Anglo-Protestant relatives in Charleston and Sa-vannah are cold, petty, and humorless. The author makes some effort to trace the rise of the Fenian movement, but her treatment of the Irish is disturbingly simplistic. Scarlett's cousin Colum is a Catholic priest and a gun-running terrorist, a tension that is virtually unnoticed. Ripley's handling of the Irish has an irritatingly quaint tone, like a package tour of Eire for middle-aged tourists.

In one sense, gender poses less of an issue. Mitchell's Scarlett seems thor-oughly modern in her career-mindedness, and she continues her enterprising ways in Ripley's novel. The problem is that that is about the only way she is recognizable as the same person. "I'm Scarlett O'Hara, an Irish lass with a free-swinging skirt and a secret red petticoat," she says at one point, and one wonders if Ripley is even making a pretense to retain Mitchell's character anymore.[79] This Scarlett adores her new child—expressing her opposition to day-care[80]—and conquers her ambivalence by becoming a purveyor of self-help: "Mother was wrong. Being a lady like her isn't the only way to be. It isn't even always the best way to be. Not if it doesn't make you happy. Happy is the best way to be because you can let other people be happy too."[81] Rhett, by contrast, becomes a hopeless mama's boy, completely devoted to the mother he had so thoroughly rejected in GWTW. He has some passionate sex with Scarlett, but he seems deflated, with little of the masculine power or fascination he holds in Mitchell's novel.

So what are we left with? Most of those willing to buy the book probably do not care much about the race or class dynamics. What they do care about is gender, specifically, the resolution of that ending: Will Scarlett win Rhett back? Or, to put it a little differently, Will she finally get what she wants?

This, I think, is a key question, one that can finally suggest a reason for the persistent power of Gone with the Wind. Mitchell herself said the book is about survival, and one can hardly doubt the power of lines such as "As God is my witness, I'm never going to be hungry again" for audiences during the Great Depression.[82] Yet there was more to it than that. Even in her darkest moments, Scarlett O'Hara wants to do more than survive; she wants to thrive, to become fabulously wealthy (her voracious appetite is a telling metaphor for this). Above all, she has a dream of true love with Ashley Wilkes. This dream is flawed, even childish, and at the very moment she can finally get what she wants, Scarlett loses what she had: Rhett. The book ends with her again thwarted, again longing, and again seeking a goal that she sees as attainable.

In her own way, Scarlett O'Hara is a kind of Jay Gatsby. (Mitchell began writing the book shortly after The Great Gatsby was published in 1925, and she was a great admirer of F. Scott Fitzgerald.)[83] Scarlett lacks his subtlety and elegance, but like Gatsby, she has an intense, even insane drive to get what she wants, subscribing to a powerful—and often crude, cruel, contradictory, and amazingly persistent—national myth that anything is possible with effort. Growing up in the age of the New Woman, Margaret Mitchell wrote her book at a time when it finally seemed that modernity might allow women to escape, or at least restructure, the bonds of womanhood that had circumscribed their hopes for so long. She found, as many women have then and since, that it was not that easy.

In trying to figure out why, Margaret Mitchell looked to history. The Civil War became a canvas upon which she could imaginatively depict the personal, political, and historical forces that had shaped her own life, and a means for connecting with the people for whom she cared deeply. As I hope I have made clear, there is much in her art I find distasteful; her strident hostility toward African Americans, chauvinistic class attitudes, and misanthropy rank among the worst uses of the Civil War ever made. Nonetheless, her passion and discipline—her gumption—remain a model for those who would fashion an alternative.

Chapter 4

Reconstructing Dixie

Confederate Mythology
in Rock 'n' Roll

The South has had its full share of
illusions, fantasies, and pretensions, and
it has continued to cling to some of them
with an astonishing tenacity that defies
explanation. But the illusion that
"history is something unpleasant that
happens to other people" is surely not
one of them—not in the face of
accumulated evidence and memory to the
contrary.

C. Vann Woodward, "The Irony of
Southern History"[1]

Picture yourself at a midsized concert arena at any one of dozens of locations in the United States in the late 1970s. The hall is dark, dotted by the glow of disposable lighters and filled with the sounds of hollering young men in souvenir T-shirts they purchased illegally in the parking lot before the show. Smoke from various drugs abounds in the air, and the floor is sticky with overpriced beer from discarded plastic cups.

Up on stage, a seven-piece band led by an enormous Tennessee fiddler named Charlie Daniels thanks the audience for its support. He plays a phrase on his fiddle, and the group launches into its most famous song, a breezy tribute to good times and Daniels's fellow performers of Southern rock. It is called "The South's Gonna Do It Again."

The crowd goes wild. It is a song fans have been playing on their turntables for years, and hearing it live in some way confirms, even validates, their experience. Many members of the audience know the lyrics and sing right along, without really hearing what Daniels is saying.

Just what is Daniels asserting the South is going to do in "The South's Gonna Do It Again"? Enslave blacks? That seems unlikely. Secede? No. In fact, Daniels went on to show himself an ardent nationalist in the early 1980s, scoring Top 40 hits with the celebratory "In America" and the Vietnam-veteran anthem "Still in Saigon." He might say that he is just repeating a popular slogan, the kind found on bumper stickers, such as the one where a whiskered old Confederate veteran clutches the Stars and Bars above the caption "Hell No, I ain't forgettin'!"[2] What is not being forgotten—or, for that matter, what exactly is being remembered—is never made clear. Doing so would probably prove difficult, sticky, painful, or impossible to state.

Nevertheless, an urge to remember and a simultaneous urge to forget have been irresistible impulses for white Southerners since 1865. Of course, people in all times and places have engaged in a similar process of selective memory. What makes the Southern case so striking in the context of U.S. history was an experience of defeat coupled with ongoing access to present its side of the story for large, receptive audiences. *Gone with the Wind* is only the best-known example of this access. That I, a suburban adolescent who had never been south of New Jersey, would go to see Charlie Daniels (twice, no less) is another.

For well over a century now, Confederate partisans have been especially attentive to and skillful at making history, even in adverse circumstances. The Southern Historical Society was founded in 1869 to offset what was perceived as a pronounced Northern bias in accounts of the Civil War, owing

to the destruction or confiscation of Southern records by conquering Yankees insistent on promoting their view of the conflict. The SHA and allied (if occasionally squabbling) organizations such as the Sons of Confederate Veterans and Daughters of the Confederacy carried out their mission with notable effectiveness well into the twentieth century. In addition, as the broad influence of professional historians such as John Burgess, John Dunning, Charles Ramsdell, and James Randall attests, Southerners have been well represented and influential inside the academy. Even those outside it, such as Shelby Foote and Margaret Mitchell, have shown themselves to be meticulous purveyors of Confederate perspectives.

Perhaps even more striking than the efforts of these self-conscious guardians of the white Southern past are the effects of those who have invoked it reflexively, drawing on images and slogans all the more powerful because they represent shared assumptions rather than scholarly arguments. That much of this mythology is wrongheaded and dangerous is beside the point. (As I have tried to show in the preceding chapters, the best-documented history can be wrongheaded and dangerous, too.) It still requires careful attention by non-Southerners, along with alternative mythologies invoked to contest it.

"The South's Gonna Do It Again," along with some of the other rock 'n' roll music produced by musicians in the same generational cohort as Charlie Daniels, represents one such aspect of collective memory that has gone relatively unexplored. Although explicit references to the Civil War in this music are relatively infrequent, a few of the occasions where they have surfaced tell us a good deal about the state of the union after World War II.

There are a number of reasons why rock 'n' roll, especially post-1960s rock 'n' roll, is a uniquely useful vehicle for making such an inquiry. First, for all its dizzying variety, rock music is grounded in a very specific place: the former Confederacy. The very factors that shaped rock music—a tradition of slavery and distinctive cultures arising from it, the presence of blacks and whites in relative proximity, a strong sense of (and belief in) regional identity—are precisely those that helped bring on the Civil War. That event, however directly or indirectly, looms over the best music of the United States, giving

Lynyrd Skynyrd, one of the most important Southern rock bands of the 1970s, on stage in its heyday. The Confederate flag backdrop was a fixture of its shows in the region, providing a historical context for the band's music. (Michael Ochs Archives, Venice, California)

it texture and depth even as it has responded to and has been shaped by subsequent struggles.

Second, the best rock music is thoroughly interracial. Virtually all American musical forms, of course, draw on a number of racial and ethnic elements, though usually one has dominated at any given time. For example, the music that developed in southern Appalachia in the nineteenth century relied on the banjo, an African instrument. However, when Appalachian music emerged from the mountains in the mid-twentieth century as bluegrass and country, it was made and listened to most widely by whites. Similarly, the blues was formed when blacks in the South adapted a European musical scale, and they used the blues largely for their own purposes, at least until the twentieth century. However, rock 'n' roll, which drew on both these streams, represented a far more conscious and synthetic attempt to fuse them. The result was a relatively unstable compound—centrifugal tendencies outlined below made it difficult to sustain a truly interracial form—but an extraordinarily powerful and historically resonant one.

Finally, rock 'n' roll arrived (I argue below that this was not coincidental) at the very moment that the racial legacy of the Civil War became a pressing national issue for the first time in a century. As we have seen, the interwar years were a time of great ferment for many in the United States, North and South, who explored the Civil War for explanations and solutions for contemporary problems. After Pearl Harbor, the Civil War was supplanted as a theme of primary interest in popular culture while national attention focused on the struggle at hand. Ironically, however, World War II made the legacy of the Civil War increasingly important in the 1940s and 1950s. The mass migration of African Americans to Northern cities, the acceleration of industrialization in the South, and the rise of a national economy all created pressures for a second Reconstruction. That massive undertaking, which involved a transformation of the federal government, the legal system, and social mores, and also influenced a variety of other political efforts (e.g., the antiwar and women's movements), was one of the most important events of twentieth-century U.S. history.

Revolutions are generally followed by reactions, and the Civil Rights revolution of the 1960s was no exception. In its aftermath, those disoriented or thrown on the defensive by the event tried to come to terms with it by means of a variety of strategies. Some of those strategies—I call them modes—are vividly captured in the music I will be discussing in this chapter.

In the previous chapter of this book, I traced how the struggle for (and ambivalence over) women's political rights became a critical context for Margaret Mitchell's exploration of the Civil War. In this chapter, I will look at how the struggle for (and anxiety about) African Americans' political rights became a critical context for understanding rock 'n' roll explorations of the Civil War. The ensuing sections will portray a handful of performers in the aftermath of the Civil Rights movement who tried to make sense of their past—a past that included the 1860s as well as the 1960s. They are performers of widely different temperaments and styles; only one group, Lynyrd Skynyrd, fits squarely into the genre of Southern rock, which I will describe more fully below. However, they are all people who invoked their heritage and in so doing often unconsciously echoed a century of explanations, rationalizations, and justifications of other white Southern men—who, historically, have the most to answer for.[3]

Notes from the Working Class

> They prefer books which can be easily procured, quickly read, and which require no learned researches to be understood. They ask for beauties self-proffered, and easily enjoyed; above all they must have what is unexpected and new. Accustomed to the struggle, the crosses, and the monotony of practical life, they require strong and rapid emotions, startling passages, truths or errors brilliant enough to rouse them up, and to plunge them at once, as if by violence, into the midst of the subject.
>
> Alexis De Tocqueville on Americans
> and their literature, 1840[4]

> Rock & roll is a combination of good ideas dried up by fads, terrible junk, hideous failings in taste and judgement, gullibility and manipulation, moments of unbelievable clarity and invention, pleasure, fun, vulgarity, excess, novelty and utter enervation, all summed up nowhere so well as on Top 40 radio, that ultimate rock & roll version of America.
>
> rock critic Greil Marcus, 1975[5]

If rock 'n' roll grew out of Civil War tensions, the fact that it did not emerge until the next century suggests that other factors must also have been at work.

Certainly, rock is far from the only music to have come out of the South since 1865; the blues, gospel, jazz, bluegrass, and country help constitute a heritage that makes music perhaps the nation's most singular cultural achievement. This heritage has proved to be a rich source of material and sounds that have contributed to the success of rock music. But the rise of rock music and its massive worldwide influence can be attributed to other factors that, strictly speaking, are nonmusical (and even antimusical).

One of these factors is capitalism. Capitalism sped the rise of rock 'n' roll in the United States in two ways. First, it provided the impetus for the development and sale of new technologies such as radio and records, which gave musicians new outlets for their work and access to ideas outside their immediate geographical areas. Second, capitalism developed a structure for mass distribution to create new markets, and thus new communities, for its products.

There was another aspect to these developments that suggests the power of history in shaping culture. In the United States, the development of hardware for film, radio, and television (projectors, transmitters, stereos) outpaced the development of software (movies, programs, songs). This created a vacuum in which an emerging future reached into the past for material. Thus, for example, early television drew on vaudeville, drama, and stand-up comedy for its first shows. Recombinations and innovations among these forms soon created a distinctive television sensibility (e.g., the situation comedy), but not before these earlier forms received a new lease on life.[6]

A similar process took place in popular music. One can find no better example than in Elvis Presley's first release. On the A side he recorded "That's Alright," a relatively obscure blues tune by the even more obscure Arthur "Big Boy" Crudup, a Mississippi Delta bluesman whose name may have otherwise disappeared into the cultural silt that has helped nourish so many other performers before and since. On the B side, he sang "Blue Moon of Kentucky," Bill Monroe's bluegrass standard. The record is a perfect metaphor for Presley's career: making blues and country two sides of the same coin, etching them with a sense of style all his own, and interfacing with an emergent popular culture infrastructure of records, television, movies, and so forth.[7]

Above all, that style was seen as youthful. To this day, rock music is stereotypically associated with teenage infatuation and other preoccupations of the young. In one sense, this perception is odd: The musical antecedents of rock music (blues and country) were anything but adolescent in transmitting age-old sorrows and joys for working-class people. However, the prevailing demographics of the 1950s and 1960s led the music industry to channel rock music toward white teenagers, whose disposable incomes were geared for the purchase of records, those most nonutilitarian—and easily marketed—of consumer products.

Unlike modern jazz, for example, rock obtains its strength from its lack of sophistication: Deriving from standard blues chord progressions and repetitive, driving rhythms, it is a relatively easy form of music to play and to appreciate. In this regard, it is a form of folk music with a strong participatory element. But rock is not really folk music, because unlike other folk forms, it rests too heavily on industrial technology and marketing for its dissemination and too heavily on consumption over production for appreciation. Indeed, a discrete musical genre of folk music that emerged in the 1950s was in large measure a nostalgic, pastoral, middle-class *reaction* to rock.

At its best, rock's simplicity is a form of democracy, a truly working-class form of art. Consider the following: "I know that rock and roll changed my life. It was something for me to hold onto. I had nothing. Before then the whole thing was a washout for me. It really gave me a sense of myself, and it allowed me to become useful, which is what I think most people want to be."[8] These are the words of Bruce Springsteen, the son of a bus driver and a secretary. "I grew up in a house where there was never any books or I guess anything that was considered art or anything," he told his biographer.[9] As an adult and a self-educated master of the rock idiom, Springsteen eventually read some books, created some art, and became immensely wealthy. His experience is not common, but it is not unique, either. Certainly, success in rock 'n' roll has created some painful contradictions and tensions—as the lives of Chuck Berry, Janis Joplin, Jimi Hendrix, and others attest. But it also created opportunities and offered meaning in the lives of these performers and others, whether they actually became rock stars or not. In its simplicity, availability, and even opportunity, rock is art for the masses.

This democratic element in rock 'n' roll had another dimension that was more elusive but important nonetheless: a tendency toward equality that had potentially powerful political implications, especially when one considers the rise of rock in the 1950s. In the United States, rock 'n' roll has been the music of integration par excellence, and if that integration has been uneven, unfair, and incomplete, it shows how well rock has reflected the culture at large. It also seems more than coincidental that Martin Luther King and Elvis Presley arrived on the national scene simultaneously. Both, in their own way, were proponents—and living symbols—of integration. King represented a legal, moral, Apollonian side of integration; Presley an emotional, expressive, Dionysian side. Both had profound effects on American consciousness. Moreover, both had common enemies. Some of the opposition was passive, an elite resistance to the messiness of cultural and political agitation by lower orders (one thinks of elite disgust with Jacksonian politics, and of contemporary denunciations of rap). And some of the resistance was more visceral, violent, and massive. One good example of this hostility can be seen in the career of Alan Freed, the disc jockey who disseminated so much of the music in the North. Freed was labeled a "nigger lover" who played "jungle music" on the radio, and his television show was canceled after he aired a scene in which black singer Frankie Lymon danced with a white woman. Later, of course, Freed became a victim of the payola witch hunt—which had at least as much to do with his musical taste as it did his business practices.[10]

Of course, Martin Luther King did far more for civil rights than Elvis Presley ever did, and the cultural contributions of rock to the movements of the 1950s and 1960s proved to be far less decisive than its more naive prophets hoped. Perhaps this simply reveals the limits of culture in political reform. In the end, simply buying a Motown record (literally or figuratively) was not enough.[11]

Some performers were much more self-conscious about the political dimensions of their work. The most obvious example here is Bob Dylan. If Presley's art was grounded in the black music that moved up from the Mississippi Delta, Dylan's drew its vitality from the white folk music and the radical protest tradition embodied in Woody Guthrie. By the early 1960s, this music—typified by a spectrum that ran from the Kingston Trio to Joan Baez to Pete Seeger—was a staple of college campuses, a symbol of hipness for white college students who fused their brand of intellectual leftist politics with the simple music of the people.

If Presley in the 1950s achieved an integration of blues and country, Dylan in the 1960s achieved an integration of rock and folk music (at least after his controversial appearance at the Newport Folk Festival of 1965). In drawing new attention to politics and verbal wordplay, Dylan paved the way for a whole generation of performers, including the Beatles (who in a sense integrated Presley and Dylan into one potent package), Simon and Garfunkel, the Jefferson Airplane, and many, many others. For these people, rock was a vehicle—or at the very least, the soundtrack—for a cultural revolution that would end racial strife, imperial wars, and the ineffective lifestyle choices of the previous generation.

By the end of the 1960s, however, the cultural diffusion and fragmentation of rock—a diffusion and fragmentation that reflected that of a wider culture engulfed by war, civil unrest, and adolescent self-absorption—created a pro-found sense of disorientation throughout U.S. society that was by no means limited to those over thirty. One of the first people to sense this was Dylan. He suffered a near-fatal motorcycle accident in 1966 and was off the scene for two years. When he returned, the unpredictable demigod did the unthink-able: He went country. *John Wesley Harding*, recorded in Nashville, was released in 1968 and was followed by *Nashville Skyline* (on which Charlie Daniels appeared) in 1969. The acerbic, byzantine, raspy folk-rocker was writing and singing un-ironic songs celebrating the joys of rural living.

By the early 1970s Dylan had spawned a whole generation of singer-songwriters from more privileged backgrounds—James Taylor, Jackson Browne, Joni Mitchell, and others—who emphasized acoustic sounds and personal themes. Meanwhile, the powerful cultural energies integrated by figures such as Presley, Hendrix, and the Beatles passed from the scene. Record companies such as Motown and Stax, which had crossed musical lines and built biracial audiences, lost their cachet. And radio resegregated as mainstream rock became increasingly white, leaving black music confined to "urban" programming formats.

Times had changed. Richard Nixon was in the White House; he made it there in 1968 with the help of a "Southern strategy" that allowed him to break the post-Reconstruction Democratic hold on the region completely by 1972. For Nixon, the white South was a key component of the "silent majority" that formed his political base and was a symbol for the resistance to the reform movements of the 1960s. His compilation of an "enemies list" and acts of harassment typified by the immigration problems of John Lennon shows how seriously he took the cultural dimension of the political left and reveals the lingering power it retained as he headed into his Watergate quagmire.[12]

Yet even for those who loathed the silent majority and everything it stood for, the South exerted a compelling symbolic appeal by the late 1960s. For some, it could be seen as a place apart, relatively free of the corruptions that had corroded modern life—sterile suburbs, mindless consumption, scarred landscapes at home as well as abroad. This is a very old trope in life in the United States, one that runs from the plantation novel of the 1830s through the Agrarian essay collection *I'll Take My Stand* (1930) and into *Nashville Skyline*, three very different cultural manifestations of a similar underlying regional nostalgia. The South could also represent an experience of defeat, one that could take on metaphorical connotations—or, with the pall of Vietnam hanging over the nation, more direct ones. Here again, Dylan played a part, for in performing periodically with a group of men who called themselves The Band in the mid-1960s, he gave national prominence to a group of people who demonstrated the ongoing power of lingering Confederate mythology around which many in the United States, North and South, came to rally.

Mode: Tragic

The Soul of White Folk: The Band

> Never was nobler duty confided to human hands than the
> uplifting and upbuilding of the prostrate and bleeding
> South—misguided, perhaps, but beautiful in her suffering,
> and honest, brave and generous always.
>
> Henry W. Grady, "The New South,"
> a speech delivered to the
> New England Club in New York, 1886[13]

The Band had a long foreground even before Dylan discovered it. Its origins can be dated back to Ronnie Hawkins, an Arkansas rockabilly[14] singer who went to Canada in the late 1950s in search of the fame and fortune that had eluded him in the States. Hawkins recruited a number of musicians to play behind him in the ensuing years, including Levon Helm, a drummer who also was from Arkansas, and four Canadian musicians: pianist Richard Manuel, organist Garth Hudson, guitarist Rick Danko, and a fifteen-year-old roadie-turned-guitarist named Robbie Robertson.[15]

The living was rough for Hawkins's band, not only because of the venues they played—"Those places were so tough you had to show your razor and puke twice before they'd let you in," Hawkins later joked[16]—but also because their leader was a stern and obsessive taskmaster. The band underwent a series of permutations with and without Hawkins, in Toronto and near Helm's hometown of West Helena, Arkansas, in the early 1960s. In 1964 the group took a tour of East Coast clubs and provided an electric blues-based backing for an album by folk musician John Hammond, Jr. Hammond boasted of their talents to his friend Bob Dylan, who was looking for an electric band with which to smash his folk image. Helm was not interested, but the rest of the band accompanied Dylan to the Newport Folk Festival of 1965, where he infuriated the faithful with his now-fabled performance there.

The group continued to perform with Dylan until his motorcycle accident of 1966. While recuperating at his home in the upstate New York town of Woodstock (which was actually sixty miles away from the site of the legendary festival held three years later), he invited band members to come up and play with him as he metamorphosed again, this time from chaotic rocker into rustic traditionalist. In this period of mutual influence, the Canadians and Dylan recorded regularly in the basement of a rented house in the nearby town of West Saugerties; their 1967 collaborations were released as *The Basement Tapes* in 1975 (band members also made contributions to *John Wesley Harding*). When Dylan went off on his own again, the four musicians coaxed Helm back into the fold and began making their own album as The Band, an audacious sobriquet if ever there was one. The result of their efforts, *Music from Big Pink*, was released in the summer of 1968.

In the context of the musical scene of the late 1960s, *Music from Big Pink* seemed to come from a different time—or, to put it more accurately, it seemed timeless. There was nothing precisely antiquarian about it. Guitars and keyboards were amplified. None of the songs was anachronistic, nor were they topical. Though country flavored, this was not the sound of Charley Pride, Merle Haggard, or George Jones; though blues derived, the music bore little resemblance to anything Muddy Waters or B. B. King might play. Lyrically, many songs were elliptical, even incomprehensible. Other songs consisted of vignettes almost Melvillean in irony and ambiguity. "Long Black Veil," for example, tells the story of a murder suspect who will not give his alibi because he was with his best friend's wife. The woman returns each year to sprinkle roses on his grave—from where he tells his story. Still, for all the dark elements on the album, it closes with Dylan's "I Shall Be Released," a testimonial to the strength of human will enduring oppression. Without any specific reference to current events, the song nevertheless seemed powerfully relevant (and became a staple of Amnesty International rock benefits in the 1980s).

Music from Big Pink attracted the attention of critics and musical cognoscenti, though it was not an especially popular record. In the fall of 1969, the group's next album, recorded in Los Angeles and eponymously titled *The Band*, was released. This was a commercial as well as a critical success and sealed The Band's reputation for years to come (the group was featured on the cover of *Time* in January of 1970).[17]

Like *Music from Big Pink*, *The Band* managed to suggest a rich national past that was integrated with the present. Ed Ward, who later became a rock historian, recalled his experience of the record:

> The amazing thing about the album was that, without quoting or making direct reference, verbal or musical, to country music, 19th century parlor and military music, or any of the patriotic poets like Whitman, Sandburg or Lowell, it seemed to evoke all these things and more, entirely on its own terms. . . . If my experience is anything like typical, I would say that The Band helped a lot of people dizzy from the confusion and disorientation of the Sixties feel like the nation was big enough to include them, too.[18]

It was not only the 1960s—or those in the counterculture—that were being included. The Band was reaching beyond the moment to connect with an older, broader, more mythic nation. One sign of this was "King Harvest (Will Surely Come)," the album's closing track, sung from the point of view of a desperately hopeful farmer who will turn to factory work—and a union—if his crop fails. However, the most explicit effort to connect with this past was "The Night They Drove Old Dixie Down."

"The Night They Drove Old Dixie Down" was written by Robertson but sung by Helm, whose mournful vocals merge with his intentionally slapdash drumming and a lumbering piano line to give the song its distinctive character. The lyrics are written with a clarity of the kind one might find in a short story: A former Confederate named Virgil Kane explains that in the winter of 1865, he was fruitlessly trying to protect rail lines from Union cavalry attacks. In the barren aftermath of the war, he remembers the pervasive despair of Richmond's surrender that spring. This sense of loss stays with him as he chops wood in his reduced circumstances. But it is his emotional impoverishment that bothers him most, as he explains in the final verse:

> Like my father before me, I'm a working man
> And like my brother before me, I took a rebel stand
> He was just eighteen, proud and brave
> 'Til a Yankee laid him in his grave
> I swear by the mud below my feet
> You can't raise a Kane back up when he's in defeat
> The night they drove old Dixie down.

This is the Southerner's Civil War rendered in the tragic mode. We are given the story of a man caught up in a struggle not of his own making, for which he and his family pay a terrible price. The outside world rarely impinges: There is no mention of slavery (it is unlikely this man could afford any slaves) or secession (nothing indicates that he cared much for anything but defending his home), only a passing glimpse of Robert E. Lee, that archetypal fallen leader who endures humiliation with grace. Instead, we hear a painful recollection—which is not altogether accurate because Richmond fell in April, not May as Kane asserts, though that hardly matters—and are asked to contemplate the costs of war.

The appeal of a song such as this can be suggested not only by the fact that Joan Baez was able to make a huge hit of it in 1971, but also in the analysis of Greil Marcus, in his essay on The Band in *Mystery Train:*

> It is hard for me to comprehend how any Northerner, raised on a very
> different war than Virgil Kane's [he is referring to Vietnam], could listen to
> this song without finding himself changed. You can't get out from under the
> singer's truth—not the whole truth, simply *his* truth—and the little
> autobiography closes the gap between us. The performance leaves behind a
> feeling that for all our oppositions, every American still shares this old
> event; because to this day none of us has escaped its impact, what we share
> is an ability to respond to a story like this one. [19]

Marcus's analysis is fine as far as it goes, though it seems unlikely that all Northerners will be as moved as he is. However, he—like The Band—makes this argument by evading politics. In effect, both Marcus and The Band suggest that we suspend all our skepticism about the Confederate cause as irrelevant and that we immerse ourselves in the human drama of Virgil Kane. Whether or not they actually intended to make a current political argument, one could use their logic to argue that we should suspend our skepticism about the innocent GIs who went to fight in Vietnam, only to find horrors beyond their imaginations. In both cases the stories of other victims—slaves, the Vietnamese—are at best conflated with the characters in question and at worst are ignored altogether. The attempt to understand a Virgil Kane will presumably yield compassion, if not approval, and unite us in a common tragedy, however we may feel about the wars we fight.

If this rhetorical approach sounds familiar to the student of the Southern past, that is because it has a century-long history. One can find it in "Battles and Leaders of the Civil War," a series of articles published in *The Century,* a genteel late nineteenth-century magazine that stressed "contemplation of sacrifice, resourcefulness, and bravery in foes." The strategy is also apparent in the efforts of New South prophets such as L. Q. C. Lamar and J. L. M. Curry to promote sectional reconciliation. Putting the past in a new kind of order was more than a matter of noble sentiment; emphasizing unity was useful for newly capitalistic Southerners for everything from the negotiation

of loans from Yankee banks to crowd control at Confederate memorial celebrations. In any case, avoiding discussion of slavery or secession did not imply
a rejection of old assumptions. Far from it. Ironically, a sober contemplation
of Southern defeat shaded, almost imperceptibly, into a celebration that did
little to examine the underlying causes of that defeat by anything other than
overwhelming numbers. Despite all this—or because of it—a lingering de-
fensiveness on the part of many white Southerners remained well into the
twentieth century.[20]

There is nothing very celebratory, or defensive, about "The Night They
Drove Old Dixie Down." Still, viewed from this angle, the song draws on an
old tradition. The ease and clarity with which The Band (probably unconsciously) evoked a mythic past suggests how attuned it was with the Southern
past and how well the group was able to provide a reassuring rendering of it at
a time—the late 1960s—when the present was becoming a bit much to take
even for those who were theoretically committed to change.

Indeed, there are ways of interpreting "The Night They Drove Old Dixie
Down" that have less to do with Southern politics than with a wider sense of
cultural enervation. As I have already suggested, the song could be read as a
parable of Vietnam, providing a kind of melancholy nostalgia that could
soothe those enmeshed in a frustrating war. More generally, the song could
speak to a larger sense of defeat for the left, a feeling of disappointment of
early promise that had gone unfulfilled. That Joan Baez—widely seen as a
voice for liberalism at the advent of the 1960s—made a hit of the song in the
early 1970s suggests that many people could identify with its tone if not its
actual content. What all these ways of reading the song share, however, is a
retreat from public struggle into private loss—a retreat, ironically, that then
becomes a kind of collective lament of victimization. This strategy is central
to the Vietnam movies discussed in the chapter that follows.

Perhaps one should not be too hard on those who sought solace in contem-
plating personal costs (which became a mania in the singer-songwriter era of
James Taylor, Jackson Browne, Joni Mitchell, and others in the early 1970s).
As the twentieth-century French communist Regis Debray—a man of decidedly different sentiments than the Southern rebels of the 1860s—put it
after Che Guevara's failed coup attempt in Bolivia a century after the Civil
War: "It is not individuals who are placed face to face in these battles, but
class interests and ideas; but those who die are persons, are men. We cannot
avoid this contradiction, escape from this pain."[21]

It may be that the impulses behind songs such as "The Night They Drove
Old Dixie Down" are best understood not as faulty solutions to the lingering

problems of the past but as complexities that resist easy resolution. The attempt to make sense of people like Virgil Kane falls in the province of culture—history, literature, popular music—which, in facing an insurmountably difficult task, is constantly forced to rewrite the past. At different times, and in different ways, some of these rewrites will be better than others. Much better.

Mode: Defiant

Look Away: Lynyrd Skynyrd

> I wish I was in the land ob cotton,
> Old times dar am not forgotten
>
>   Dan Emmett, "Dixie"[22]

One of the more notable aspects of rock 'n' roll in the 1970s was the rise of what became known as Southern rock. As with most subcultural movements, this one had no fixed membership. In the 1970s, for example, the Charlie Daniels Band was clearly a part of it—"The South's Gonna Do It Again" is a kind of tribute to and inventory of its practitioners—but by the 1980s Daniels had migrated back into the country camp, where overlapping lines of rhythm guitars, dense drumming, and the prominence of African American musical elements were more muted. Country music has its own Confederate tradition, typified by "If the South Would Have Won (We'd Have Had It Made)" by Hank Williams, Jr., but the absence of such musical elements made the music less fraught with the tensions and contradictions that run through Southern rock.[23]

Despite the absence of a fixed definition, it is possible to talk of Southern rock of the 1970s as a recognizable entity, populated by a group of people who shared a similar background, a similar musical approach, and a sizable national audience. "At a time when most rock music was suffering from laid-back ennui," explains critic Joe Nick Patoski in his intelligent essay on the form, "the Dixie contingent offered a refreshing, no-frills return to the basics. Like the purest rock & roll of the Fifties, it relied for inspiration on country and western and rhythm and blues, two types of music that were still readily available to white teenagers living below the Mason-Dixon line." Southern rock also relied heavily upon jazz-styled improvisation, "an idea initially advanced but poorly executed by the San Francisco psychedelic bands of the sixties."[24]

In some ways, Southern rock of the 1970s was more genuinely counter-cultural than it might appear. Unlike many liberals—especially those who had attained legitimacy in the academy and were paid well to chronicle the lives of women, blacks, and members of ethnic groups—these people were solidly working class and were more skeptical of consumer culture than those leftists of the 1970s who became yuppies in the 1980s. Living out a myth of the outlaw rebel, they played hard, drank too much, took too many drugs, and had a deeply ingrained distrust of authority, especially that of outsiders. It was easy—perhaps too easy—to ridicule their myth; those who did so re-vealed their own class and regional biases. Given the political impoverish-ment and economic uncertainty of the 1970s, their fusion of the Old South and the Old West was genuinely alternative, if not necessarily appealing.

In the early 1970s the premier Southern rock band was the Allman Broth-ers Band. The group was led by Duane Allman, an enormously gifted guitarist who had done studio work for black performers such as Wilson Pickett and Aretha Franklin. In the late 1960s Allman sought to front his own band, using a distinctively Southern style. At their best, the Allman Brothers were that rarest of all species: white musicians who could credibly perform black-influenced music in a mold recognizably their own (something that the members of The Band at their best were also able to accomplish).

The creative reign of the Allmans proved brief, however. Duane Allman died in a motorcycle accident in 1971, followed by the death of the group's bassist a year later. The band continued under the leadership of Allman's brother, Gregg, and guitarist Dickey Betts, whose 1973 hit "Ramblin' Man" typified the macho, go-it-alone ethos of Southern rock. The group never recovered its initial musical momentum, though it continued to exist inter-mittently into the 1990s.

By the late 1970s commercial ascendancy devolved upon Lynyrd Skynyrd, which began its reign with "Freebird," its 1973 ten-minute tribute to the macho, go-it-alone ethos—and Allman. (The band's name, incidentally, is a sarcastic derivation of the guitarist's high school gym teacher, Leonard Skin-ner.)[25] "Freebird" was an inescapable musical presence for rock fans of the 1970s. So was the other major song associated with Lynyrd Skynyrd, "Sweet Home Alabama," a Top 10 hit for the band in 1974 and a staple of rock radio ever since.

"Sweet Home Alabama" is one of the most vivid examples of a lingering Confederate mythology in Southern culture. Although the song makes no explicit reference to the Civil War or the persistent ideology of states' rights,

both loom large over the song and any attempt to understand it. That attempt to grasp Lynyrd Skynyrd's music and message—and the underlying
ironies on which it rests—is best begun by looking outside the South and, for
that matter, the United States. Though the band ostensibly played down-
home music, Lynyrd Skynyrd's style relied on the heavy-metal approach
developed by British performers such as the Kinks, the Who, and in particular, Eric Clapton, a white blues musician whose fluid guitar style continues to
give him a devoted following. One of Clapton's most famous recordings is his
version of "Crossroads," the signature tune of the legendary Delta bluesman
Robert Johnson. Lynyrd Skynyrd also recorded the song, which follows Clapton's version so closely as to be a pointless imitation. Nothing better illustrates the British penchant, typified by the Beatles, for selling American
black music to white Americans.

"Sweet Home Alabama" was written as a rebuttal to an attack on the South
made by Canadian Neil Young. Young rose to fame as part of Buffalo Springfield and Crosby, Stills, Nash and Young in the 1960s, but in the 1970s he
went off on his own to start a successful solo career. At his best, Young has
demonstrated the expressive potential of traditional rock. Relying on simple
instrumentation and a voice that can be most charitably described as distinctive, he has been able to use both to create a powerful effect, perhaps most
notably on *Freedom* (1989), a scathing attack on U.S. complacency in the
wake of the collapse of communism. Like many of the singer-songwriters who
flourished in the early 1970s, Young could—and did—write personal, acoustic meditations on relationships, but his music has always been intriguingly
idiosyncratic and has lacked the self-involvement that plagued the work of so
many such performers. Moreover, Young's angry streak has never been far
from the surface. In 1970 he released what many consider his best album,
After the Gold Rush. Nowhere on that album is his fury more focused than on
one of his most famous songs, "Southern Man." Amid howling guitars and
with a cracking voice, Young delivered one of the most passionate denunciations of the white South that has ever been recorded:

> Southern man, better keep your head
> Don't forget what your good book said
> Southern change gonna come at last
> Now your crosses are burnin' fast . . .
> I heard screamin' and bull whips crackin' . . .

Four years later, Lynyrd Skynyrd responded with a defense of the South in
"Sweet Home Alabama," which generated at least as much attention as

Young's song. "We thought Neil was shooting all the ducks in order to kill one or two," Lynyrd Skynyrd's lead singer, Ronnie Van Zandt, who wrote the song, later told a reporter.[26]

As a defense of the white Southern way of life, "Sweet Home Alabama" works on a number of levels. Before examining them, it is worth keeping in mind that Lynyrd Skynyrd gained its reputation as a live band. This is true even for those who never saw Lynyrd Skynyrd perform, as its most successful album, One More from the Road (1976), was recorded live in Atlanta. In its live shows—and on that album's cover—Confederate flags were displayed as a backdrop for the band and provided an important visual cue for its music. In the South, the group opened its shows by pumping a big band recording of "Dixie" through the public address system ("We don't do that up North," Van Zandt said).[27] Thus, a song such as "Sweet Home Alabama" was richly contextualized before the band ever played a note.

Superficially, "Sweet Home Alabama" sentimentally celebrates love of place. The narrator is returning home from a sojourn outside the state and is looking forward to seeing his family and immersing himself in his beloved region. In the second verse, however, he gets down to business.

> Well I've heard Mistuh Young sing about her
> Well I heard ole Neil put her down
> Well I hope Neil Young will remember
> A Southern Man don't need him around anyhow
> Sweet home Alabama . . .

Here "Sweet Home Alabama" emerges as a song written in the defiant mode. The response to Young's polemic against Southern racism is dismissive, so dismissive that it makes no direct attempt to rebut his charges. Yet the very act of including him in the song suggests a need to even the score.

It is crucial to note that the suggestion that Young get lost echoes a century of similar advice that those north of the Mason-Dixon line should mind their own business. One thinks again of Grady, who argued that the "Negro Question" of post-Reconstruction be left for Southern whites to resolve on their own. "There it can be left with the fullest confidence that the honor of the Republic will be maintained, the rights of humanity guarded, and the problem worked out in such exact justice as the finite mind can measure or finite agencies administer," he wrote.[28] However, even as the seemingly mild tempered Grady made these promises, he implied that there were limits to just how much well-intentioned people such as himself can do. One can almost hear him say that we are, after all, human, and all of us make mistakes.

"Sweet Home Alabama" picks up this historical thread in the next verse:

In Birmingham they love the Governor
Now we all did what we could do
Now Watergate does not bother me
Does your conscience bother you (now tell the truth)
Sweet Home Alabama . . .

The governor of Alabama in 1974, of course, was George Wallace of "Segregation now, Segregation tomorrow, Segregation forever" fame. Wallace successfully ran for re-election that year, and so pleased was he with "Sweet Home Alabama" that he made the members of Lynyrd Skynyrd honorary lieutenant colonels in the state militia.[29] After noting Wallace's popularity, the singer says he has done all he can—about integration?—before reminding the listener that the rest of the nation has plenty to answer for. (The role of the "solid South" in securing Nixon's elections is not mentioned.) Again, this stance echoes the familiar antebellum Southern strategy of claiming that the industrial North, with its grimy factories and immigrants, has much more to answer for than the pastoral South.

The members of Lynyrd Skynyrd never suggested that "Sweet Home Alabama" is a song about white supremacy. In fact, they claimed to disavow the governor. "I support Wallace about as much as your average American supported Hitler," bassist Leon Wilkeson told Rolling Stone on behalf of the group. Yet even this was hedged. "I respect him, not as a politician—but as a man who hasn't given up what he was after. That's how we all feel."[30]

Maybe Van Zandt of Lynyrd Skynyrd did not intend to write a song about white supremacy. And it seems likely that many, if not most, of the millions of people who have heard the song over the last twenty years have understood it simply as a celebration of regional pride not all that different than, say, "New York, New York." But a closer look at the text and context of the song makes it hard not to hear the dark echoes that resound within it.

Which makes for one final, supreme irony. Derived from a standard blues chord progression, using vocal techniques that can be traced back to gospel and a piano line that harkens back to ragtime, the music of "Sweet Home Alabama" rests on an African American musical foundation. Like so much of white Southern music—including "Dixie," that classic song of blackface minstrelsy written by a Northern man[31]—Lynyrd Skynyrd's song derives its distinctive identity from the very cultural experience it seeks to deny or escape.

Mode: Liberal

Tom Petty and the Heartbreakers: Equal Opportunity Rednecks

> They aren't lavender-and-lace-moonlight-on-the-magnolias people. . . . And they were the bossiest, hard boiledest bunch of old ladies I ever saw. And they could be so plain spoken upon occasion that they could make the brashest flapper blush. But they never got too old to be attractive to the gentlemen.
>
> Margaret Mitchell
> on Southern women[32]

By the end of the 1970s Southern rock as a unified movement had largely disintegrated, absorbed, like so many other trends from punk to disco, into a musical mainstream reflected in *Billboard*'s Top 40. Yet even as this was happening, amid the swirl and sprawl of forms ranging from rap to punk, there was sporadic evidence of an attempt to capture both regional flavors and a sense of national character in rock.

This regional movement—though it was never called one as such—can be seen in the music of John Mellencamp, for example, who used traditional instrumentation to re-create a Midwestern sound on his albums *Scarecrow* (1985), *The Lonesome Jubilee* (1987), and *Big Daddy* (1990). At times, the work of performers such as Mellencamp seems to be the clearest sign yet that a rural, regionally distinct nation is gone; the nostalgia of such records suggests a glow possible only in hindsight—and with the help of sophisticated technology. Nevertheless, in the hands of other performers, a regional basis for American music could still be made compelling and fresh. The best example here is the East L.A. Chicano band Los Lobos, whose work in albums such as *How Will the Wolf Survive* (1985), *By the Light of the Moon* (1987), and *Kiko* (1992) brilliantly evokes a multicultural Southwestern landscape peopled with living history and current events. Performers such as Los Lobos demonstrate how regionalism and a purist conservatism need not be one and the same. Indeed, Mellencamp himself uses his music as an agrarian polemic against corporate capitalism, and song titles such as "We Are the People" evoke the spirit of Sandburg. Similarly, Bruce Springsteen's *Nebraska* (1982) resurrected the spirit of Woody Guthrie to protest the not-so-hidden injuries of class in the Reagan era.

Perhaps the most interesting example of a mainstream performer invoking a Southern past is Tom Petty. The son of a Florida insurance salesman, Petty quit high school to join local rock bands before leaving for Los Angeles in the early 1970s. With his band the Heartbreakers, he enjoyed consistent commercial success throughout the 1970s and 1980s with a straightforward blend of folk-rock and blues. In its own low-key way, his music can be quite affecting; albums such as *Damn the Torpedoes* (1979) and *Hard Promises* (1981) and individual songs such as "Free Fallin'" (1989) and especially his marvelous "American Girl" (1976) feature gritty characters who exhibit a quiet determination to wrest dignity from less-than-fortuitous situations.

In 1985 Petty released *Southern Accents*, an album that represents his self-conscious attempt to explore his cultural heritage. By most standards (including his other work), *Southern Accents* is an unremarkable record. The album owes at least as much to the slick musical standards of Los Angeles as it does to the South, although one song, "The Best of Everything," features Garth Hudson and Richard Manuel of The Band and was coproduced by Robbie Robertson.[33] Not surprisingly, it is one of the most evocative songs on the album.

In any case, Petty remained determined to evoke a Southern way of life that links past and present. On the title track, he declares that his way of life, like his language, is marked by a Southern accent. The phrase sums up his approach to the South: as a place whose way of life is separate—but equal—to that of anywhere else.

By far the most suggestive song on the album, however, is the opening track, "Rebels." Petty begins it in a voice so garbled one can barely make out the words. The narrator is drunk and is pleading with his lover not to walk out on him. The persona is that of the unreconstructed redneck, telling his woman to put up with his nonsense. He also asks for some understanding, because although he knows he can be difficult, he is also faced with things he has difficulty handling because he was born a rebel.

Central to the song is an assumption that the Confederate rebellion that looms over the song was a preeminently working-class struggle (though one has a hard time, for example, imagining this as the credo of Jefferson Davis or Robert E. Lee). Petty's is a highly arguable position, of course, but one with persistent appeal to many Southern whites. More fundamental, in any case,

is the singer's assertion that history is destiny, that this character has somehow inherited a penchant to rebel that can justify and explain everything
from his failures as a lover to his arrest for drunken driving. But against what
is this rebel rebelling? Here we are back to the question Charlie Daniels
prompts in "The South's Gonna Do It Again."

Petty deals with it by means of a pluralist gesture. In the second verse, the
narrator's companion bails him out of jail—and then screams at him on the
way home before throwing him out of the car into a thicket. He never
thought she was so wicked, he says; but she is a habit he cannot quite kick. In
short, she is a rebel, too. To be sure, this interpretation has its limits—after
all, we are dealing with a woman who picks up after her man, just as countless
women always have—but the listener is still supposed to believe that we are
dealing with one tough cookie who gives as good as she gets. Literally and
figuratively, they come from the same place.

The music of "Rebels" follows a standard rock progression, but the use of a
horn section with martial phrasing adds some color to the song and makes
more explicit its historical frame of reference. Lest there be any doubt, Petty
makes the memory he invokes clear in the final verse:

> Even before my father's father
> They called us all rebels
> . . . .
> I can still feel the eyes
> of those blue bellied devils
> When I'm walkin' round at night
> Through the concrete and metal

There is something convincing about Petty's voice when he sings these words
(particularly his sneering "blue bellied devils"), and one can almost imagine
the past lingering so forcefully as to hover over the glass and steel of the
Newest South. Ultimately, however, his bid to evoke the ghosts of the Confederacy falls short. Part of the problem is musical; Petty's songwriting insufficiently traces the lineaments of Southern musical traditions. In any case, it is
hard for a careful listener even to sympathize with the attempt to evoke those
ghosts. Like The Band and Lynyrd Skynyrd, Petty fails to resolve the problems inherent in trying to uphold the memory of the Confederacy. A song
like "Rebels" is written in the liberal mode—that is, it seeks to conserve
through reform (here by a greater effort at inclusion). However, the attempt

still does not address the core problems of the Confederate spirit. That attempt, it seems, calls for a somewhat different approach.

One intriguing hint of how an inclusionary sensibility *could* work, in gender terms anyway, is suggested by "Dixie Chicken," a classic song by the interracial Southern band Little Feat. Recorded in 1974 and written and sung by the late Lowell George, "Dixie Chicken" tells the story of a visitor to a Memphis hotel lured by the charms of a Southern belle with whom he shares an unforgettable evening (albeit one clouded by alcohol). Even more unforgettable is the love song, "Dixie Chicken," she crooned to him, a lovely tune that remains with him long after she has left. A year later, he returns to Memphis and tells his story to a bartender who says he knew her well. The visitor starts to sing his special song—only to be joined by the rest of the men at the bar.

Part of what makes this song so amusing and rich is its appropriation of male promiscuity for a woman empowered, but not punished or even scolded, for her sexuality. To put it more simply, the song's approach is ironic. The artistic potential only hinted at in Little Feat's music was tapped more fully, and revealingly, in the more historically minded music of Randy Newman.

Mode: Ironic

It's Great to Be an American: Randy Newman

> In moral and social condition they had been elevated from
> brutal savages into docile, intelligent, and civilized
> agricultural laborers, and supplied not only with bodily
> comforts but with careful religious instruction.
>
> Jefferson Davis
> on enslaved African Americans[34]

Of all the work by performers discussed in this chapter, only Randy Newman's spans the entire period between the end of the 1960s and the end of the 1980s. The original lineup of The Band continued making intermittently interesting music until 1976, when it gave a farewell concert captured in Martin Scorsese's *Last Waltz* (1978). A plane crash in 1977 killed key members of Lynyrd Skynyrd, and the group broke up at its commercial peak (surviving members have periodically regrouped). Although Tom Petty is still active, he did not make his first records until the mid-1970s. Newman has never been as successful as any of these performers, nor is he nearly as well known. But he is probably among the most talented and incisive figures of the rock world, even if he merely inhabits its fringes. Newman is also the only one of these performers whose commitment to exploring the Southern past has been relatively consistent. Born a Southerner but also Jewish, he was in that world (briefly) but never quite of it, which at various times seems to be his particular curse and blessing. Few contemporary artists manage to ride the line between detachment and engagement as strikingly as Randy Newman.

Newman was born in 1944 in New Orleans. His family moved to Los Angeles when he was a child, and he grew up in a sophisticated musical milieu; his uncles Lionel and Alfred wrote musical scores for television and movies, as Newman himself later did in films such as *Ragtime* (1981), *The Natural* (1984), *Parenthood* (1989), and *The Paper* (1994). He attended the University of California at Los Angeles and majored in composition before dropping out in his senior year to join a publishing company. There he wrote a number of hits for singers ranging from Ray Charles to Judy Collins, including the number one hit "Mama Told Me Not to Come" for Three Dog Night in 1970. By this point, however, Newman was getting restless writing for others and had begun recording his songs in his own distinctive voice. He was helped in this pursuit by childhood friend Lenny Waronker, a record producer and executive who later became the president of Warner Brothers Records. Given what Newman went on to do, one wonders if he would have been able to sustain a recording career at all without such a powerful friend.

Newman's performing style has been influenced by New Orleans blues singers and piano players such as Professor Longhair and Fats Domino. Greil Marcus explains the nature of Newman's debt to these people:

> What Newman has taken from black singers is not what most rock & roll singers have taken: assertiveness, aggression, melancholy, sexual power. His somnambulant personality determined his choice of a lazy, blurred sound, where words just slide into each other, where syllables are not bitten off, but just wear out and dissolve. The blues practice of dropping a key word off the end of a line, to hint at ominous sexual mastery or knowledge too strong to put into words, becomes with Newman a wonderful throwaway, a surface lack of seriousness that at first hides, and after a few listenings intensifies, a sense of Newman's commitment to his material.[35]

This emphasis on the blues is overlaid with Newman's classical training, which leads him to compose songs of deceptive simplicity and polish. In some cases, to call them rock 'n' roll at all is a misnomer, though if one is going to classify Newman anywhere, it is best done there—rock is nothing if not elastic.

The hallmark of Newman's work is the sense of irony that pervades his lyrics. This irony takes two major forms. The first is broad satire. Perhaps the best example is "Political Science," an Archie-Bunkeresque meditation on national frustration with U.S. involvement in foreign affairs included on his 1972 album *Sail Away* that advocates nuclear bombing as the solution for bringing recalcitrant enemies (and friends) into line. Another example of this kind of humor, also from *Sail Away,* is "Burn On," a mock-sentimental tribute to Cleveland. To say that Newman is playing for laughs in songs like these is not exactly accurate; certainly, many listeners find them funny, but there is a bitterness pervading them that subverts the jokes. "Political Science," like Stanley Kubrick's *Dr. Strangelove,* asks troubling questions about deadly serious matters even as they make one laugh. Not the least of those questions is "Why is this funny?"

The other form of irony Newman uses, related to this one, relies less on humor and more on a repugnant narrator who explains his point of view to the listener. The approach is most clearly embodied by the narrator of "Suzanne" from *Twelve Songs* (1970), a rapist who stalks a woman whose name he finds written in a telephone booth. When he sings longingly of putting his arms around this woman, his very tenderness is a chilling threat, turning the warm, folksy, singer-songwriter style on its head. In this regard, Newman evoked—or, more accurately, anticipated—a strain of 1970s popular culture that explored presumably deviant personalities to suggest that such people were actually representative of a pathological national character. One can see this tendency in movies such as Martin Scorsese's *Taxi Driver* (1976), albums such as Sly and the Family Stone's *There's a Riot Goin' On* (1971), and television shows such as those produced by Norman Lear. A decade later Newman anticipated the religious fundamentalism and crass materialism of 1980s culture with *Born Again* (1979), which included "It's Money That I Love" (a variation on which, "It's Money That Matters," received some airplay in 1988).

Newman's approach is most powerful when he blends it with a historical consciousness. Given his musical style, it is hardly surprising that his gaze fell on the Southern past: hence "Sail Away," from the album of the same name, perhaps the most unforgettable song of his career. "Sail Away" is a song sung from the point of view of a Southern slave trader in Africa who tells the natives about the virtues of bondage. "In America you'll get food to eat," he explains in a gruff voice as sweet strings swell behind him,

> Won't have to run through the jungle and scuff up your feet
> You'll just drink wine and sing about Jesus all day
> It's great to be an American . . .
> Sail away—Sail away
> We will cross the mighty ocean into Charleston Bay

Does the narrator believe what he is saying? Is he lying to himself? There are times when he is truthful, albeit in a tortured way: "In America every man is free," he explains, "to take care of his family." He is describing a dream and a nightmare that includes many and excludes many, too. That's America.

The historical dimension of "Sail Away" is only one on an otherwise thematically varied record, but Newman's next release, *Good Old Boys* (1975), is an album-long excursion into Huey Long's Louisiana. Actually, the reverberations of *Good Old Boys* go in both temporal directions. When the Depression-era narrator of "Birmingham" proudly asserts that "you can travel 'cross this entire land / But there ain't no place like Birmingham," the listener's experience of the song is leavened by the knowledge of what would happen in the city in 1963; similarly, when the protagonist of "Rednecks" proclaims "we're keeping the niggers down," he is echoing a sentiment that was a pillar, if not the only pillar, of a would-be nation a century before. The album's resonance, then, is not so much timeless as *timeful*, with a sense of historical resonance even greater than that of The Band.

In any case, there remains the question of where Newman—as opposed to his characters—stands in all of this. Even in his most obnoxious characters, some detect a sympathy they find troubling. The classic case in point is Newman's one and only Top 10 hit, "Short People," which reached number two in the fall of 1977. Compared to rapists, racists, or imperialists, the ostensible target of this singer's wrath, short people, seems ridiculous (one can even argue that Newman was consciously angling for a hit, given the song's jaunty Los Angeles polish and relatively tame target). But in the singer's blunt assertion that short people have no reason to live, more than a few were offended. The song was banned from a number of radio stations, program directors claimed it was "disturbing to little children," and organizations of short people made protest.[36] One can only wonder what the reaction would have been had "Sail Away" or even "Political Science" received more airplay.

There are times when Newman does seem to have sympathy for his repellent characters. In "A Wedding in Cherokee County," one of the rednecks from *Good Old Boys* describes his wedding night and at the end of the song confesses his impotence. "Why must everybody laugh at my Mighty Sword?" he asks, as horns and strings embroider his absurd lament. One cannot help but hear an invitation to laugh, but also to commiserate.

Indeed, this brings us to the ultimate issue at the heart of Newman's music. For in the end, it matters less what Newman thinks of his protagonists than what his audience does. His best songs, as Greil Marcus has argued, implicate the listener.[37] When the singer of "My Old Kentucky Home" sings "Turpentine and dandelion wine / I've turned the corner and I'm doin' fine / Shooting at the birds on the telephone line / Pickin' 'em off with this gun of mine," one is tempted to laugh, but one wonders whether one should. Does finding this funny reveal smug complacency? In "Davy the Fat Boy," the narrator promises Davy's parents he will take care of the child after their death but promptly turns him over to a circus show. It is hard not to laugh at the pathos of the lyrics and satire in the (circus) music, but doing so risks complicity in this bitter joke.

Sometimes, there are not even any jokes. This is particularly true of Newman's most recent work, where at times the irony is virtually imperceptible. "Follow the Flag," from his 1988 album *Land of Dreams*, describes nationalism as the joy of believing in something bigger than oneself. Whereas "Suzanne" includes a tinkly, unnerving organ line that serves as a cue that there is something not quite right about the rapist narrator, "Follow the Flag" is simply a man and a piano offering a seductive fascism all the more frightening for its plausibility and even attractiveness. The listener is on his or her own to face the risks Newman's work offers, one of which is that you will learn something about yourself that you do not particularly like. Another risk is that you will take Newman at face value. Part of his power derives from his characters saying the unspeakable in compelling ways. Tom Petty's and Lynyrd Skynyrd's presumably bold assertions are tame indeed compared with statements such as "We're keeping the niggers down"—a pronouncement that (as Southern historian Ulrich Phillips has more subtly argued) has been the central theme of Southern history.[38]

Through it all, what makes Newman's work all the more remarkable is his ability to convey the appeal of a lingering Confederate fantasy even to outsiders. Perhaps the best example of this is "New Orleans Wins the War," an apparently autobiographical rendering of a childhood memory. Newman describes scenes from the segregated city ("Momma used to take me to Audubon Park / Show me the ways of the world / She said 'here comes a white boy, there goes a black one, that one's an octoroon'") before relating a story:

> In 1948 my daddy came to the city
>
> Told the people that they'd won the war
>
> Maybe they'd heard it, maybe not
>
> Probably they'd heard about it and just forgot
>
> 'Cause they built him a platform there in Jackson Square
>
> And the people came to hear him from everywhere
>
> They started to party and they partied some more
>
> 'Cause New Orleans had won the war
>
> (We knew we'd do it, we done whipped the Yankees)

At this point the music—a truly lovely Dixieland arrangement—takes over, and it is hard not to be momentarily swayed by it along with everyone else. But when his father's voice returns, it is to inform us that the family is moving. "People have fun here, and I think that they should / But nobody from here ever come to no good," he explains, and although he may be overgeneralizing, it is not hard to understand why a Jewish father might not want to keep his son in a place where "they're gonna pickle him in brandy and tell him he's saved." (In "Dixie Flyer," another song on the album, Newman sings of "tryin' to do like the Gentiles do / Christ they wanted to be Gentiles too / Who wouldn't down there wouldn't you? An American Christian—God damn!")

"The ironic interpretation of history is rare and difficult," writes C. Vann Woodward in his classic essay "The Irony of Southern History." "In the nature of things the participants in an ironic situation are rarely conscious of the irony, else they would not become its victims. Awareness must ordinarily be contributed by an observer, a nonparticipant, and the observer must have an unusual combination of detachment and sympathy."[39] It is hard to imagine C. Vann Woodward listening to Randy Newman records. It is even harder for me to imagine that if he did, there would not be some very fundamental understanding in the meeting of the minds.

The Burden of American History

> It is not that the present South has any lack of conspicuous
> faults, but that its faults are growing less conspicuous and
> therefore less useful for purposes of regional identification.
> They are increasingly the faults of other parts of the
> country, standard American faults, shall we say.
>
> C. Vann Woodward,
> "The Search for Southern Identity"[40]

Admittedly, the view one gets of the Civil War from rock 'n' roll is fragmentary. In the larger scheme of rock's own history, the subject is rarely explored, and even when it has been, references have been fleeting and indirect. (Or simply uninteresting; I have not even bothered to mention some songs about the war.) And although, as I have tried to suggest, many of these performers have evoked voices from the past, one should not assume harmony among them. Henry Grady, for example, would probably have been appalled to be compared with people of the likes of Lynyrd Skynyrd, and there are vast differences in their respective worldviews.

Nevertheless, I am struck by the continuity of certain ideas about the Southern past, ideas that get deployed in very different contexts and are appropriated unconsciously but have an ongoing connection nonetheless. In this chapter I have tried to trace some of those connections and to show the ways Civil War battles continue to be fought in what might seem the unlikeliest of places. In uncovering and recognizing the records of such events, one simultaneously catches a glimpse of the bonds between past and present as well as the distinctive accents that mark even opposing ideas as belonging to a particular time.

In his provocative 1990 collection of essays *Time Passages: Collective Memory and American Popular Culture*, George Lipsitz employs the concept of collective memory to suggest how history functions as an important force for making meaning in a time of postmodern fragmentation. For Lipsitz, the crucial factor in collective memory is what he calls "counter-memory," the mass remembrance of alternative ways of life that dominant interpretations must take into account to make their own versions seem credible. Yet accounting for opposition, however marginally, risks legitimating it, giving popular culture vibrance and hope. In short, the past has the power to save the future.

Lipsitz's work is an important tool for recognizing how powerful a force history can be for making social change. However, it is clear that collective memory works in other ways, too, and that it can be used to resist change and provide explanations very different from those that would promote alternative social arrangements. Perhaps this is just another way of saying what scholars of popular culture have been saying for the last two decades: It is a site of struggle between warring views of the world. It is a struggle that seems to go on no matter who wins wars, what laws are passed, or what ideas appear to be discredited. This is our blessing as well as our curse.

At the end of his checkered life, living off interest from a vast talent squandered in Hollywood and Las Vegas, a declining Elvis Presley performed a piece he called his "American Trilogy."[41] It was a medley of three classic songs: "Dixie," "Battle Hymn of the Republic," and the slave spiritual "All My Trials." With a barbershop quartet and a swelling orchestra backing him, it is hard not to be amazed, if not offended, by the way Presley conflated some of the most emotionally charged music in U.S. history and packaged it for tourists in the Nevada desert. And yet for all the squalor of its execution, there remains something compelling about the concept of integrating these three songs. Despite the best (and worst) intentions of some very determined people, the things for which this music stands—slavery, freedom, despair, redemption—remain connected. Even in the most careless (or willfully ignorant) moments, our shared history of division marks our national psyche like a scar that gives a face its distinctive cast.

Chapter 5

A Few
Good Men

Glory
and the Search
for a Just War

The war for our Union, with all the
constitutional issues which it settled, and
all the military lessons which it gathered
in, has throughout its dilatory length but
one meaning in the eye of history. It
freed the country from the social plague
which until then had made political
development impossible in the United
States. More and more, as the years pass,
does that meaning stand forth as the sole
meaning.

William James, 1897[1]

At one point in Toni Morrison's 1987 novel *Beloved*, Sethe, a former slave in post–Civil War Ohio, is late arriving at the restaurant where she works as a cook. It is the first time in sixteen years that this has happened, but the owner of the restaurant, Mr. Sawyer, is annoyed. He warns her not to do it again, but Sethe continues to be late, spending time with the daughter against whom she had committed an act of horrific desperation before the war. So Sawyer fires her.

It is possible to see Sawyer as a typically insensitive white man, quick to anger when things are not done his way and unwilling to tolerate any deviation from his dicta. But Morrison suggests that there may be more involved. Though his countenance is now stern, Sethe considers his hiring her despite her criminal record as an act of kindness. "He used to be a sweet man," she reflects. "Patient, tender in his dealings with the help. But each year, following the death of his son in the War, he grew more and more crotchety. As though Sethe's dark face was to blame."[2]

Reading these words at the end of the twentieth century, there is a sense in which one can only hope Sethe's dark face *was* "to blame." Given the staggering cost in human life, the change in status of African Americans, however tenuous and incremental, is the most concrete and important good to have come from the Civil War's evils. Although the first objective of the war was union—an issue given almost mystical appeal in the prose of Abraham Lincoln—one is forced to wonder if such an end justified the means. Would two (or many) United States have been such a bad thing? We will never know. But any measure of racial justice that has been achieved in this country since 1865 springs directly from one of the war's lasting legacies: emancipation.

Unlike many other conflicts in U.S. history, there is no myth of effortless victory surrounding the Civil War. The war did mark the burgeoning of industrial capitalism in the North, with an attendant rise in Darwinian complacency. However, for most people in the United States, the direct costs of the war were emphatically evident, not only in terms of blood and grief, but also in terms of the devastation of the Southern economy, which chained freedpeople to tenant farming and turned the region into a colonial outpost

"These men, these faces in these uniforms, is finally the iconography this movie presents," said director Edward Zwick of his 1989 film Glory, *a fictionalized account of an African American Union regiment in the Civil War. "If there's a certain degree of liberal fantasy in that, well, so be it." (Photo courtesy of Tri-Star Pictures, Culver City, California)*

for Northern capital. If there were obvious winners in the Civil War, it is equally obvious that there were losers, losers who were not necessarily—or even predominately—Confederates. This truth is one among many that Morrison's *Beloved* makes clear.

Not until this century, with the Vietnam War, did the nation face loss on anything resembling a comparable scale. Unlike the Civil War, Vietnam wreaked no havoc on the nation's landscape (though the inflation of the 1970s and the receding interest in the War on Poverty could be considered casualties). The psychological scars have proved lasting, however, cutting across the ideological spectrum. For those on the right, the war shattered the myth of invincibility, a loss that seemed all the more galling for having been generated by "traitors" from within. For those on the left, Vietnam symbolized the corruption of American ideals, the nation as the villain in a heroic Third World struggle for independence. For those in between, Vietnam was painful in both ways to varying degrees, and this ambivalent confusion became the backdrop for Richard Nixon's fitful, protracted withdrawal of troops from the Vietnamese countryside.

In the years since the war's end, the slogan "No more Vietnams" has been heard repeatedly regarding flash points around the world—Grenada, Nicaragua, Lebanon, Kuwait, Bosnia, and others. For the military and its partisans, this means no fighting without unconditional civilian support for a war effort. For pacifists and skeptics, the phrase also means no fighting without unconditional civilian support, but with the implication that such support should rarely, if ever, materialize. For U.S. policymakers, this situation has resulted in tenuous efforts to bridge these two camps through action and rhetoric, perhaps most revealingly in George Bush's 1989 invasion of Panama to crush the U.S.-made monster Manuel Noriega—an effort named, without irony, "Operation Just Cause."

It is perhaps one of the strange contradictions of human nature that even the most ruthless despots wrap aggression in the mantle of morality. It seems there are never mere assertions of power; all wars are somehow just causes undertaken for God and country (which always seem indivisible). In the United States, a nation presumably governed by mutual consent and free choice, the need to persuade the citizens that any wars we fight are *good* wars takes on a particular kind of importance. Unlike that of other nations that can rely on executive fiat or religious order, U.S. martial ardor depends on mass mobilization through a variety of media that include the press as well as popular culture.

However, in the half-century since World War II—the last war widely considered morally justified—the most meaningful and lasting national struggle, the Civil Rights movement, has been waged at home. Although this conflict is an ongoing one, even the most committed conservative will concede, if only to argue that enough has been done, that the old segregated racial order in this country was immoral and that those fighting to change it had a just cause. No other issue in the last half-century has the same stark clarity as that crystallized by Rosa Parks on a Montgomery, Alabama, bus in December 1955, which helped bring about one of the most important social revolutions in the United States in the twentieth century.

As I tried to suggest in the last chapter, this revolution provoked resistance that had powerful consequences in U.S. politics and culture. To a great extent, the history of the nation in the 1970s and 1980s was a reaction to the tide of reform in the 1960s, one visible everywhere from busing controversies in Boston to Southern rock in Alabama. Whatever future historians may say of the period, contemporaries experienced it as an age of conservatism marked by a rolling back of the Great Society, a new commitment to the economic myth of laissez-faire, and an attempted restoration of "traditional" values (often 1950s mores that were assumed to be the norm for all Americans at all times). The specter of Vietnam lurked behind all these efforts, a symbol of the crippled confidence the ruling Republican coalition sought to restore.

Not everyone considered himself or herself conservative in these years, of course, but even a person radically committed to challenging the prevailing assumptions of the Reagan era was forced to respond to them in a climate far different from that of the 1960s. At the same time, many people, even those who *did* consider themselves conservatives, felt a yearning for the kind of good fight that World War II and the Civil Rights movement symbolized for many. It may have been a half-hearted yearning, often inchoate, and perhaps one that was too easily satisfied (witness the almost obsessive parading in the wake of the Persian Gulf War). Yet it surfaced from time to time, awkward and almost palpable when George Bush spoke of "the vision thing" and "a thousand points of light" in his successful quest to become caretaker of the Reagan coalition in the presidential election of 1988.

The most compelling evidence of the impulses I am describing is discernible in the popular culture of the period.[3] For my purposes, the 1989 Civil War film *Glory*, a rendering of an 1863 African American–led attack on well-defended Confederate Fort Wagner, is a particularly apt example of the political crosscurrents shaping the presentation of history at the twilight of the Reagan era. By returning to the very roots of the Civil Rights movement—and portraying it as a good war—*Glory* reshaped the parameters of Vietnam conventions and reintroduced a notably absent moral worldview into popular discourse. It did so in a way that seems highly characteristic of a conservative era: portraying a moment of social redemption but using war as the vehicle for it; depicting collective action by African Americans as effective, if supervised by whites; and arguing for the necessity of progress but minimizing the ironies and contradictions that surround it.

Nonetheless, I believe that the overall thrust of *Glory* was reformist; in a culturally significant way, the movie evoked a restless mood that anticipated the political rejection of Bush in favor of Bill Clinton in 1992. In its attempt to heal and unite a divided black community, to build bridges between blacks and whites, and especially to connect past and present, I also believe the movie is an important example of the communion motif I discussed at the beginning of this book. For these reasons, I think the film represents one of the most notable uses of the Civil War in twentieth-century popular culture.

There are two separate contexts that can help illuminate how *Glory* works. The first is recent academic historiography of African American men in the Civil War and scholarly efforts to uncover the choices and conflicts they faced. One of the most important results of post–World War II prosperity and the upheavals of the 1960s in the academy was a broadening of the kinds of people that inhabited it. In the 1970s the racial, class, and gender analyses that had challenged the status quo in the decades before became, at least to some degree, a part of it. This meant that many of the people, events, and perspectives that had not been previously deemed worthy of study received new—or unprecedented—attention. In some cases, *Glory* among them, such scholarship furnished the raw material for popular cultural representations. (The new demographic order in the academy also fostered popular/academic divisions, which will be discussed in the next chapter.)

The other important context I will discuss is the Hollywood war film since Vietnam. War films of the last generation have either been dark commentaries on U.S. failure or hollow celebrations of ersatz success. Such tendencies can be seen in popular music, fiction, and television, notably M*A*S*H—a movie and subsequent television series about the Korean War that is essentially a parable of Vietnam.[4] But in terms of lasting impact, particularly with the advent of home video, film seems to be the form best suited to mass exploration of the Vietnam War, perhaps because of the panoramic possibilities it offers to express what became highly interiorized feelings (more on this below). In any case, by the late 1980s the Vietnam movie had evolved into a distinct subgenre that influenced not only films about the conflict itself, but also other would-be war movies that were indirectly forced to respond to it. Similarly, although there were a number of other film conventions upon which Glory drew—the "buddy" film of the 1970s and 1980s and the larger iconography of African American film history, to name two—these can been seen as operating in a particular way within the paradigm of war films.

After surveying these contexts, I proceed to a close reading of the film that analyzes how it functions ideologically. I conclude by showing that Glory is actually part of a long tradition of commemorating the simultaneously doomed and inspiring attack on Fort Wagner and ask how we can make sense of these varied meanings.

The Black Badge of Courage

> I think that the proposition to make soldiers of the slaves is the most pernicious idea that has been suggested since the war began. You cannot make soldiers of slaves, or slaves of soldiers. The day you make a soldier of them is the beginning of the end of the revolution. And if slaves seem good soldiers, then our whole theory of slavery is wrong.
>
> Former U.S. senator and Confederate general
> Howell Cobb of Georgia[5]

"The American negroes are the only people in the world, as far as I know, that ever became free without any effort of their own," wrote W. E. Woodward in a 1928 biography of Ulysses S. Grant. "They twanged banjos around the railroad stations, sang melodious spirituals, and believed some Yankee would soon come along and give each of them forty acres and a mule."[6]

These remarks were quoted by James McPherson in The Negro's Civil War, a 1965 collection of primary source documents that refutes Woodward's description of African Americans.[7] One of the most important themes of Civil War and Reconstruction historiography since the 1960s has been an effort to recover the lost contributions of black people fighting for their freedom. This theme intersects with one of most notable methodological developments in the discipline, social history, in the work of scholars such as Herbert Gutman,

Eugene Genovese, and others. In shifting their gaze away from prominent leaders and thinkers toward ordinary people and the conditions of their lives, these historians have offered us a wealth of new insights into the past. This effort is captured most powerfully in *Freedom: A Documentary History of Emancipation*, an ongoing project to unearth documents from the national archives of the United States that reveal the dramatic and often moving acts of courage by blacks all over the nation during and after the Civil War.[8]

From these and other studies, there is now a fairly clear picture of the military activities of African Americans during the war, which can be summarized as follows.[9] The outbreak of war in 1861 led men all over the country to volunteer for military service, and African Americans were no exception. But they were almost always turned down. Ironically, black men experienced some of their greatest success in the Confederacy, though they were generally put to work building fortifications or other kinds of tasks requiring heavy labor, perhaps in the hope of being looked upon with favor in the event of Southern victory. A desperate Confederacy did not officially sanction black combat participation until the very end of the war, and by then it was too late to have any effect.

These studies document the work of Northern black soldiers in greater detail, largely because more records survived. Despite a federal ban on black recruitment for the army, unofficial African American units were organized in Kansas, South Carolina, and Louisiana, and these soldiers saw action in the early years of the war (indeed, blacks had been participants in the guerrilla warfare over "Bloody Kansas" for years). Moreover, the U.S. Navy had long been a multiracial institution.[10] Meanwhile, intractable rebel resistance, military defeat, and growing difficulties in meeting manpower needs from white volunteers impelled the Lincoln administration to widen its war aims and turn the political screws on the Confederacy. It did this with the Emancipation Proclamation, conceived by Lincoln in the summer of 1862. Around the same time, the president and Congress removed legal barriers to blacks in the armed forces. By the end of the war, approximately 180,000 African Americans served in the United States Armed Forces. Although less than 1 percent of the North's population, African Americans constituted roughly 10 percent of the Union army.[11]

Although some works portray this situation in relatively optimistic terms, the most exhaustive studies show that the struggle for black enlistment was not altogether affirming.[12] Many Northerners supported the effort not because they believed it to be a crucial dimension of emancipation but because they would rather have had blacks die than whites. Indeed, white eagerness to have blacks serve in the army reached vicious proportions. Civilians and

government officials soon realized that enlisted blacks could be credited toward conscription quotas, and coercion and terror were often the result, as
some black men were literally abducted from their homes and forced into the
army. Northern states sent agents to enlist "underemployed" men of the
occupied South for a fee, and they wandered the countryside in search of
recruits, often impeding military operations and demanding food, forage, and
transportation from their "hosts."[13]

Virtually all recent accounts describe how even those blacks who entered
the army freely and enthusiastically quickly encountered situations that clari-
fied the predicament of blacks: Although the government was committed to
freedom, it had no intention of promoting equality. Once black enlistment
became official policy, the government ordered that all black units should
have only white commissioned officers, barring advancement for enlisted
African Americans. Many blacks who were already officers were hounded
into resigning their commissions.

Another widely noted problem was a controversy over pay. Despite promises of receiving the same amount of money as whites, black soldiers were paid
only about half of what their white counterparts were, and the government
dragged its heels in living up to its stated policy. Some black units refused
their pay in protest, at great personal cost to themselves and their families,
and still others threatened to lay down their arms. Some were shot or jailed
for their protests; 80 percent of U.S. soldiers shot for mutiny were black.[14]
When Congress finally acted to correct the situation, it did so by making an
invidious distinction between those who had been slaves before the war and
those who had been free. Such a policy impaired morale within these regiments and exacerbated tensions between Northern and Southern blacks as
well as the previously enslaved and previously free.[15]

Finally, these works note that African Americans were often given a dis-
proportionate amount of fatigue duty. Ordered to dig ditches, build fortifications, clean latrines, or do other dirty work, they were often denied the
opportunity to drill or perform the more esteemed tasks of soldiering. Such
practices not only bred resentment, but also contributed to the higher disease
rate among blacks, many of whom should not have been in the army in the
first place or who were overworked by their officers. Whereas two white
soldiers died of disease for every one who died in battle, for blacks the ratio
was about ten to one. One in twelve whites in the Union army died of disease
in the war; one in five blacks did.[16]

By the end of the 1980s, then, Civil War historiography had done a great
deal to fill in aspects of black life that had been neglected by previous
historians. Yet this story was not well known outside the confines of the

academy—or for that matter, to those who were not Civil War or Afro-American scholars. *Glory*, which gives a fictionalized rendering of a Massachusetts regiment in Georgia and South Carolina, is the first account most people have heard of black soldiers in the war. As such, it can be seen as part of a trend toward greater racial awareness in U.S. movies with historical subjects ranging from Kevin Costner's *Dances with Wolves* (1990) to Spike Lee's *Malcolm X* (1992).

But *Glory* is not only a story about race. It is also a story about war, and as such is part of a long film tradition. It is difficult to get a full sense of the movie's texture without this war movie context.

Warring Sentiments

> America it is to thee
> Thou boasted land of liberty
> It is to thee I raise my song
> Thou land of blood, of crime, and wrong
>
>   James M. Whitfield, 1852[17]

The United States film tradition includes both pro- and antiwar strains, and as often as not, contradictory attitudes coalesce in the same movie. Thus, although there have been plenty of movies in the spirit of *The Kaiser, The Beast of Berlin* (1918), there have also been pacifist manifestoes such as *All Quiet on the Western Front* (1930) and movies that affirmed war while frankly portraying its costs, such as *The Big Parade* (1925).[18]

Nevertheless, opposing views on war do not cancel each other out, and at different times one mood is usually dominant. During the world wars, for example, prowar exhortations were commonly produced by Hollywood and the U.S. government, urging the nation to throw its collective weight behind the efforts. Indeed, to show war in any other light would have been looked upon with governmental disfavor—or even, in the case of the Creel committee set up by the Wilson administration, repression.

The aftermath of conflicts were sometimes marked by an antiwar mood. Certainly this was true of the First World War. To some degree it was even true of World War II; the Academy Award–winning best picture of 1946, *The Best Years of Our Lives*, captured the anxiety and skepticism of soldiers returning from war to their families, prefiguring the issues facing veterans a quarter of a century later. In the next decade, Stanley Kubrick made a career of directing caustic antiwar movies, including *Paths of Glory* (1957) and *Dr. Strangelove* (1964). Although neither film directly concerns the Second World War, one can imagine from Kubrick's stark portrayal of inept and bloodthirsty military and civilian leaders that his view of the war would have looked far different from that in Frank Capra's *Why We Fight* films produced for the government during the war.

Still, however significant one deems these examples, they constituted a minority view until the advent of Vietnam, when growing skepticism and protest over that war led to a more critical stance toward World War II in the film versions of Kurt Vonnegut's *Slaughterhouse Five* (1972), Joseph Heller's *Catch 22* (1970), and *A Bridge Too Far* (1977). In the twenty-year period between *Casablanca* (1942) and *The Longest Day* (1962), however, the conflict was almost always portrayed as an essential—and triumphant—struggle of good over evil. Humphrey Bogart may be a little more reluctant than John Wayne, but there was never any doubt who the good guys and bad guys were (and we are talking about *guys*). Wayne himself virtually defined the subgenre of heroic World War II movies, with appearances in *The Fighting Tigers* (1942), *The Fighting Seabees* (1944), *The Sands of Iwo Jima* (1949), *In Harm's Way* (1965), and many others.

It may be helpful to state the obvious here: The United States won World War II. Because of this victory, filmmakers were able to portray the outcome as the best of all possible worlds. The United States did not win in Vietnam. This alone can explain much about the predominately negative mood that pervades movies about the war there. One stark statistic tells a striking story: Whereas roughly 450 World War II movies were released during the Second World War, only one Vietnam film came out during that conflict.[19] This was *The Green Berets*, a 1967 release starring (who else?) John Wayne. Made at the height of the war, it can be considered a kind of booster film of the type made during World War II. By the time of the psychologically decisive Tet Offensive, however, doubts about the war made it difficult to sell an unalloyed celebration of the U.S. effort—or, for that matter, anything at all about the war.

It was not until the late 1970s that feature films about Vietnam began to appear, notably, *The Deer Hunter* (1978) and *Apocalypse Now* (1979). The production of *Apocalypse Now* has itself become a kind of legend. Spending ten years and $31 million, the obsessive Francis Ford Coppola mortgaged his house, his critical reputation, and possibly his sanity in making the movie, whose ending he reshot a number of times—including once after the official release of the film.[20] Visually, the movie is a stunning tour de force, with more panoramic combat and landscape scenes than perhaps any Vietnam movie since. The decision of Coppola and co-screenwriter John Milius to make the film an Americanized version of Joseph Conrad's *Heart of Darkness* was a genuine act of historical imagination. Marlow's (played by Martin Sheen) search for the ominously elusive Kurtz (Marlon Brando) becomes a parable of latent American savagery. Still, there is something about the film that remains imperial. As in the case of the *Godfather* movies, Coppola's obvious fascination with repellent characters becomes a form of oblique acceptance, even approval. At the same time, the bitter irreverence of *Apocalypse Now* prevented it from becoming the archetypal Vietnam movie.

In many ways, *The Deer Hunter* fulfills that role. Michael Cimino's three-hour epic exhibits the hallmarks of what film scholar Pat Aufderheide calls "the noble-grunt film."[21] Aufderheide considers the noble-grunt film predominately a late 1980s phenomenon, but many of the pieces are in place here. The fundamental strategy of this subgenre is suggested in the most basic description of the story line: Three men from Pennsylvania (or possibly Ohio) leave their mill town and experience the horror of Vietnam. There is no mention of strategic objectives, national goals, or even brotherhood within any military unit (even when the three are prisoners with other GIs). It is as if the only way to salvage the Vietnam movie as a credible form is to marginalize the big picture and project a small one. As Aufderheide explains, movies such as *The Deer Hunter* are best seen "as reconstructing the place of Vietnam in American popular history, away from a political process and toward an understanding of the war as a psychological watershed. Indeed, they speak more eloquently to the psychological plight of the average moviegoer than any reality of the war years."[22]

This may be why so many movies about Vietnam—from *Coming Home* (1978) through *In Country* (1989)—focus on the domestic scene, whether during the war or after it, and on the scars of the Vietnam veteran and his loved ones. For the regular moviegoer in these years, a veteran who was not taciturn, self-pitying, and potentially violent seemed like an aberration. What makes these people sympathetic characters is not the cause that sent them overseas (they were lied to), or even having seen combat (the enemy was invisible), but simply returning home. Survival becomes heroism; cynicism becomes idealism.

Ironically, however, *The Deer Hunter* slowed the flow of Vietnam films for a few years. It was a hit, winning five Oscars, including best picture and a best director award for Michael Cimino. Yet it also proved to be his undoing.

Anxious to have a hot director on its hands, United Artists gave Cimino the reins for the disastrous *Heaven's Gate* (1980). Coppola overwhelmed his own studio; Cimino destroyed United Artists.[23] For the next six years the major studios avoided Vietnam like the plague.

Key changes in the industry allowed the floodgates to open with *Platoon* (1986). By the mid-1980s large studios were acting less like producers of films than brokers of projects, which they could then distribute and exploit through cable, home video, and overseas markets at less risk. Thus, for example, the British company Hemdale financed director Oliver Stone for *Platoon*, which he had been trying to make for years, whereas Orion distributed it.[24] *Hamburger Hill* (1987), *Gardens of Stone* (1988), *84 Charlie MoPic* (1989), and others followed.

The one significant exception to the noble-grunt approach of the late 1980s is Stanley Kubrick's *Full Metal Jacket* (1987). Kubrick's caustic irony offers a bracing alternative to the rest of the pack—Matthew Modine's character is called "Joker"—but Kubrick's misanthropy ultimately undermines its power. Stone's *Born on the Fourth of July* (1989), which tells the story of paralyzed veteran Ron Kovic, is yet another victim tale, rendered in Stone's now familiar pedantic style.

By the end of the decade, Aufderheide suggests, the noble-grunt movies may have helped the nation recover "not for anything U.S. forces did in Vietnam, but simply for having felt so bad for so long."[25] Yet it was one thing to feel less bad; it was another to feel good. A number of U.S. films in the 1980s attempted to portray military involvement in a more sympathetic light, only to reveal the limitations and contradictions involved in such an attempt. The most commercially successful version was *Top Gun* (1986), essentially a 109-minute recruiting commercial for the U.S. Navy. There is a hollowness at the core of the movie, though, because there is no real adversary. "If I can't shoot this sonofabitch, let's see if we can have some fun with him," says Maverick (Tom Cruise) during an incident with a Soviet-made jet fighter early in the film. By the time he finally gets his chance for some real action, a rescue mission on a disabled communications ship that "wandered" into foreign territory, one wonders if any of these characters—or any of the filmgoers who flocked to the movie in droves—had ever heard of the Gulf of Tonkin.

Then there were the *Rambo* movies, which dwelled on the plight of the Vietnam veteran. In *First Blood* (1982), Sylvester Stallone plays veteran John Rambo, who in the opening sequence of the film goes to the hometown of his African American war buddy, only to learn that he is dead. Having established good-guy credentials in this way (here, as in his *Rocky* movies, Stallone uses friendships with black characters to build sympathy for his protagonists), one thing leads to another—a misunderstanding between Rambo and a policeman, car crashes, the arrival of the National Guard, the incineration of much of the town—before Rambo's superior officer, Trautman (Richard Crenna), finally confronts him in the empty police station. "It's over, Johnny," Trautman advises, giving Rambo the chance to put the rage that has virtually destroyed a town into words: "It wasn't my war. You asked me, I didn't ask you. And I did what I had to do to win. Then I come back to the world, and I see all those maggots at the airport protesting me, spitting, calling me baby killer and all kinds of crap. Who are they to protest me? Unless they've been me and been there?"

Rambo has a point, and it is one that no doubt represents the rage of many veterans, as well as noncombatant war supporters at home. However, his actions—and the depictions of those who oppose him—have something of a paranoid, even homicidal quality that competes with the viewer's sense of Rambo as a hapless victim ("They drew first blood," Rambo explains). These tendencies are even more pronounced in *Rambo: First Blood Part II*, which implies that the U.S. government conspiratorially avoided retrieving its prisoners of war and troops missing in action from Vietnam. *Rambo II* is one of a number of 1980s movies, such as *Missing in Action* (1986), which involve returning to Vietnam to set right some individual wrongs. Such wounded surliness also characterizes Rambo's attitude in the sequel. When Trautman proposes an undercover mission to find U.S. prisoners, Rambo asks, "Do we get to win this time?" (Of course—this is the movies.)

For many adventure-movie lovers, the first two Rambo movies were satisfying entertainment. The third movie, *Rambo III* (1988), attempted to go beyond its predecessors with a setting (Afghanistan) and message that seems to offer firmer political and moral ground. This time the reluctant Rambo's mission is more personal: to rescue Trautman. However, it is clear that the viewer is also supposed to sense the virtue of the cause to which Rambo's Afghan allies have pledged their lives; a note at the end of the movie states that "this film is dedicated to the gallant people of Afghanistan." The validity of the Afghan struggle for independence from Soviet domination notwithstanding, there is something problematic in this particular movie's affirmation of it, best suggested by Trautman's jibe at his vicious Soviet captor: "You talk of peace and disarmament to the world, but here you are wiping out a race of people." The pot is calling the kettle black here over a struggle that is necessarily remote in some very basic ways. In any case, *Rambo III* was a box-office flop.

By the end of the 1980s, then, the heroic war movie seemed to have been painted into a corner. Cut off from any sense of national unity or moral certitude, movies with military themes either exhibited a sharp strain of aggrieved resentment or an unconvincing air of celebration.

Until *Glory*.

Sixtysomething

> It is hugely difficult in any society, black or white, to come
> up with legitimate heroes.
>
>   Edward Zwick, director of *Glory*[26]

"War movies abound, yet remarkably few exist about the Civil War," *Entertainment Weekly* reported in its "complete guide" cover story published in the aftermath of the hit PBS documentary *The Civil War*. [27] This generalization is basically true, but only of the last half-century. The war was a popular subject in the age of silent film, and some of the most profitable or highly regarded motion pictures of all time—*Birth of a Nation, The General* (1926), *Gone with the Wind*—had Civil War settings. Many others—particularly Westerns such as *The Searchers* (1956)—have used it as a point of departure (e.g., *Dances with Wolves*).

All this said, the war has a reputation as box-office poison. "Forget it, Louie," Metro-Goldwyn-Mayer producer Irving Thalberg is widely reported to have told studio executive Louis B. Mayer, who had expressed an interest in acquiring *Gone with the Wind*. "No Civil War picture ever made a nickel."[28] Thalberg had overlooked *Birth of a Nation* but not *Operator 13* (1934) or *So Red the Rose* (1935), which had flopped in the years preceding the release of *GWTW*. Nevertheless, Thalberg did express the conventional wisdom, and that wisdom survived the success of *GWTW* into the years following the Second World War. Certainly, Civil War movies were made, notably, John Huston's version of *The Red Badge of Courage* (1951), William Wyler's *Friendly Persuasion* (1956), and John Ford's *Horse Soldiers*, starring Wayne (1959). But although all three films attracted critical attention (*Friendly Persuasion* received a few Academy Award nominations and is a staple of television rebroadcasts; *The Red Badge of Courage* has enjoyed the esteem of Huston's rising reputation; and *The Horse Soldiers* has a place in Ford's well-established reputation), none approached blockbuster status. Others, such as the Elizabeth Taylor/Montgomery Clift epic *Raintree County* (1957), were major critical and commercial disappointments.[29]

Whatever the reception of these and other films, the tone of virtually all Civil War movies is heroic. Significantly, those that were not, such as the low-budget *Journey to Shiloh* (1968) and Clint Eastwood's *Beguiled* (1971), were made at the height of the Vietnam War. These films, however, were exceptions to the rule. More typical is *The Red Badge of Courage*, which displays none of the subversion that lurks in the margins of Stephen Crane's novel. Even *Friendly Persuasion*, which is sympathetic toward the idea of pacifism, tips its hand somewhat in that Confederate officer John Mosby's raiders invade the family's small town, making self-defense a plausible pretext for violence.

This heroic sensibility also suffuses *Gettysburg* (1993), based on Michael Shaara's 1974 Pulitzer Prize–winning historical novel *The Killer Angels*. Writing as the Vietnam War dragged to its fitful end, Shaara, a career army officer, made *The Killer Angels* one of the few effective defenses of military culture in that era. His defense of soldiering is especially apparent in his description of Union colonel Joshua Chamberlain's heroism at Little Round Top, his deification of Robert E. Lee, and above all his vindication of James Longstreet, the defensive strategist who was vilified after the war for cooperating with Republican Reconstruction efforts. At twenty years' remove and lacking some of Shaara's nuances (Martin Sheen's Lee seems dangerously close to senility at points for insisting on attack over Longstreet's objections), *Gettysburg* retains his celebration of military valor and detail, at the expense of virtually everything else. Neither book nor film has much to say about race; to the extent it does, *Gettysburg* is evasive and even ludicrous. Although Chamberlain (Jeff Daniels) is portrayed as the abolitionist he really was, a captured Rebel infantryman insists that he was not fighting for slavery one way or another, which would have been a plausible view if it had been balanced by frank proslavery sentiments elsewhere. At one point in the movie, Longstreet (Tom Berenger) tells an English visitor that the South should have freed the slaves and then seceded—an almost laughable denial of what at least a significant part of the Confederacy was fighting for, and yet another example of the willed forgetfulness surveyed in the previous chapter and discussed again in the next one.

Heroic or otherwise, in no major Civil War movie since World War II has race played any major role, with the exception of *Glory*. Thus the film is notable not only in being the first Hollywood film in years to return to a war that had a bad cinematic reputation, but also in focusing on race, a cinematic theme with a troubled—and often conspicuously silent—history.

Glory sprang from unlikely sources. According to the press kit distributed with the movie, screenwriter Kevin Jarre—whose credits include *Rambo II*—was inspired to write a screenplay after meeting Lincoln Kirstein, cofounder of the New York City Ballet. In 1973 Kirstein had written a short essay on Colonel Robert Gould Shaw, the son of prominent abolitionists who died leading an attack of black troops on a fort outside Charleston. The essay, which accompanied photographs of a famous monument dedicated to Shaw, was published in *Lay This Laurel: An Album on the Saint-Gaudens Memorial on Boston Common Honoring Black and White Men Together Who Served the Union Cause with Robert Gould Shaw and Died with Him July 18, 1863.*

The script Jarre went on to write was also based on *One Gallant Rush*, a 1965 monograph by Peter Burchard (the book, part of the new wave of Civil War historiography during the Civil Rights movement, was reissued upon release of the movie).[30] Jarre succeeded in attracting the interest of producer Freddie Fields, who acquired rights to the film in 1985. Financial backing came from Tri-Star Pictures, which hired Edward Zwick.

Zwick became famous, along with partner Marshall Herskovitz, as the creator, writer, and director of the television series *thirtysomething* (1987–1991), a show tagged "domestic white whines" by critics and one even its biggest fans hated to love. Yet in *thirtysomething*'s cast of self-absorbed Philadelphia professionals with fashionably liberal attitudes, there were also struggles to find greater meaning in conflicts over religious rituals, marital fidelity, and terminal illness. For these people, "the good life" meant something in addition to a happy marriage, well-scrubbed kids, an exquisitely tasteful house, and a fulfilling job. "I think there is a deep political dialectic involved there," said Zwick of *thirtysomething*. It was about ambivalence, the contradictions of the human heart. "I think all popular culture is *de facto* political, so you better damn well be responsible about the images you put out into a culture."[31] Clearly, *Glory* represents a bid for political responsibility on Zwick's part (perhaps even an act of compensation).

Although Jarre ultimately received the screenwriting credit, Zwick said he played a large a role in shaping the portrayal of the main characters. He read a variety of sources to rewrite the screenplay, including Thomas Wentworth

Higginson's memoir *Black Life in an Army Regiment* (1869), oral histories of former slaves, and all 1,300 of Shaw's letters. He also talked with Shelby Foote.

In describing his vision of the project, Zwick spoke elliptically of powerful childhood experiences watching movies. "It was finally a personal agenda that bore fruit for me later," he explained. "My fantasy would be that others would have a similar experience in seeing this movie." Zwick said he sought to portray "a time when ideas had real currency that moved men and nations, a time when the force of an idea could change history." Fields put it in Hollywood jargon: "In the form of an entertainment vehicle, we tell a love story about the camaraderie between black and white men who learned and grew together. It's a story of how a black regiment and its white officers challenged history, racism and the fortunes of war."[32]

The Massachusetts 54th Volunteer Infantry is a powerful vehicle indeed on which to base a movie. Led by Shaw, the 54th became well known in part because two of Frederick Douglass's sons and two brothers of William and Henry James served under him. (All four survived.) After training in Readville, Massachusetts, in the winter of 1863, the regiment arrived on the islands off the South Carolina coast in June. This area, under the umbrella of the U.S. Department of the South, was a site of great activity for Northern women who went South to teach, businessmen who sought to aid and exploit black labor, and government officials trying to formulate postwar policy.[33] Black regiments were often assigned menial tasks, and the 54th was no exception. However, it did participate in a foraging raid in Georgia and, after a preliminary skirmish in a larger battle, was chosen to lead the attack on Confederate Fort Wagner on July 18, 1863.

Wagner was one of a series of forts (including Sumter, site of the war's first shot) guarding the entrance to Charleston. The center of some of the most fierce Confederate sympathy, the city was more a political than a military target. Protected by water and accessible only by a thin strip of sand, any assault virtually guaranteed heavy casualties for those who led it. The 54th lost about half its members in the failed attack. All told, there were 1,515 Union casualties, with 181 for the well-entrenched Confederates.[34] In retrospect, it appears that the 54th was used as cannon fodder. It is known that Shaw actively sought a combat role for the regiment and that leading the attack was considered an honor to him and his commanding officer, Brigadier General George Strong. However, Strong's superior, Major General Quincy Gillmore, is recorded as having said, "Well, I guess we will let Strong lead and put those damned niggers from Massachusetts in the advance; we may as well get rid of them one time as another."[35] In keeping with the overall tone of the film, this aspect of the story is ignored (more on this below).

After the filming of a historical reenactment of the Battle of Gettysburg using twelve thousand mock troops on July 4, 1988, the movie went into production in February 1989, with most of the shooting done in Savannah, Georgia. The Battle of Antietam sequence (Shaw was there before joining the 54th) was filmed in a rural area near Atlanta, whereas the Fort Wagner scenes were shot on Jekyll Island, off the Georgia coast. Thousands of extras and reenactors participated in these scenes, all costumed in period attire. The largest prop was the fort itself, a hollow structure made of plywood and sand.[36]

As in Kirstein's *Lay This Laurel* and Burchard's *One Gallant Rush*, the film's focus remains on Robert Gould Shaw, who is played by Matthew Broderick. The script shifts the ground significantly, however, with the addition of four fictional African American characters: Trip, a runaway slave from Tennessee (played by Denzel Washington); Rawlins, a former gravedigger who encounters Shaw at Antietam (played by Morgan Freeman); Sharts, a stuttering, illiterate South Carolinian (played by Jihmi Kennedy); and Searles, an educated free black and friend of the Shaw family (played by Andre Braugher).

The ensemble represents a notable case of racial diversity in a film that avoids cinematic stereotypes that persisted through the 1980s.[37] This point gets underlined in the movie when the 54th arrives in South Carolina and Searles literally cannot understand his fellow African Americans. At the same time, a story line centering on four personalities who must put aside any differences in the service of a larger cause amounts to a striking evocation of countless World War II movies—such as *Bataan* (1943)—in which the symbolic Jew, WASP, ethnic, and other potentially stereotypical characters find themselves thrown together. Pauline Kael admirably sums up what makes *Glory* familiar: "The principal characters are fictional, and you know it instantly, because they're the usual representative group of recruits who bicker and quarrel before they shape up and become fine soldiers."[38] In Vietnam movies such as *Platoon*, by contrast, the result of such quarreling is not unity but frustration and fragging (men on the same side killing each other).

The sympathetic portrayal of major national issues and collective struggles in the movie also represents a major departure from the Vietnam tradition and a return to a World War II sensibility. "We fight for men and women whose poetry is not yet written, but which will presently be as enviable and as renowned as any," Shaw says in a voice-over letter to his mother—a sentiment that would have been tragic in the hands of Oliver Stone and sarcastic if directed by Stanley Kubrick. When Frederick Douglass declares early in the film that the 54th "will offer pride and dignity to those who have known only degradation," he speaks with an authority meant to be accepted at face value.

That pride and dignity, as Douglass often asserted in his writings, comes from a reaffirmed sense of manhood.[39] For the characters of *Glory*, war (long considered a quintessentially masculine activity) was a key avenue for this affirmation. "Consider me your first recruit," Shaw's friend Searles tells him in Boston. The erudite Searles will have a lot to learn, but his commitment to the war and its ultimate value is never in question, even after he is wounded. "It's not true, is it?" he asks Shaw about rumors that the regiment will never be allowed to see action. "The men are all living for that day. I know I am." Clearly, he is not the only one. Words are not needed to convey the utter joy that the inarticulate Sharts feels when he is issued a uniform: His face is radiant. So, too, are those of all the recruits when they are finally issued guns.[40] They play with the guns and stage deaths like children—until a concerned and severe Shaw demonstrates to Sharts that being a good shot is not enough for fighting men.

In noble-grunt movies, becoming a soldier is usually a negative epiphany in which childhood innocence is lost. In *Glory*, the process is one of innocence lost, but it is also an affirmative ritual whereby "boys"—children and slaves— become men. One of the most moving moments in the film occurs when the regiment marches in South Carolina and encounters some slave children. "That's right . . . it ain't no dream," a proud Rawlins tells them. "We run away slaves, and we come back fighting men. Go tell your folks—our kingdom come in the Year of Jubilee!" Simply marching as a soldier represents an important political, moral, and psychological victory for many more than those who happen to be in uniform (including those, white and black, who watch the regiment march through the streets of Boston).

But manhood is not simply conferred; it must be earned. Again it is Rawlins who makes this point explicit. When Trip tells Searles he is a "nigger" who is acting like "the white man's dog," Rawlins replies,

And what are you? So full of hate you just want to go off and fight
everybody 'cause you been whipped and chased by hounds. Well, that might
not be livin', but it sure as hell ain't dyin'. And dyin' is what these white
boys have been doin' for goin' on three years now. Dyin' by the thousands.
Dyin' for you, fool. I know 'cause I dug the graves. And all the time I'm
diggin', I'm askin' myself when, when O Lord, will it be our time. The
time's comin' when we're goin' to have to ante up and kick in like men.
Like men!

You watch who you callin' a nigger. If there's any niggers around here, it's
you. Smart-mouth, stupid-ass, swamp-runnin' nigger. You don't watch out,
that's all you ever gonna be.

Trip remains a defiant figure after this dressing-down, but he carries this
rebuke with him. Later, after he has completed his journey into maturity, he
tells his fellow soldiers, "Ain't much matter what happen tomorrow, but we
men, ain't we?" They affirm him in unison.

Not only are they men, but they are men *together*. In a very real sense,
Glory is a movie about male bonding, of brothers—in the conventional and
specific African American senses of the word—bound in a common cause.
One of the most important images of the film is repeated shots of the four
men in the tent. It is a world unto itself, one endowed with its own dignity.

Zwick also employs less direct techniques to emphasize that dignity. One
good example is his use of the Boys' Choir of Harlem to provide the soundtrack for many of the scenes, most notably the final battle sequence and its
aftermath. The music exalts the fighting and provides an oblique comment
on the nobility of death in battle. Similarly, director of photography Freddie
Francis bathes his images in a warm light that exudes ripeness and acces-
sibility, particularly in the panoramic long shots of the Antietam sequence,
where a hundred years' worth of black and white photographs seem magically
transformed into color. When combined with production designer Norman
Garwood's exquisite sense of period detail, *Glory* creates an accessible and
alluring world that seems palpably real for the late twentieth-century viewer.

At the same time, one of the strengths of *Glory* is that having posited
soldiering as an affirming experience, it does not stint on the horrors of
combat. This point is made almost immediately in the Antietam sequence,
where in one of the most graphic images in a domestic war film, an officer's
head explodes at the very moment he urges his men forward. Shaw, who has
been slightly injured, is taken to an army hospital, where he learns of the
Emancipation Proclamation. Meanwhile, we hear an injured man scream and
moan as a limb is amputated, and we see blood splash on the curtain hiding
him from view. These frames not only record the hideousness of combat's
aftermath, but in their juxtaposition with the dialogue also suggest an allegory of emancipation as a necessary but torturous struggle in which the infec-
tion of slavery is surgically removed from the body politic.

Not that the rest of the country is altogether healthy. Throughout *Glory* we
are introduced to Unionists whose behavior is less than laudable: a general
who treats captured territory as a personal barony, a quartermaster who
hoards supplies, a journalist who flits from story to story without an apprecia-

tion for what the 54th is trying to do. The most sordid affair is the Union foraging raid on the town of Darien, Georgia. This sequence, which stays close to Burchard's account in *One Gallant Rush*, depicts the destruction of the town and the terror visited upon its residents by the 54th and another black regiment on the orders of Shaw's superior officer, Colonel James Montgomery. Perhaps even more appalling than Montgomery's gratuitous orders is his callous justification for his use of black troops: "You think anybody's going to put these boys into some real combat? Do you? I mean, they're little children, for God's sake, little monkey children, and you just got to know how to control them." Then, noticing a soldier assaulting a white woman, Montgomery says, "Hey, boy, take your hands off the white lady." When this order does not get immediate results, Montgomery shoots him.

The film also depicts the racism of white Union soldiers. Sometimes, this is simply a matter of slurs. "I'd rather have a hog than niggers," an unnamed white man says as the regiment marches in camp. "At least you can eat the hog." Later, Trip objects to being called "boy" by a white private, and Rawlins, who by this point has been promoted to sergeant, steps in to prevent a fight. The white man looks him over and says, "Stripes on a nigger. It's like tits on a bull!" When Shaw's friend and subordinate officer, Major Cabot Forbes (Cary Elwes), arrives on the scene and threatens to discipline the private, Rawlins dismisses the argument. "It's just a soldiers' fight, sir," he explains—subtly emphasizing just who he and Trip are.

Ultimately, insulting words are less problematic than the more systemic forms of discrimination that hamper the regiment, from delays in getting equipment to receiving less pay than white soldiers. The latter draws angry protests led by Trip. Trip himself is forced to pay dearly for the selfishness of others. After being absent without leave in search of shoes to protect his blistered feet, he is found and brought before Shaw, who orders him to be whipped. When he has been stripped of his shirt, all can see the scars of the whippings he received as a slave. Shaw, not realizing why Trip left the camp and anxious to maintain his authority, orders the whipping to proceed. Upon learning of the reason for Trip's behavior, Shaw acts quickly and decisively to procure shoes for his men from the corrupt quartermaster. But the scars will remain.

In a variety of ways, then, *Glory* develops themes common in the academic scholarship on African Americans in the Civil War since the 1960s. Yet what may be even more revealing is what it does *not* depict, the aspects of the story of the 54th that are downplayed or overlooked. As in the case of *Gone with the Wind*, comparing and contrasting versions of similar stories in different media can help one understand the distinctive cast of each. In contrast to some academic history, Glory reduces the amount of ambiguity surrounding the black military experience in the war.

One of the best examples of this cinematic simplification involves Shaw's decision to take command of the 54th. Glory depicts Massachusetts governor John Andrew's offer to Shaw as taking place at the Shaw home in Boston at a party attended by an oddly aged Frederick Douglass (he was forty-five at the time but in the film looks as though he is in his seventies).[41] Shaw, overcome by the offer, goes outside and thinks a minute but decides to accept it. Yet Burchard's One Gallant Rush describes Shaw as a man ambivalent not only about taking the regiment, but also about the entire idea of arming African Americans. In a letter dated August 6, 1862, the young soldier, then a captain, recorded a conversation he had had with a quartermaster who had talked with a general "about making use of the negroes against the Secessionists. I thought it a waste of breath."

Even the advent of the Emancipation Proclamation, issued by a president Shaw admired (and had met six months before) left him skeptical. "So the 'Proclamation of Emancipation,' has come at last, or rather its forerunner," he wrote on September 25, three days after Lincoln had acted. "I suppose you are all very much excited about it. For my part, I can't see what Practical good it can do now. Wherever our army has been there remain no slaves, and the Proclamation will not free them where we don't go." According to Burchard, Shaw's observation did not reflect the common abolitionist concern that Lincoln had not gone far enough; rather, he was afraid that the Emancipation Proclamation would make the war more fierce. "Jeff Davis will soon issue a proclamation threatening to hang every prisoner they take, and will make this a war of extermination," he wrote. One can infer that Shaw would have been even more concerned over the Confederate reaction not only to free slaves, but also to arm them.[42] When the governor actually did make his offer to Shaw in early 1863 (not, as shown in the movie, late 1862), he did so in a letter to be given to Shaw by his father, Francis Shaw. The elder Shaw traveled to his son's camp in Virginia to deliver the proposal. Shaw declined it. It was after his father left that Shaw changed his mind and telegraphed his acceptance of the colonelcy of the 54th.

The most interesting person in all of this may not have been the young soldier (or his father) but Shaw's mother, Sarah Blake Sturgis Shaw. When Shaw declined Andrew's offer, Francis Shaw telegraphed his son's decision to his wife, who then wrote the governor. "I just received a telegram from Mr. Shaw saying, 'Rob declines. I think rightly.'" Mrs. Shaw did not agree. With striking candor, she told Andrew that had her son accepted, "It would have been the proudest moment of my life and I could have died satisfied that I had not lived in vain. This being the truth, you will believe that I have shed bitter tears over his refusal." Then, in what could be construed as an unkind cut at her husband, she wrote, "I do not understand it unless from a habit inherited from his father, of self-distrust in his own capabilities."[43]

Burchard's account of Shaw's refusal stresses concerns about his fiancée, his position within his current regiment (the 7th New York), and his feeling of unworthiness for the job. What he does not argue, but which seems possible, even likely, is that Shaw was aware of his mother's attitude and that her feelings were a factor in changing his mind. "God rewards a hundred-fold every good aspiration of his children, and this is my reward for asking [for] my children not earthly honors, but souls to see the right and courage to follow it," she wrote him after learning of his decision. "Now I feel ready to die, for I see you willing to give your support to the cause of truth that is lying crushed and bleeding."[44]

Mrs. Shaw, one could argue, was the most militant member of the family. You would never know it watching *Glory*, in which she silently looks stoic and all other women seem ornamental. Nor does one have much sense of Shaw's inner torment over whether to join the 54th. It is at least conceivable that the inclusion of one or both dimensions could have added psychological (not to mention gender) complexity to the movie. It might even have made Shaw's decision to go forward despite his doubts seem even more impressive. "I finally decided that particular moment was less important than others," Zwick said of his decision not to emphasize Shaw's reluctance.[45] Whatever his reasons or intentions, the script as written puts Shaw's behavior in a much more straightforward and conventionally heroic light.

To be fair, the movie does suggest ambivalence on Shaw's part. When Rawlins receives his promotion, he tells Shaw, "I'm not sure I'm wantin' this, Colonel." A wry Shaw replies, "I know exactly how you feel." *Glory* also recognizes a gulf that exists between the races. But it does so in a way that reinforces sympathy for the colonel. Shaw is a remote and even curt officer (Burchard says that "there had always been a touch of austerity in his relations with his men"[46]), but we are to feel that he means well and that his behavior is due more to inexperience than to lack of sensitivity. Lest there be any doubt, a letter he writes that is voiced over amid scenes of black soldiers in camp emphasizes his earnestness and commitment: "Try as I may, I don't know these men. Their music, their camaraderie, which is different from ours. I am placed in a position where if I were a man of real strength I might do a great deal, but I am afraid that I will show I am of not much account. I don't want to stand in their way because of my own weakness." Shaw's anxiety and uncertainty suggest his lack of complacency and also affirm the common ground he shares with black soldiers in their own concerns about their masculinity and the cause they serve.

Perhaps the most significant omission in Glory concerns an important episode in U.S. racial history: the New York draft riots of 1863, in which angry mobs of predominantly Irish descent destroyed property and attacked African Americans in anger over federal conscription policy. These riots, which occurred just before the attack on Fort Wagner, were quelled by the time of the battle, but the government ultimately committed twenty thousand troops to enforce order in Manhattan. Shaw's mother and sisters were forced to flee their Staten Island home, and the nephew of one of the black men in the regiment was killed by rioters.[47] Yet no mention of disorder in New York—or elsewhere—is made in the movie. By contrast, Union victories at Gettysburg and Vicksburg are mentioned, though these took place weeks, not days, before. The riots could have been worked in somehow had the filmmakers considered this important; the movie's time frame had been manipulated in more arbitrary ways, such as the dates of the regiment's training. Filmmakers manage to insert such facts, however awkwardly, all the time.

The movie's silence about the race riots is not simply a matter of avoiding unpleasant racial realities that would undermine the value of the cause for which African Americans risked their lives. There are a number of scenes that do face such injustices. On the whole, however, Glory has a tendency to personalize and thus attenuate the racism it portrays in a number of ways. One of the best examples is its portrayal of an Irishman. Shaw recruits a drill sergeant named Mulcahy (played by John Finn) to get the troops in shape. He is a foulmouthed man who takes special pleasure in insulting his charges, and although such verbal abuse is the stock in trade of drill sergeants, the racial dimension of his approach gives his words a sharper bite. "You've never had a master like me," he yells, repeatedly calling each "boy" and singling out the educated Searles for particular attention. "You know the Irish are not known for their fondness for the coloreds," Shaw's friend Forbes observes with some amusement. Later, Shaw takes Mulcahy aside and asks if he is not being a little too rough with Searles. "We grew up together," Shaw explains, encouraging Mulcahy to speak frankly. "Let him grow up a little more," the Irishman says. Mulcahy later tells Searles "there's no shame" in the sergeant's ability to knock him down, and as the man assigned to flog Trip, even he pauses before

the scars on the runaway's back. Ultimately, however, it is Mulcahy's toughness, not his kindness, that makes the difference. Though no one comes out
and says so, it is clear that his drilling has helped shape the 54th into a
splendid fighting unit capable of handling the worst the rebels have to offer.

Indeed, there is a patronizing subtext in Glory in that it is whites who make
the most dramatic contributions to the black cause. The best example is
Shaw, who is portrayed as a racial avenger. His role is best symbolized by the
training camp scene where he slashes watermelons from his horse (anachronistic, to say the least—watermelons were not exactly common in
nineteenth-century New England winters). His family connections allow him
to threaten to expose the illegal activities of the general who refuses to let his
regiment fight, and his righteous anger is finally what gets shoes for the men
from the corrupt quartermaster. "You really think you can keep seven hundred Union soldiers without proper shoes because you think it's funny?" he
asks as he rampages through the warehouse. "Now where would that power
come from?" In the movie, though not in life, the question is rhetorical. On
matters where he lacks power, Shaw casts his lot with his men. Thus, when
the regiment tears up its pay in protest of not getting the same as whites,
Shaw also rips up his (the most symbolic of gestures from a man who hardly
needs government money). "Let's hear it for Colonel Shaw!" yells Rawlins,
and the rest of the men shout in approval.

A viewer versed in African American history might view this scene more
ambivalently. However jubilant real-life soldiers might have been over Shaw's
solidarity, it was another year before the government actually equalized pay
(the regiment turned down an offer from Massachusetts to make up the
difference, insisting on federal fairness), and by the time it happened, the
officers of the 54th had been ordered to shoot and wound two soldiers who
had refused to obey orders. One soldier in the Massachusetts 55th was executed for near-mutiny.[48] Even those who performed meritorious service experienced prejudice. Sergeant William Carney of the 54th received the Congressional Medal of Honor for bearing the regiment's colors during the retreat
from Fort Wagner despite bullets in his head, chest, and arm—thirty-seven
years late.[49] These events occurred after Shaw's death and, not surprisingly,
are not recorded in the movie. What is in the movie suggests a steady, if
gradual, sense of racial progress. (It is worth noting that it was not until 1948
that the armed forces actually began to be desegregated by presidential edict.)

Perhaps the most significant revelation of Glory's underlying racial politics
involves the narrative treatment of Trip's character. From the start he is
clearly the rebel, calling Searles "Snowflake," mocking Sharts, and disregard-

ing Rawlins's considerable moral authority. Yet he is also something of a charmer, a man with wit and a political critique that seems no less real because it is not formally articulated. As such he is what Pauline Kael calls "the Brando-Bogart figure."[50] Because of this, however, he also has a lesson to learn, and the viewer's sympathy for him will not be complete until he has learned that lesson.

Trip is an angry man. Unlike Searles, he is more than willing and able to take on Mulcahy, though Rawlins holds him in check. He is also critical of Shaw. "He a weak white boy," Trip asserts, adding, "Only reason he in charge is that his mommy and daddy fixed it." True enough, but the movie subtly undercuts Trip's credibility by having him incorrectly claim that Shaw will not die in battle. Similarly, his bullying of Searles becomes misplaced when "Snowflake" later saves his life in combat. Later, in a contrived but dramatically important moment, Trip has a scene with Shaw, who asks him to bear the regimental colors. Trip declines the honor.

TRIP: I ain't fightin' this war for you, sir.
SHAW: I see.
TRIP: I mean, what's the point? Ain't nobody gonna win, it's just gonna go on and on.
SHAW: Can't go on forever.
TRIP: But ain't nobody gonna win, sir.
SHAW: *Somebody's* going to win.
TRIP: Who? I mean, you, you get to go on back to Boston, big house and all that. What about us? What do we get?
SHAW: Well, you won't get anything if we lose. (*Pauses.*) What do you want to do?
TRIP: I don't know, sir.
SHAW: Stinks, I suppose.
TRIP: Stinks bad. And we all covered up in it, too. I mean, there ain't nobody clean. Be nice to get clean, though.
SHAW: How do we do that?
TRIP: (*Smiles to himself*) We ante up and kick in, sir. But I still don't want to carry your flag.

Trip gets in a dig at Shaw here ("We *all* covered up in it"). But what is striking is the way in which the "all" includes himself. Perhaps even more striking is the way in which these two scenes echo—and invert—a famous letter of Abraham Lincoln's to an Illinois constituent a few days after the Wagner assault: "You say you will not fight to free negroes. Some of them will fight for you; but no matter. Fight you then, exclusively to save the Union." Lincoln goes on to exhort greater effort on a nonracial basis but at the end of the letter turns to the subject of African American soldiers. "There will be some black men who can remember that, with silent tongue, and clenched teeth, and steady eye, and well-poised bayonet, they have helped mankind on to this great consummation; while, I fear, there will be some white ones, unable to forget that, with malignant heart, and deceitful speech, they have strove to hinder it."[51]

This black man will do the right thing and fight. Trip begins by making his peace with his black brethren. "Y'alls the onlyest family I got," he tells the regiment awkwardly in a prayer and song session on the eve of battle. "And, uh, I love the Fifty-fourth." So after these men march down the beach to the cheers of their fellow whites—"Give 'em hell, Fifty-fourth!" shouts the man who had made the "stripes on a nigger" comment—we should not be surprised that Trip *does* end up carrying the flag, leading the attack when Shaw falls. We all, black and white, are covered up in it, but we all can (will?) redeem ourselves.

It would be easy from the examples discussed here to simply dismiss *Glory* as a manipulative movie. Yet to reject it on that basis overlooks not only the extent to which all history is an act of manipulation, but also the value in this particular historical movie. Morgan Freeman touches on this issue indirectly when replying to critic Roger Ebert's charge that the movie focuses too much on the white point of view. "I don't have a problem with that," he said. "He [screenwriter Kevin Jarre] wrote it from a place he could write a story from, the only place he could get a grip on it from. You cannot reasonably ask a white writer to do it differently. Now, if we're going to start citing some unfortunates, it might be unfortunate that a black writer didn't write it, but if a black writer had written it, there's a good chance he wouldn't have found a producer. So there you are. This is a movie that did get made, and a story that did get told, and that's what is important."[52]

"Let's not choose up sides," Freeman continued. "The real message in this movie is that we as people, black and white, have shared it all." So speaks a voice of moderation, a moderation that perhaps unwittingly suggests the limitations of not only the movie, but also the society in which it was produced. By the end of the twentieth century, African Americans such as Spike Lee and John Singleton are getting their films written and produced, yet this still seems remarkable. Clearly, we have not quite shared it all.

Nevertheless, there are some things that have been shared, not the least of which is popular culture, and although popular culture tends to confirm its audience's prejudices, it also challenges them. There is also always the hope that it can overcome them. *Glory* sidesteps some hard racial truths, but to some extent it, like other examples of popular culture, is an effort to *resist* history, not succumb to it.

Glory was not the first attempt to wrestle with the legacy of the 54th. It is only the most recent chapter in a long (and, one hopes, ongoing) story.

Monumental Gestures

> I ask no monument proud and high,
> To arrest the gaze of passers-by
> All that my yearning spirit craves
> Is bury me not in a land of slaves
>
> Frances Ellen Watkins Harper, 1854[53]

In art and in life, Robert Gould Shaw led the 54th Massachusetts in the attack on Fort Wagner and was one of its first casualties. "Considering his position at the head of the assault, it was miraculous that he even reached the Rebel works, although he had sustained multiple wounds," writes Joseph Glathaar in his history of the black military units in the Civil War. "As Shaw reached the top, he called on his men to move forward, when a ball crashed into his chest and toppled him backward dead."[54]

The next day, the Confederate commander rejected a truce offer, claiming that he had plenty of medical supplies to tend the wounded and plenty of soldiers to bury the dead, Union and Confederate. According to John T. Luck, a Union surgeon captured while tending to the wounded, "All the officers killed in the assault were decently buried, excepting Colonel Shaw. His remains were thrown into a trench with those of his privates, and then covered up." A remark attributed to a Confederate general soon began to circulate in the North: "He is buried with his niggers."[55]

Shaw's death sent waves of shock and grief through the New England abolitionist community, and condolences flooded in from figures such as William Lloyd Garrison, Lydia Maria Child, and Henry Ward Beecher. Some initial effort was made to recover Shaw's body, but his family made it clear that they preferred it to remain buried with the men of the regiment. The family gave money for the restoration of the pillaged town of Darien, Georgia, and when local hostility prevented the erection of a memorial to their son in Charleston, funds for that project were used for the establishment of a school for African American boys.[56]

In the years that followed, Shaw received numerous tributes. Whether in verse, granite, or some other form, they took one of two basic approaches. The first was a celebration of the elite's contributions during the nation's hour of crisis. "There is no class of men in this republic from whom the response of patriotism comes more promptly and surely than from its most highly educated class," wrote Thomas Wentworth Higginson in a preface to *Harvard Memorial Biographies* published immediately after the war. Shaw's cousin, the historian Francis Parkman, was fond of noting his achievements—but never noted that he led black troops.[57]

Ralph Waldo Emerson, decrying the "age of fops and toys," commemorated Shaw in his poem "Voluntaries":

> So nigh is grandeur to our dust
> So near to God is man
> When Duty whispers low *Thou must,*
> The youth replies *I can.*[58]

Emerson's poem, which touches on a widespread Brahmin anxiety of affluence, taps into a more enduring meaning for Shaw's actions: sacrifice for a worthy cause. This was important to many abolitionists, particularly those who in the years before the war had nurtured pacifist sentiments. "The high soul burns on to light men's feet / Where death for noble ends makes dying sweet," wrote James Russell Lowell in his 1863 poem "Memoriae Positum R.G. Shaw." For many of his family and friends, the cause for which Shaw died provided spiritual solace for personal loss.

After years of delay, the famous sculptor Augustus Saint Gaudens finished a monument to Shaw, and in 1897 formal dedications were held in Boston. The structure, still standing at the corner of the Common near Beacon Hill, was unveiled in the presence of a number of luminaries, including the governor of Massachusetts, Booker T. Washington, William James, and survivors of the 54th and New York 7th regiments of which Shaw had been a member.

In reading over their tributes, one is struck by a subtle change in the sense of loss. In these post–Civil War writings, it seems, what is being mourned is not so much the loss of the men of the 54th as the lack of an overriding societal commitment to make sacrifices comparable to Shaw's. "The full measure of the fruit of Fort Wagner and all this monument stands for will not be realized until every man covered by a black skin shall, by patience and natural effort, grow in moral responsibility, where no man in all our land will be tempted to degrade himself by withholding from his black brother any opportunity which he himself would possess," said Washington characteristically. "Until that time comes, this monument will stand for effort, not victory complete. What these heroic souls of the 54th regiment began, we must complete."[59]

James was more direct. "Our present situation, with its rancors and delusions, what is it but the direct outcome of the added powers of government, the corruptions and inflations of war?" he asked.[60] (One feels a sense of eerie prescience in reading these words in the aftermath of Vietnam and the Iran-Contra scandals.) On the eve of the age of Theodore Roosevelt—and the Spanish-American War—the philosopher, an opponent of Roosevelt's policies, was somewhat unusual in seeing war as the problem rather than the solution. But Roosevelt himself and many others shared James's sense of national malaise.

In later years the 54th was used as a symbol to measure the distance between this sense of malaise and a bright, shining moment of moral achievement and certitude. Perhaps the most famous example is Robert Lowell's poem "For the Union Dead," which surveys a Boston landscape of outward indifference and inner enervation:

Parking spaces luxuriate like civic
sandpiles in the heart of Boston.
A girdle of orange, Puritan-pumpkin colored girders
braces the tingling Statehouse,

shaking over the excavations, as it faces Colonel Shaw
and his bell-cheeked Negro infantry
on St. Gaudens' shaking Civil War relief,
propped by a plank splint against the garage's earthquake.[61]

Lowell felt that the monument had become like a fishbone in Boston's throat. He was writing these words in the early 1960s, a time of great hope for many in the Civil Rights movement, who went about their work with the fervor of nineteenth-century abolitionists. Whatever the reasons for his despair, at least one observer was no more optimistic in the next decade. Lincoln Kirstein obviously drew some spiritual sustenance from the St. Gaudens monument in his 1973 essay, but clearly the disappointments of the 1960s were on his mind. "In a time when military heroism is suspect and a thousand images of melodramatic violence have polluted the subject, to adequately recount the actual battle at Fort Wagner, where Shaw and almost half the regiment were killed, would call for the exaltation of an ancient Greek or Welsh bard," he wrote.[62]

Whether or not Glory amounts to an adequate recounting of Fort Wagner is something the viewer can decide; the point here is that by the late 1980s enough fairly influential people thought it was possible without being an ancient Greek or Welsh bard and lent their talents and capital to bring such an effort to the screen. In so doing they reintroduced a point of view to popular discourse that had been missing for many years. For Zwick this was not a detached act of antiquarianism. "One hopes one is not making a quaint historical pageant. You are making drama that you hope has contemporary elements," he said in an interview. At the same time, however, he recognized the symbolic and even wishful dimensions of his work. "Pop culture's all about iconography. These men, these faces in these uniforms, is finally the iconography this movie presents. If there's a certain degree of liberal fantasy in that, well, so be it."[63]

Glory occupied an interesting place on the cinematic landscape in 1989–90. It was sandwiched between, and ultimately overshadowed by, the blockbusters Driving Miss Daisy and Born on the Fourth of July. The former, a story about a rich Jewish dowager and her wise but self-effacing chauffeur—played, interestingly enough, by Morgan Freeman—is an even greater racial fantasy than Glory. Essentially, it amounts to a gender and ethnic rewiring of Huck and Jim, with Freeman continuing the redeeming, salt-of-the-earth black man tradition that extends back to Uncle Tom. It is a sharply observed, beautifully executed piece of cinema—and it is also popular culture at its confirming worst, which is probably why it received the Best Picture Oscar.

Oliver Stone's Born on the Fourth of July is another "we were betrayed" picture drawn on a somewhat broader canvas than Platoon and other noble-grunt films. This, too, is a fairly accomplished piece of work, overdrawn and didactic, but deliberately so. Yet for this very reason it irritated sympathizers and repelled anyone who saw the war in terms other than Stone's. In this light, it also was confirmative, preaching to the converted and driving away skeptics.[64]

Those who saw *Born on the Fourth of July* and *Glory* in close proximity were presented with an intriguing set of messages. To usefully oversimplify, those emerging from Stone's movie were likely to say to themselves something like, "My God, what an awful war. Why did we ever get involved in it?" But after seeing *Glory*, one was likely to think, "My God, what an awful war. Too bad we had to fight it."

Glory, then, is not simply a movie that portrays a cause worth dying for. It is also a movie that portrays a cause worth killing for, which makes it more complicated. It suggests a yearning for moral, collective commitments in the twilight of the Reagan era. At the same time, it evokes a militant fervor that has often been distorted and exploited by unscrupulous leaders and careless voters. This is the risk a free society takes, and it is hard to see how it can be avoided.

One of the best suggestions on how to balance such risks comes from William James. "The lesson that our war ought most of all to teach us is the lesson that evils must be checked in time before they grow so great," he told the crowd at the dedication of the 54th's monument. For James, Shaw's moment of glory was not the storming of Fort Wagner, but rather the decision to take command of the 54th in the first place. "That kind of valor (civic courage we call it in peace times) is the kind of valor to which the monuments of nations should most of all be reared," he said.[65]

As the story of a few good men whose actions helped change the fate of a nation, *Glory* offers challenges to a society still distrustful of and complacent about the possibilities of positive social change. Such changes have been made before, albeit at great cost and with some moral ambiguity. They can be made again. But there are other ways of doing this than by war. And when we find—and rediscover—such ways, perhaps we really will be free at last of the oppressions and longings that continue to haunt us.

Chapter 6

Patriotic "Gore"

Jonathan Clarke's
Civil War

> It's our duty, imagining each other.
>
> Lucy Marsden, narrator of
> Allan Garganus's *Oldest Living*
> *Confederate Widow Tells All*[1]

It was difficult to see Private Jonathan Clarke of the 2d Rhode Island Infantry through the smoke of Rebel artillery as he marched up a well-defended hill. Federal troops were advancing from their position near Bull Run Creek in what was supposed to be a surprise attack on the Rebel left. The Confederates were prepared for this maneuver, however, and were initially successful in holding back the badly disorganized Union regiments that attacked them piecemeal. (The 2d Rhode Island, which led the assault, quickly ran out of ammunition and was ordered to leave the field.) But lacking the sheer numbers the Federals were throwing at their line, the Rebels were forced to retreat to a more defensible position. There, augmented by reinforcements, strategically placed artillery pieces, and the inspiration provided by General Thomas J. "Stonewall" Jackson (who earned his famous sobriquet by solidifying the Confederate line at this battle), the Rebels successfully counterattacked, driving the Yankees—and interested spectators who had come to witness the first major land battle of the Civil War—back to Washington, D.C.

Or so it would seem. Actually, although many would indeed be driving back to Washington, others would be heading elsewhere—Massachusetts, Louisiana, Kansas, even Canada. (North-south traffic could be seen moving on a road near the field at the height of the battle.) Whereas the first battle of the Civil War had been fought on a hot July day in Manassas, Virginia, this event was taking place on a cool August morning nine miles away. At First Manassas, the 2d Rhode Island did in fact lead the assault, but Jonathan Clarke was not a member of it. In fact, he never existed; the private is an amalgam of two soldiers who were encamped in North Carolina at the time. Actually, the man who represents Jonathan Clarke is not a man at all; "he" is a woman who works in a Rhode Island factory.

Jonathan Clarke—her real first name is being withheld at her request—was one of an estimated two thousand participants and fourteen thousand spectators who attended the 130th anniversary reenactment of First Manassas[2] held at James S. Long Regional Park in Haymarket, Virginia, in 1991. Numerous other reenactments are held each year, ranging in size from small skirmishes to the twelve thousand soldiers and one hundred thousand spectators at the 125th reenactment of Gettysburg in 1988 (scenes of this reenactment were used in Glory).[3] The reenactment described above was the tenth battle hosted by the Prince William County Park Authority, which sponsors the event, and was the first staging of First Manassas since the 125th anniversary in 1986. The event has grown in size since then; in 1993 the nearby Manassas Museum and the U.S. Park Service joined the effort, making it a three-day festival of concerts, lectures, and exhibitions at a series of sites,

including the actual battlefield. The centerpieces of these weekends are particular Virginia battles reenacted at Long Regional Park, with smaller ones occurring throughout.

The spectacle spills beyond enclosed borders on these late August weekends in Manassas. Motels along Route 234—a key thoroughfare during the actual battle—are booked with visitors, and media representatives come from near and far to observe the event (an ABC News truck was seen at the 1991 reenactment). It is not uncommon to see women in Victorian dresses and parasols on line at McDonald's or to observe Confederate soldiers driving pickup trucks.

For administrators of the Prince William County Park Authority, the reenactment is the highlight of its annual calendar. Planning begins in October and intensifies after March. At the 1991 reenactment, seventy volunteers, some of them employees who attended the event without pay, registered the reenacting groups that came from all over the country, supervised parking for spectators ($10 per car, used to finance park projects), and answered questions from both spectators and reenactors. Emergency medical personnel, dressed in Union and Confederate uniforms, hid among the trees to make sure that those who were "shot" by blanks were not really hurt and to respond quickly to those, such as the Confederate cavalryman knocked from his horse during a charge, who were injured. (He was later able to ride from the field accompanied by the applause of the crowd.)

The battle itself, staged in two parts in the morning and afternoon, constituted only a small part of the entire affair. Although the park was open to the public only on Sunday, reenactors began arriving Friday night. They had the park to themselves on Saturday, setting up camp, talking with friends made at other events, and staging a non–Civil War battle whose result depended more on tactical skill than the script worked out by historically minded commanders of reenactments. Before and between battles on Sunday, soldiers and costumed civilians staged "living history" demonstrations for the public—hospital operations, a fashion show, a Southern army church service—and answered the questions of visitors (What did soldiers eat? How

Civil War reenactors meet in hand-to-hand "combat" at a reenactment of the Second Battle of Manassas held in Prince William County, Virginia, in 1992. By the early 1990s these annual events attracted upwards of fifteen thousand spectators and reenactors each August to the park. (Photo by Mark Milligan, courtesy of the Prince William County Park Authority, Manassas, Virginia)

did the cavalry replace lost or killed horses? Why does the regimental flag look the way it does?).

These questions were answered by people with little academic training in Civil War history. Nevertheless, they were often able and willing to offer listeners precise regimental histories, explain technological developments in weaponry, or render authoritative judgments on individual generals. Many believed the hobby served a pedagogical function. "It's something we do for family, to educate people," a Confederate soldier explained to a television crew at the battle site. "Reenactors research their roles by studying old documents, letters, and photographs," reads a brochure advertising the event. "Every detail of life from the 19th century is taken into account to make the individual reenactor look, sound, and act like someone from the Civil War era."

Just what is learned at these events is impossible to quantify, although some of the most striking lessons are learned by children. "You can never be part of a unit until you learn how to obey orders," an exasperated father told his son at a reenactment in Massachusetts. Another child at the same reenactment, excited by the prospect of battle, yelled "Kill 'em North!" to the men in blue. But he seemed genuinely frightened by the sight of a man falling nearby, anxiously asking him, "Are you all right? Are you all right?" Others came to different conclusions. "I can kill somebody!" a very young child dressed in pink said at the Virginia reenactment, brandishing a wooden gun.

Reenactors consider the hobby a learning experience for themselves as well. "It's important to me because it's something I missed," said a Connecticut man dressed as an Alabama Confederate. "What does it mean to be a man?" he asked, suggesting that he—and the two sons he brought with him—got some answers by wearing authentic clothing and sharing the same sensory experiences as Civil War soldiers.

More scholarly minded observers may well question the quality of the educational experience offered by reenacting. But for better or worse, most people pick up their history in fragments from non-experts, whether they are school teachers, magazine editors, or television writers. Hobbies such as reenacting provide influential views on history. And although many of those who absorb such sensory experiences are simply weekend warriors or novelty-hunting tourists, there are some, like Jonathan Clarke, who approach the Civil War with diligence and passion.

Civil War reenacting represents one facet of a hobby known as living history, which also includes reenactments of other conflicts, such as the

Revolutionary War and World War II. Active militia units that dress in period clothing for Memorial Day parades, civilian community celebrations, and similar events represent other forms of living history, as do professional reenactors at sites such as Old Sturbridge Village, a Jacksonian-era living history museum in central Massachusetts. In all these cases, people perform "impressions" for themselves and others that are meant to recreate vanished experiences or ways of life.

Despite this fundamental similarity, there are important differences between Civil War reenactment and other forms of living history. First, these reenactors generally do not have affiliations with local chambers of commerce, the military, or museum administrators the way parade marchers and museum workers often do. Second, actors or militiamen are often paid for their work, whereas Civil War reenacting is an amateur affair. Finally, reenacting is portable; although in recent years local events have proliferated, reenactors often go great distances to practice their craft on or near the site of actual battles.

Judging from some anecdotal evidence, there are also differences between Civil War and Revolutionary War reenactors. One of the most important is age. Whereas Civil War reenactors tend to be around thirty years old, the Revolutionary War crowd is typically older. This means Revolutionary War reenactors tend to be less interested in the physical exertion involved in much Civil War reenacting. Also, since colorful Revolutionary War garb is much more expensive than basic Civil War clothing, Revolutionary reenactors are less willing to subject the clothes to the wear and tear of battle. This in turn leads to greater informality in drilling, reveille, and so forth. Finally, the American Revolution happened much longer ago than the Civil War. Most contemporary reenactors identify with the winning side, and reenactments have less drama as a result.[4] In any case, Civil War reenacting seems to have the largest, most broadly based constituency of any form of battlefield reenacting, perhaps because the Civil War looms larger in the national imagination than any other conflict in our history.

Each of the previous chapters in this book analyzes documents produced for mass consumption. As such, they tend to focus on artists rather than on audiences, although the major figures—Carl Sandburg, Margaret Mitchell, Southern rock performers, and the makers of Glory—are interesting to me because they identify so intensely with the people they address. All artists begin their careers as members of (often shadowy) audiences whose members and attitudes may be difficult to identify and understand. The best succeed in part because they are able to express the views of their fans and in so doing reveal new perspectives to those who may or may not be sympathetic toward those views.

Reenactors, however, make culture for themselves and interact directly with their audience, often on a one-to-one basis. Although it remains difficult to obtain a comprehensive view of the hobby, it is possible to catch intriguing glimpses of the lives of these people by watching and listening to them. This chapter is the result of such an effort, which I conducted during 1991 and 1992.

Reenacting represents one facet of an entire world of amateur history: genealogists, collectors, antiquarians, discussion groups, and so forth. Although reenactors occupy a singular place in this world, they share assumptions with practitioners of other Civil War hobbies. Therefore it may be helpful to supply some context, which I will do before surveying the history of reenacting, contemporary practices in the hobby, and the ideas and values that shape Jonathan Clarke's Civil War.

Nights at a Round Table

> We are simply people who are interested in the Civil War,
> and long to hear about it. We do have a very few experts,
> but the majority of us are simply listeners and learners.
>
> A member of the Decatur, Illinois,
> Civil War Round Table, 1968[5]

As I discussed in Chapter 2, the profile of professional scholars in U.S. history in general, and Civil War history in particular, grew more prominent in the years following the Second World War. In their shadow, amateur historians continued their work and were occasionally even recognized by academics who too often looked on them with disdain.

The activities of amateur historians are difficult to trace because there are few widely available records of their activities, and they are difficult to observe easily because their work tends to be intensely local and private. Relic hunting on battlefields and memorabilia collecting, to cite two examples, are hobbies that have strong followings around the country. One can learn about these activities by talking with individual participants or by looking through specialized periodicals such as *North-South Trader's Civil War* or *Civil War Book Exchange and Collector's Newspaper*.

Such hobbyists are also likely to read more commercial magazines that cater to Civil War enthusiasts, such as *Blue and Gray*, *America's Civil War*, *Civil War News*, and *Civil War Times* (which runs its stories in the present tense; "Yanks Cheer Lincoln in Richmond," reads the cover of the January/February 1991 issue). Judging from advertisements, classified ads, and stories—often written by Civil War buffs themselves—these magazines reach people who commit time and energy to the war in a variety of ways.

Another common activity is tracing genealogy. Like many hobbies, the tracing of Civil War genealogy parallels that of the American Revolution. No Civil War organization has the profile or prestige of the Sons/Daughters of the American Revolution. But the Sons of Confederate Veterans (heir to the United Confederate Veterans and brother to the United Daughters of the Confederacy) continues its work.[6] Organized in 1896 "for the purpose of preserving and defending the principles of the Old South," the SCV continues to serve "as a means for a gentleman to honor his Southern ancestry with memorial, historical, and educational activities," according to a 1990 advertisement.[7] "Why not join in preserving and defending the memory, songs and symbols of those who fought for Southern independence?" it asks rhetorically.

Then there are discussion groups. One of the more famous of these is the Abraham Lincoln Association. Formed in 1908 as the Lincoln Centennial Association to prepare for the national celebration of Lincoln's 100th birthday, the organization also launched a program of research and publication in Lincoln studies. The capstone of this effort was the eight-volume *Collected Works of Abraham Lincoln* published in 1953 under the editorship of Executive Secretary Roy Basler. The association disbanded after the publication of the *Collected Works* but was reactivated in 1962 to work with the state of Illinois in restoring the old state capitol (site of Lincoln's "House Divided" speech). Since then, the group has continued to grow, holding annual dinners to honor Lincoln in Springfield and starting a journal published by the University of Illinois.

The national Lincoln organization acts as an umbrella for a number of Lincoln groups, such as those of Boston; New York City; Washington, D.C.; Florida; and Kansas. Lincoln groups have also sprung up in Ontario and even Taiwan. A volume of Lincoln's writings on democracy supervised by the association was published in the United States and abroad in 1990, and over thirty thousand copies—twice the original printing—were distributed in Poland amid the collapse of communism in Eastern Europe.[8]

Indeed, although the organization has a local grass-roots constituency, the Abraham Lincoln Association has always maintained a relatively high profile. Early members included a number of luminaries, including Booker T. Washington, Henry Cabot Lodge, and William Jennings Bryan. (Lincoln's appeal seems limitless.) Later, noted Lincoln scholars such as Paul Angle and Benjamin Thomas were among the distinguished participants. In recent years, members have included William Safire and Mario Cuomo, who wrote an introduction for the *Lincoln on Democracy* collection. At the same time, the *Journal of the Abraham Lincoln Association* includes the work of some of the most respected academic historians in the profession; the 1991 edition, for example, included pieces by James McPherson, Richard Current, and Don Fehrenbacher.

Perhaps more broad in appeal are Civil War round tables. The membership and practices of these organizations are hard to gauge because in many cases they are informal and even ephemeral. The oldest known Civil War round table was founded in Chicago in 1940. During the centennial years of 1961–65, it was estimated that the number of round tables had grown to approximately two hundred, only to fall off to about sixty by the mid-1970s. Since the nation's bicentennial, however, interest has grown again, and by the early 1990s there were again about two hundred groups. The actual number of members in these round tables varies; some comprise only a handful; one Alabama round table boasts two hundred members. There are also round tables in England, Germany, Belgium, and Australia.[9]

Round table programs typically include presentations by local members, lectures by guest speakers, or discussions of a particular book or event. Locales can range from private homes to local libraries or public halls. Members also arrange field trips to battlefields or conferences and organize panels or exchanges with other groups. The focus is generally on military history. The president of a round table in California, one of eight in the state, estimated that membership is mostly white, 70 percent male, and ranges in age from thirty to seventy years. (It also seems largely middle to upper middle class, made up of people who have had college educations, judging from my own attendance at Rhode Island's Round Table.)

Until the 1970s the only national link for round tables was a national assembly held once a year. In an effort to promote more groups and further contacts among them, Arkansas political consultant Jerry Russell founded the Civil War Round Table Associates in Little Rock in 1968. The CWRTA serves as an information center for those trying to organize groups (almost three dozen have started under its auspices), publishes a newsletter, and since 1975 has held an annual congress.

Despite all the contact between and among different hobbyists and professionals, the field of amateur history remains a fragmented one, linked by networks that tend to be more personal than organizational. Moreover, although there is a natural fit between, for example, collecting memorabilia and relic hunting, many activities remain foreign to those pursuing others. There is even a whiff of snobbery toward those who are not considered serious. Reenacting in particular has been described as "superficial" and practiced by those who are "largely play acting," to quote an Abraham Lincoln Association figure and round table official. Although there is surely some truth to this perception, reenacting has a longer history and exhibits more complex dynamics than even some of its most ardent champions recognize.

Nineteenth-Century Spectacles

> Once again we have the "serious historians" telling the "living historians" that what we do is really not to be taken seriously. I contend that most Reenactors are first and foremost serious students of history. And that not being satisfied with merely reading about what happened and visiting the scene where it happened, they want to go one step further. They want to *feel* what happened, know what it means to have some thoughtless officer leave them at support arms for too long, sit in a dog tent during a driving rain and hope against hope that most of what you own will stay dry, and yes, I will admit, feel the exhileration [sic] of a spontaneous charge toward the enemy's works. If there is something sinful or disrespectful about "doing it for fun," then I guess those who visit national Battlefield Parks, attend Round Tables, or do anything in their individual pursuit of history for the pure joy of it are guilty of the same crime. For most of us, history is a hobby, not a job, and people select hobbies because they are enjoyable, even fun.

> Bill Holschuh, publisher of *Camp Chase Gazette,*
> on a *New York Times* article that quoted
> Vermont officials critical of reenacting[10]

The roots of Civil War reenacting date back to the late nineteenth century. Although there are, of course, important differences between the way it was practiced then and the way it is now, the most striking aspect of the activity is the degree of continuity that marks the rituals and assumptions that surround it.

The first reenactments were staged by Civil War veterans, especially those who were members of the Grand Army of the Republic, a fraternal organization that attained considerable clout in the closing decades of the nineteenth century. Individual GAR chapters ("posts") would hold "encampments" where members would wear old uniforms, sleep in tents, and recreate the trappings of their soldier days. In 1878, 1881, and 1883, a New Jersey encampment of Union veterans engaged in sham battles with the state's National Guard unit. Such activities became increasingly frequent as the GAR grew in size and commanded more attention in government, community life, and the press.[11]

Presumably, such encampments were designed to recapture the flavor of wartime life, an effort marked by a series of ironies, not the least of which is that wartime life was not always something a veteran would have liked to relive. Another irony was that Union veterans began showing increasing regard for their former enemies, who would appear at such events and would be treated with growing respect as the century wore on. (Actually, this practice was discernible even before the war ended and survived in reenactments straight through the twentieth century.)[12] Finally, a powerful impulse for meticulously re-creating the particulars of camp life coexisted with a highly sentimentalized view of the war. As GAR historian Stuart McConnell has noted of these events, "Orders from headquarters always arrived on time and were followed, sentinels stopped every intruder, soldiers said their prayers and abstained from drink, privates had constitutional rights and their turns being officers, space was orderly and movement controlled, marching was strictly for show, and of course no one was ever killed."[13]

Actually, there is an underlying logic in all these apparent contradictions: Encampments offered participants opportunities to affirm a sense of communion that was likely to be missing from the rest of their lives. War may have indeed been hell, but it was also a time of intense passion and attachment to one's fellow soldier. Furthermore, if the enemy had mistaken principles, he understood a soldier's situation far more easily than women, children, or mere civilians could. Although encampments may have been stylized, to say the least, they did affirm a sense of community all too lacking in more conventional social arrangements.

Such communal impulses could, and did, transcend the confines of the GAR. In the first few decades of the twentieth century, the most obvious manifestation of them were historical pageants. These community celebrations, which were extraordinarily popular, featured people dressed in period costumes turning history into ritual. (The comic possibilities of these scenes are affectionately depicted in Meredith Willson's 1957 play *The Music Man*, which depicts an event of the pre–World War I era in small-town Iowa.) Pageants typically represented scenes from early in a town's history— tableaux with Native Americans were common—although some Civil War scenarios were staged. Pageants declined in popularity after the Second World War, however, as immigration, urbanization, and the growth of national media fragmented shared community pasts and alternative ethnic traditions took their place (and were themselves weakened by assimilation). Indeed, it is possible to see pageants as attempts to forestall these very developments.[14]

Another analogue for reenacting is the living history museum, the best known of which are Michigan's Greenfield Village and Virginia's Colonial Williamsburg, which were developed in the 1920s to sate the nostalgic appetites of Henry Ford and John D. Rockefeller, respectively. Museums such as these (and Old Sturbridge Village, which opened in 1946), feature meticulously—but selectively—re-created moments from the community's past peopled with actors in period garb.[15] Such living history sites continue to be extraordinarily popular.

Meanwhile, Civil War reenacting continued to have a life even after veterans' events passed from the scene. In 1935 the Fredericksburg Battlefield Park Association and the National Park Service cosponsored a reenactment of the Battle of Chancellorsville in which the U.S. Marines, cavalry, and cadets of the Virginia Military Institute participated. The army also carried out a series of reenactments for its own purposes before the Second World War, which attracted unexpected interest on the part of spectators.[16]

Reenacting in its modern form emerged during the Civil War centennial of the early 1960s. A series of commemorations organized by the federal government and local communities heightened public interest in the war and helped spur the growth of tourism as visitors flocked to National Park Service sites that had become virtual shrines. Actually, it was this attitude of veneration that triggered a major controversy over reenacting, revealing a good deal about tensions between amateur and professional history that continue to survive, albeit in different forms, to this day.

At issue was reenacting on actual Civil War battlefields. At first, this was a matter of relatively little contention. The army gave logistical support to several reenactments during the centennial, and the first major event, a 100th anniversary reenactment of First Manassas, had the support of Ulysses S. Grant III, the grandson of the Civil War general, who served as chairman of the United States Civil War Centennial Commission created by Congress. The federal government permitted the site to be used for the event, and the state of Virginia provided some early funding. There were some who felt the reenactment would be too much of a celebration rather than the re-membrance of a tragedy, but such skepticism was not widely shared.[17]

In any case, the reenactment seemed to be a success. Fifty thousand specta-tors attended the meeting of the two "armies," who concluded the reenact-ment by joining together to sing "God Bless America," yet another example of the romance of reconciliation. Thousands of reenactors paid their own way and went long distances to participate, and they came away with varied lessons. (One felt the reenactment served as a "solemn reminder of a time when men fought for principle without the inducements of the G.I. Bill," apparently unaware of bounties for joining the army or the intense GAR lobbying for pensions in the 1880s and 1890s.)[18]

But in the aftermath of the event, critical voices, particularly in the press, grew more harsh, and cautious public officials beat a hasty retreat away from involvement with reenactments. Allan Nevins, who replaced Grant as the Civil War Centennial Commission chairman after a segregation fiasco marred a commission meeting in South Carolina, felt reenactments were "trashily theatrical" and that if any commission participated in any further reenact-ments, it would be over his dead body. National Park Service director Conrad Wirth also sought to reduce the role of reenactments in centennial commem-orations, placing an emphasis on less dramatic forms of pageantry selected and enacted by park service personnel. Such an approach, he explained, would leave history more in the hands of trained interpreters and ensure that the centennial would be "a dignified and impressive commemoration com-pletely beyond reproach."

So spoke presumed voices of moderation. Nevins (author of an eight-volume history of the Civil War era)[19] held a particularly ironic position in the reenactment controversy given his own view of himself as a champion of historical democracy in his editorship of American Heritage, a magazine he founded to combat what he saw as academic pedantry.[20] Wirth's position suggests that although the National Park Service was presumably founded to give the nation's citizens access to their heritage, only professionals could really be trusted to understand and present the past.

That is not to say that reenactments always exhibited laudable sentiments. A chummy affirmation of North-South unity could—and did—obscure real and important differences in the early 1960s, when the Civil Rights movement was giving the war a new and pointed relevance. Conversely, there were cases where Southerners were all too willing to affirm sectional identity. Historian John Bodnar notes that "at a time when citizens of Montgomery could read about attempts by whites to limit the political power of blacks in the state [of Alabama], they could also attend a reenactment of the arrival of Jefferson Davis in the city."[21] In general, the South embraced reenactments with more fervor in these years, leading Bodnar to conclude that the centennial was more a regional than national event there.

Yet as I have tried to show repeatedly throughout this book, it is not only misguided amateurs who have made judgments that could legitimately be questioned. In a spirit of easy reconciliation similar to that of reenactors, centennial commission chairman U.S. Grant III accepted a Washington, D.C., Civil War Round Table medal from John C. Pemberton, the grandson of the man who surrendered to Grant after the fall of Vicksburg. (An army official present at the ceremony applauded their unity in the face of the communist threat.) Grant also condoned hotel segregation at the centennial commission's national assembly in Charleston, South Carolina, in 1961; it was the resulting furor that led to his replacement by Nevins.[22] Nevins himself exhibited an disdainful elitism toward reenactors that belied his commitment to historical democracy. It should be said, however, that even many reenactors now believe that holding events on actual battlefields is inappropriate, though it is still sometimes done (Jonathan Clarke "fought" on the 1864 site of the Battle of Cedar Creek in Virginia on a number of occasions in the 1980s, though she herself is uneasy with the practice).

In any case, Civil War reenacting, like Civil War round tables, appears to have retreated into the background from the mid-1960s straight through the 1970s. Perhaps this is because the contentious events of the period challenged previously held assumptions about patriotism, and the sense of affirmation underlying reenactments was difficult to sustain. Whether or not the hobby actually declined in numbers of participants is impossible to confirm, though public attention to the practice became less marked after the Civil War centennial ended in 1965.

It was during the 1980s, and 125th anniversary celebrations, that reenacting really came of age. Beginning in 1983, for example, a variety of organizations in Gettysburg began hosting Civil War heritage days, week-long festivals, encampments, reenactments, and collector's shows. In 1986 *Time* magazine took note of the hobby in a two-page spread and estimated that as many as fifty thousand people were involved in various forms of living history. This includes Revolutionary and Civil War reenacting together; a 1989 article in *Travel-Holiday* pegged the Civil War figure at twenty-two thousand.[23]

As with other Civil War hobbies, figures fluctuate and are uncertain; reenacting, too, is very much a localized phenomenon. There are national organizations such as the National Regiment, which sponsors events, and publications such as *Camp Chase Gazette*, "The Voice of Civil War Reenacting," which carries announcements and advertising of interest to enthusiasts. The magazine runs "Event Reports" by participants at major reenactments as well as features such as "What Would Your Father Say?" (interviews with sons of veterans who approve of the hobby) and "Lithuania and the Confederacy: Thoughts on the Meaning of Secession."[24] Still, despite such outlets for information and communication, most reenactors are "unattached others" who belong to "gypsy" units that operate independently. Indeed, there is some skepticism, even distrust, of the mere idea of a national organization. "How can you have one set of rules for so many people doing things for different reasons?" asked a Rhode Island reenactor whose whole family participates in the hobby. The man's wife and one of his daughters are civilians; the other plays a vivandière—a woman who carries the flag during battles in a noncombatant role.

This reenactor, an active member of the National Guard in Rhode Island, was referring to the different levels of intensity in Civil War reenacting. In the early years of the hobby, reenactments were fairly casual affairs that were not very concerned with period detail. Although this is still true of some participants, recent years have seen increasing verisimilitude and a perception of three tiers of reenactors. Those with the least interest in precision are called "farbs," a term of uncertain origins that connotes a lack of seriousness and a vulgar interest in guzzling beer and raising hell. The second tier, one that includes most contemporary reenactors, is that of the "authentic" reenactor. Authentic reenactors pay careful attention to details, though they do cut some corners and allow twentieth-century comforts to seep in, such as sleeping bags or cans of soda. Finally, there are the "hard-core" reenactors. These people are the most precise practitioners of the hobby; they eat hardtack and salt pork, remain in character for entire weekends, and frown upon anything that compromises accuracy.

Although reenacting tends to be overwhelmingly a hobby for white males, this is not an ironclad rule. There is, for example, a Massachusetts 54th regiment, and African Americans are often welcome to join others. Women

and children can also be reenactors, usually as civilians or as nurses, laundresses, or other noncombatants. As in real war, the question of women in
combat is more problematic, particularly for hard-core reenactors. There
seems to be genuine diversity in class composition. In Company K of the 2d
Rhode Island, for example, there is a banker, a certified public accountant,
and an antiques dealer, as well as Jonathan Clarke and a coworker at the
factory. Doctors often play the part in camps and even perform mock
amputations.

The first step for anyone who wants to enter the hobby is acquiring the
proper clothing and hardware. For soldiers, this includes a sack coat, trousers,
a cap, insignia, and leather gear (a belt, belt plate, cartridge box, and shoul-
der sling). Brogans, or shoes, are not essential but are a good idea. The most
expensive item is a musket, which costs about $400. Muskets can be supple-
mented with bayonets, swords, and scabbards. These items can be purchased
through mail-order catalogs and advertisements published in magazines and
from sutlers who attend reenactments. A person can be outfitted for roughly
$1,000 to $1,200, though creative reenactors can sometimes make items for
themselves. In virtually all cases, objects are replicas; even those collectors
who own authentic Civil War clothing or weapons generally do not bring
them to the battlefield. Artillery units also must acquire cannon replicas;
cavalry units provide their own horses.[25]

The next step is mastering drills. Units often practice before events but
sometimes gather locally, particularly in the spring, to polish skills and inte-
grate newcomers. Safety is strongly emphasized. Although reenactors load
their guns with powder, they shoot blanks; there are no known cases of live
ammunition actually being used. Safety is also discussed before events to
protect not only participants, but also the reputation of reenacting as a
whole.

Most reenactments are weekend affairs. Units typically gather on Friday
night, paying anywhere from $2 to $7 (for expenses such as insurance, meals,
and battlefield preservation), setting up camp, touching base with friends,
and generally getting into the spirit of the event. Saturday morning is usually
devoted to rehearsal, with drills, reviews, and preparation for the battle. That
afternoon, the battle proper is typically staged. At big events, thousands of
spectators will gather over the course of a weekend.

Usually, reenactments are simplified versions of actual engagements, cho-
reographed in such a way as to make them practical for the numbers and types
of people involved. There are also "tacticals," more open-ended affairs that
allow participants to test their strategic mettle in trying to outflank or other-

wise outmaneuver the "enemy." Sooner or later, the din of firing erupts, sometimes culminating in hand-to-hand combat. And when it does, there will be casualties. "Death" can come to reenactors in any number of ways: if one would have undoubtedly been shot or impaled; if the "script" of the battle calls for heavy casualties (a commander may tell odd- or even-numbered people to fall); if one runs out of ammunition; or if pure exhaustion leads one to drop. Sometimes, a lucky soldier will be carried away on a stretcher; otherwise, the "victim" heads for camp at an appropriate moment.

As the First Manassas example suggests, the battles themselves take up relatively little time for individual participants. The rest of the weekend is spent in camp along with other soldiers, civilians, or visitors. This is where reenacting most resembles living history museums such as Old Sturbridge Village. Participants are expected to remain in character for wondering children or adults who will ask questions about what the war was really like. At night, with spectators gone, soldiers often continue their roles, sitting around a campfire, playing Civil War music, or discussing a battle.

Reenactments take place rain or shine. Since they are usually in the summer, and often in the South, it can get quite hot, particularly for people wearing wool uniforms (though once soaked with sweat, wool can actually be cool). Yet exposure to such elements is precisely what appeals to reenactors. In sleeping on the ground, eating bad food, and feeling some of the crushing fatigue that Civil War soldiers did, they hope to recapture, in the most direct sensory way, an experience that fascinates yet eludes them.

The primacy of the senses creates camaraderie for those who experience it, as seems to have been the case during the war itself. Furthermore, although many reenacting units are typically named after or patterned on the one closest to home, others may resurrect the banner of those farther afield (a New Jersey group reenacts a different company in the 2d Rhode Island than Clarke's, and her unit joins it at larger events), and some reenact units of their erstwhile enemies. Thus, although the reenactor quoted above and his company generally reenact as the 7th Rhode Island, they also on occasion represent the 15th Alabama. To some extent, their motives are pragmatic: "There's not as many Southerners in the North," he explains, which can give his group advantages at local events. But there is more to it than that. "I think of them as outstanding people," he says of the Confederates. "People have a lot of respect for the other guy. The more you do it, the more respect you get." The stance here evokes the position held by Lynyrd Skynyrd band members on George Wallace: He did not necessarily represent their views, but they "respected" him nonetheless.

The immediacy and verisimilitude of reenacting may explain the appeal of the hobby compared to reading a book or holding a discussion, but the question remains as to why these people long to recapture the experience of the Civil War in the first place. To put it more simply, what do reenactors (or, for that matter, any amateur historians) get out of the hobby? The answers, as one might expect, are diffuse. Many explain that they have always been Civil War buffs and that this is a way of taking their interest further. But why the Civil War? For some, it is not a particularly relevant question. "Why do people ski or collect coins?" responds one committed reenactor. It is not that he is hostile to the question or unwilling to try to answer it, but simply that it is not something those in the hobby usually spend much time exploring.

Jonathan Clarke did not really have an explicit answer, either. She, too, prizes the sensory appeal of reenacting. Yet it appears that there is something more involved, something that binds past and present, the personal and the collective. By becoming someone else a few days each year, it seems, she gets a better sense of who she really is.

Making Memory

> They were explicit—no women doing soldiers. I mean, what
> is this? This is America! What's the matter with you? And I
> felt that if I could do a good job and pull it off and really
> melt in, then I feel that I had every right to be doing it.
> And if I can honor and remember my people who did this, I
> think I have the right to.
>
> Jonathan Clarke[26]

She thinks her mother had a lot to do with it. Six generations of children had grown up in the Narragansett house, near the bay. Her mother told stories to her and her sister and showed them memorabilia. There were the letters from her great-great-grandfather, for example, who had joined the artillery and had worked as a cook. Later she copied them into spiral notebooks in blue pen, so that she could read them over and over again without worrying about whether they would fall apart. The letters filled three notebooks, and she found herself making his spelling mistakes long afterward.

Her paternal name is Italian. Her father rode the rails for the post office from Boston. He was the son of Italian immigrants, but she never learned much about them. Indeed, although nominally a Catholic, growing up in a Catholic neighborhood, she and her older sister "were exposed to" Protestants. Jonathan herself chose no religion. "I've had people say to me, 'No, you weren't brought up like an Italian,'" she explains. "My father's relatives are up in Massachusetts. What influence I have is basically from the heritage my mother passed on. So I have that strong force that was there, I guess from just being brought up with the stories."

Jonathan attended public schools, where, from the way she talks, one suspects that she was subject to what educational reformers call "tracking"—a subtle process of channeling students into hierarchies that can have a strong impact on their sense of themselves. "I don't have a good background in fourth- through eighth-grade education because we were in the dumb class, the C class," she explains. "We were more riled-up kids, we were more immature, and we didn't learn as easily." She was also something of a tomboy.

She graduated from high school in 1969 and enrolled in the local community college for an associate's degree in biology ("I always liked the outdoors and nature," she explains.) Here the sense of pride and identification with the country her mother had done so much to inculcate was challenged. "That was about the time of the student riots, and they said, 'Well, if you go to class, this is what you believe and this is what you think of the [Vietnam] war,'" she recalled. "I said, 'Hey, look, I paid a lot of money and I'm going to get what I can out of it. I went to class. You're not going to tell me that I think this way because I'm going to class.'" But although Jonathan kept her distance from the antiwar movement, she was still affected by it. "I was never really in the crux of the protesting and things like that, and yet with it going on, you questioned. And yeah, maybe there really was something very wrong." Nevertheless, she was not inclined to see fundamental, structural problems with U.S. democracy. "I could never not be patriotic, because it has a good foundation. It's the people who are elected and who run it that don't always do it justice," she concludes.

After getting her degree, Jonathan took up a trip across the country on horseback—she says it revived her love of the country—before trying to join the navy as a Wave (women accepted for volunteer emergency service). But she failed the math test. She remains a strong believer in combat roles for women in the military and was particularly pleased with their performance in the Persian Gulf War. "I'm very proud, very glad," she says of them. "I think the women in our country have always been tough, because you can't tell me that those women who went out west with those men were not tough. You can't tell me that they couldn't pull their share, and they weren't strong and couldn't do what they had to. Sometimes I don't think they're given enough credit. Nowadays you hear more and more, because more of it is coming out."

Jonathan was never an active member of the women's movement but does, almost reluctantly, cite its impact on her life. "I guess in some ways I'm a feminist, but I'm very independent, a loner type," she explains. She feels the women's movement made it easier for her when she got her job in 1973 and became one of the first women in a predominately male area of the factory floor two years later. "The opportunities were there because I was there at the right time, the attitude was changing, things were being opened, and they really had to start putting women into these positions," she explains. "It's an awful thing to say that they had to do it, rather than willingly do it. But sometimes, that's what it takes." The security of the job allowed her to buy a house for herself in 1979 in the small rural town of Exeter, where she was able to keep the horse she rode across the country until it died in 1987.

In 1982 a coworker told her about a Civil War reenactment. Jonathan was intrigued. She had always been interested in history, particularly U.S. history (it had been her minor at the community college). "It just happens to be the Civil War that I got into for living history," she speculated nine years later. "It could have been a colonial thing or Plymouth Rock or Williamsburg, who knows? But I just happened to get into this. I like learning the detail of one particular period of history, to the point where I can almost feel I live it."

The fact that there were family ties also made it appealing. Jonathan's great-great-grandfather on her mother's side was Ethan Dudley Pendleton, who was thirty-three when he enlisted in the 1st Rhode Island Light Artillery and was designated a cook. Pendleton's wife, whose maiden name was Nye, had two younger brothers who joined Pendleton under the command of Rhode Island general Ambrose Burnside in New Berne, North Carolina. It was there, in 1861, that the younger of those brothers, Jonathan Nye, died of fever. The family could not afford to take his remains home, and so he was buried in New Berne.

Shortly after he left for the war, Pendleton's wife had a daughter, Agnes New Berne Pendleton, who later married a man named Joshua Clark. They had a son, Harry Clark, who married Nellie Clarke. Their daughter, Barbara Clarke, was named after Nellie's mother, complete with the "e." Barbara Clarke is Jonathan's mother.

When she joined the 2d Rhode Island Company K as a soldier, Jonathan needed a man's name. She chose Jonathan Clarke—Jonathan in honor of her uncle, and Clarke for her mother's family and her Yankee heritage. Most of the people in the 2d Rhode Island know her as Jonathan; they do not know her real name. This is as she prefers it, not only because she likes the privacy, but also because then people cannot make mistakes during reenactments.

"When we first formed the group it was hard, because you didn't know how you were going to be taken," she recalls. She was especially unusual in that she did not join with a husband or boyfriend, as most women in living history do. At first, members of the company suggested that she do a woman impression, which she rejected. "I said, 'I don't want to stick out, I don't want to be noticed; I just want to melt in and take in the whole of Civil War reenacting.'" But why not be a woman—a plantation mistress, nurse, or even vivandière? "I would be bored," she replies. "I don't want to stand around looking pretty! That's boring." At the same time, she insisted on joining an infantry, not a cavalry or artillery unit. "The main crux was the man on foot, the foot soldier," she explains. "He was to me the heart of the armies."

Jonathan has found acceptance in the 2d Rhode Island, not only locally, but also with Company B in New Jersey. From the very beginning, however, she has encountered objections that she has quietly ignored. At her very first reenactment, for example, a pamphlet distributed to participants stated that women were prohibited from participating in the event. At a reenactment of the Union attack on Fort Wagner, members of the company talked with members of the sponsoring regiment, which had barred women from combat roles, and learned that it was a commander who was primarily responsible for the order. "We happened to be in line for rifle inspection, and the commander comes up and he didn't know what was going on," she remembers. "He looked at me right in the face, and he didn't know if I was a young kid or a girl. And he was so flustered trying to get things organized that he didn't know what was going on all weekend. No problem. Never heard a another word about it." Yet it was perhaps the epilogue to the story that amused her most. "I had to go in the girls' room the next day—whoops!—and I said [to the surprised women], 'No, I'm a girl.' 'You're on the field fighting?' [they asked.] They couldn't believe I had the *nerve* to buck this guy. But then again, I think basically most women are brought up to let the guys intimidate them, you know?"

Women have become more common as combatants in living history events, much to the chagrin of some hard-core reenactors. In 1989 an Arlington, Virginia, woman who does an impression of a male soldier filed suit against the U.S. Department of the Interior for her ejection from living history events at Antietam National Battlefield in Sharpsburg, Maryland, after it was discovered she was a woman. As part of her case, she documented dozens of known instances of women who secretly fought as men during the Civil War. In 1993 a federal judge ruled in her favor.[27]

Critics of women in battle roles argue that their position has nothing to do with discrimination; rather, they say, an interest of accuracy demands that women be kept off the battlefield. When it is pointed out that hundreds of women did secretly fight for both armies, the response is that these women were able to fight precisely because it was a secret—which it no longer is for the women who publicly contest such a rule.[28] Jonathan has little patience for such arguments. "Either you discriminate or you don't," she asserts. Nor does she accept the accuracy position. "You can go into any encampment and find something that's farbish," she says, including, presumably, the most scrupulously hard-core encampment. Ultimately, however, the question of women in living history is a distraction for those actually participating in reenactments. "I didn't do it to break any barriers," she says. "It's just something I wanted to do, only because I love history."

That love of history has some very specific contours. "I kind of transcend into that period of time," she says, describing a typical experience.

> Everybody talks a lot of history, and tactics, and other battles you've been at, and then at night you sit around the campfire with a pipe. You may have music, you may have singing, we have a couple people that play harmonica who just sit there and look up at the stars and it's quiet. Sometimes I go off and think, "Well, what was it like, what did these people think, what made them stay, what were they made of?" And you get it from the letters. I think of my grandfather. I see him sitting around this little stove that he talks about cooking on. . . .
>
> Then the next day comes the battle, and so you're in line and you practice and you drill for this scenario that you're going to be putting on for the public and you stand there and you look, and, I know at New Market [a reenactment held in Virginia] a few times there were a lot of Rebs that come up that hill at you with the shoes and the mud, and you could almost get scared if you think these are bullets coming at you.

Sometimes Jonathan *does* get scared. She particularly remembers seeing a "wounded" man at Gettysburg covered with "blood." "It was all acting, but for that moment, for a quick moment, I thought, 'My God, I'm in this real situation where people are dying!' It was just a quick moment, but I can remember it."

Other times, she experiences a kind of awe, as in this memory of Gettysburg:

All the units were lined up, and one wave would go in, and you'd cheer 'em on and say "Rah!" and I'm thinking, "God, here are these men. These men actually did things like this. They went in and faced another group of men, in the open, lined right up and shot at each other, and killed and fought with each other and you cheer 'em on and send in the next wave of them to die." Things like this go through my mind. You know, try to picture the reality of this happening, that our people stood there and went in, as the Southerners went in, to die and fight, and the way they fought was the end of the old wars and the beginning of the new wars. Because the whole thing evolved. These things cross my mind.

Clearly, there is more involved here than the kind of momentary thrill of an amusement park. Jonathan seeks—and feels she gets—a truer understanding of the past than she finds in books, an understanding that emphasizes not only the personal stake she has in the war, but also those of countless other citizens. "You remember Lee, you remember Grant, you remember [Union general Joshua] Chamberlain, you remember all these people. But these are the little people nobody remembers. These are people who have families, they *do* know them like I know and have that tie," she explains. "I think that's why a lot of people do it. They have that tie and it brings something together for them."

"What I get out of this is that I feel I'm doing something patriotic to remember the high price we paid for what we have in this country," she says. "To remember the people, whether it's Revolutionary or Civil War, who sacrificed for this country, why they sacrificed, to really remember them— what this country means to me. I do it because of family. I know who my family is; I feel a part of the evolution of the whole country."

In 1989 Jonathan and her mother journeyed to New Berne, North Carolina, to visit the national cemetery there. They found the grave of Jonathan Nye, and the two generations laid flowers there, becoming the first family members to pay him homage. Jonathan has pictures of the site.

She continues to work at the factory. In January 1990 she was promoted after receiving certification for developing new skills. "Our jobs have changed drastically," she says. "It wasn't done nicely," she says of the company. "They left a lot of hard feelings. Some people didn't want to change. At [the factory], once something came in, a month later it would go away. But this isn't going away because we wouldn't survive. We've never had the competition we have today. I like change; that's part of life. It's an opportunity. If I lost this job, the more I know the more I can do—it can only help me get another job. Education is something I value. I've always respected it."

She feels her passion for the past has served her well:

Because of history I can understand today much better what is happening in today's world. A lot of people I know, they can't look at history and relate to today, where I find ties somehow. It repeats. Technology changes, the way we do things, the areas we do things, the areas we deal in. Now it's a world economy, as opposed to our economy. You can see this evolve all through history. You can see it happening, right where I work. . . . It's like another industrial revolution of the technology that we created. . . . History has cycles. It repeats. Man has not basically changed. His mind has created the technology. But he's basically the same.

"I don't consider myself a leader or a follower," she concludes. "I just happened to be at the right place at the right time and the challenge was there. I happened to be the first one to grab at it. And maybe it's because of my independence and the way I am. It's America, you can achieve whatever you want. Unconsciously, that's how I feel, I guess. It's been bred in me or something."

Making Judgments

> In fact, of course, "living history" is a contradiction in
> terms, and being able to eat and dress like a nineteenth
> century person provides little in the way of insight into what
> a nineteenth century person was thinking or how he or she
> behaved.
>
>   Richard O'Sullivan,
>   a Confederate reenactor in England[29]

I have made some effort here to report the ideas and attitudes of a few reenactors and other amateur historians on their own terms. My goal has not been to place the attitudes or behavior of these people in some analytic category (although that is possible) or to argue that they are representative of most amateur historians (in some ways, they surely are), or even to demonstrate that their lives illustrate a particular facet of change over time (there are ways of doing that). These are all venerable traditions in historical writing and remain useful avenues of inquiry. What matters to me here, though, is that these people have ideas about the past, ideas that I wish to take seriously. They are not necessarily representative ideas, but they are intelligible to outside observers and can be analyzed.

This, as Jonathan Clarke might say, is the crux of the matter. For I am not simply content to report ideas; I feel compelled to judge them. I suppose I am granting some degree of legitimacy to reenacting simply by giving my attention to it. Actually, I *am* willing to grant it legitimacy, because for people such as Jonathan Clarke, reenacting really does seem to be a sincere and meaningful cultural act.

I do have some reservations, however. For example, one of the most striking things about talking with an amateur historian of any variety is his or her mastery of detail. The typical Civil War buff, whatever the hobby, is likely to have accumulated an impressive amount of factual information on any number of pertinent subjects—where a regiment was at a particular moment, who supplied weapons for either side at a given time, the career trajectory of relatively obscure officers, and so on. On questions such as these, the typical buff is likely to know at least as much as—no, more than—the typical professional.

However, it also seems that amateur historians tend to lose the war through the battles. A thorough mastery of military events may coexist with little knowledge of political, cultural, and social movements before, during, and after the war. Although there is a place in reenactments for death and injury, some important complexities—the chaos, brutality, and uncertainty of wartime, and the disillusionments of its aftermath—are missing. It is tempting to think this is because the passage of a century has necessarily cut contemporary reenactors off from these experiences and perhaps has led them to trivialize what really happened. As Stuart McConnell shows, however, Civil War veterans themselves indulged in a similar whitewashing of the past in their own GAR encampments.[30] In an interesting way, such historical fictions resemble science fiction, where verisimilitude and fantasy also coexist to serve what might be considered a deeply human, anthropological need for myth.

Of course, professional scholarship generates myths of its own. But it often does so in ways that can challenge, and perhaps even change, amateur myths. When Jonathan Clarke speaks about the toughness of women on the frontier, and that "nowadays you learn more and more, because more of it is coming out," one suspects that, however indirectly, professional scholarship has influenced her understanding of women's history. That, in turn, may have played a role in her decision to become a reenactor.

Nevertheless, amateur historians generally overlook historiography. In a way this makes sense—why should amateurs care how professionals have argued among themselves? However, there is a static quality to the study of the past without an awareness of how opinion has shifted in light of new discoveries or emerging issues. Again, this sense of stasis seems to have been common among GAR veterans, who believed that Union victory in the Civil War represented a permanent vindication of federal principles for all time.[31]

One of the great strengths of a hobby such as reenacting is that it can give participants a vivid, even visceral, experience of the past on a very personal level. One by-product of this is enhanced respect for the "other guy," still another relic of nineteenth-century attitudes. It is an understandable and perhaps even appropriate one. Yet, for me, academic research has brought the past to life in no less real a way—and has, more than ever, confirmed my Northern sympathies. Nineteenth-century issues have become clearer than ever when placed in context and have new relevance, even urgency, in twentieth-century society.

At the heart of issue is slavery. One might think that the Southern wartime position would give some contemporary Northerners and Southerners pause in "respecting the other guy," however valiantly he fought. In many cases, it probably does. However, no person interviewed for this chapter would agree that slavery was central to the conflict, and nobody seemed all that interested—or comfortable—talking about it. "People think it was all slavery, but it was politics," said a Confederate cavalry officer from Maryland at the First Manassas reenactment, pointing to the growing congressional representation of Northerners in the years preceding the war. "The South just felt, 'This just isn't going to work out.'" Many others, North and South, saw union, secession, or more generally fighting for one's home and family as the primary cause—and meaning—of the conflict. In one sense, this is hardly surprising; such explanations have been common from the very beginning. Yet one is struck by the gap between some professional historians, who have emphasized the importance of African American issues since the 1960s, and the amateurs, who are generally willing to note (but not emphasize) the importance of the slavery issue in particular and the role of African Americans in general.

One plausible explanation for this discrepancy is that the academy is a very different place than it was prior to the 1960s. Unlike some other institutions in U.S. society—such as, for example, the Senate—the professoriate is no longer an almost universally white male domain. Although hardly a perfectly integrated institution in any sense of that term, the ivory tower is much more varied in terms of race, class, gender, ethnicity, and politics than it ever was before. The upheavals of the 1960s—and the continued presence of those who participated in them at many colleges and universities—have distanced the academy from those segments of U.S. society, such as those most likely to participate in reenactments, who are seemingly unaffected by the changes of the last four decades.

But they have not been unaffected. Indeed, that seems to be the point of their Civil War.

The White Badge of Courage

> All attempts to make history are an attempt to form internal consensus.
>
> Ken Burns[32]

> [A]n appropriately idealized version of the past may also allow a group of human beings to come closer to living up to its noblest ideals.
>
> William McNeill, "Mythistory, or Truth, Myth, History and Historians"[33]

In the twentieth century, fascination with the Civil War has been a white affair. Of course, African Americans have been interested in the war, have participated in the excitement surrounding works such as the Ken Burns documentary, and have made distinguished contributions of their own. Black writers from Frances Ellen Watkins Harper to Alex Haley have dealt with the war in their work to varying (but almost always partial) degrees.[34] However, although African Americans have created a wide variety of internationally famous works of popular culture, the Civil War does not leap out as a common theme.

In white culture, by contrast, some of the most famous popular cultural works of all time—such as *Birth of a Nation* and *Gone with the Wind*—have focused on the Civil War. Other works directly or indirectly about the war, such as *Glory* and *Roots*, have included the work of black writers, actors, and other contributors but have white directors and producers who are primarily responsible for bringing them to the large or small screen. More importantly, given the demographics of the United States, the huge audiences for these works are overwhelmingly white, embraced by the vast "middle America" so ardently pursued by marketing experts and publicity departments.

And so we are faced with perhaps the most fundamental question hovering over this book: Why, for whites at least, does the Civil War continue to exert its persistent power in U.S. life? I cannot give a definitive answer, of course, but the one I shall offer relates to the usability of the past.

In each of the chapters of this book, I have tried to provide some historical context for the works being discussed. In each case, there has been social or political stress that has shaken the confidence of the creators—and, I think it is safe to say, the audiences—that the United States can offer the comfort and satisfaction stated or implied in its creation and subsequent revisions (of which the Civil War was the most dramatic example). For Carl Sandburg, this crisis was the Great Depression. For Margaret Mitchell, it was uncertainty about women's roles in a South on the cusp of increasing turmoil. For Southern rock performers, it was the Civil Rights movement and the fear and guilt that movement engendered in white men. For Edward Zwick and his fellow creators of Glory, the crisis was Vietnam and its crippling effect on the moral confidence of liberals.

What is the source of unease in the case of reenactors? I believe that it is the fear that in this increasingly diverse society, events such as the Civil War (which so many European Americans hold near and dear to their hearts, and in which they have such personal, familial, or assimilationist interests) may become less relevant. In this light, reenacting becomes a ritual—I think it is possible to argue that Burns's Civil War is another—by which a majoritarian United States reassures itself that it, too, has a past, and that that past is as dramatic, interesting, and important as the alternative, multicultural pasts that are increasingly competing with it. Once again, the Civil War has become a banner around which millions can rally, a point of reference that can shore up a center that fears it may not hold.

I must confess that I write these lines with some unease: unease because I am not sure this is the best use of the Civil War, and unease because as someone with a deep feeling for it, I do not want to condemn that interest as a veiled form of racism. However, I think we have to be as honest as we can about our motives, which are rarely pure. By the same token, I think it is possible to identify aspects of that interest—such as Carl Sandburg's efforts to make the war a precedent for a more just society—that are deserving of our attention and emulation. And so I hope we can continue to engage with our past and use it to touch and strengthen the better angels of our nature.

Conclusion

The Art
of History

It is no argument against the use of analogy to say that it is dangerous. So is the historian's use of evidence, comparison, imagination, or, for that matter, metaphor. Analogy is itself an abridged metaphor. History is a perilous craft. History without analogies, however, would be a meaner thing, no more than a social science, perhaps one that speaks of analogies as "models" and misconceives their uses. Of course analogies never prove anything. They only provoke things. They can even provoke thought.

C. Vann Woodward[1]

It was time to kill Abraham Lincoln, a moment Ken Burns had long been dreading. He had visited dozens of Civil War sites, many of them places of great sorrow, in the process of assembling his monumental Civil War documentary. However, there was something about Lincoln's death that seemed almost too much to bear. Indeed, when he needed footage of Ford's Theater, where the assassination had taken place, the director sent a film crew ahead without him. But he was mixing the soundtrack for the film, and he had to face the murder. "Just as the pistol was about to ring out in the studio, I looked at my editor, who had tears in his eyes, and yelled 'Stop!'" Burns recalled. "The engineer hit the panic button and the rolls of film and tape came to a halt just a fraction of a second before the sound of the gunshot."[2] The filmmakers paused; then, reluctantly, Burns allowed Abraham Lincoln to be shot. His death and its aftermath, which constitutes a major portion of the last episode of *The Civil War*, are among the most affecting moments of the documentary, and it is a measure of Burns's achievement that he was able to take a very familiar story and once again imbue it with tragedy and dignity for yet one more chronicle of the Civil War.

Indeed, the difficulty of managing such a feat has led some historians to eschew even trying. The last chapter of James McPherson's *Battle Cry of Freedom*, published two years before the premiere of the Burns documentary on public television, ends with Lincoln outlining his position on Reconstruction in Louisiana. John Wilkes Booth solemnly declares, "Now, by God, I'll put him through. That is the last speech he will ever make." McPherson's epilogue then begins with Lincoln already dead.[3]

The respective narrative decisions of Burns and McPherson are striking in the way they echo those made by Carl Sandburg and James Randall roughly a half-century before. Sandburg made the Lincoln assassination a major dramatic element of his Lincoln biography, employing literary techniques that gave his account an almost cinematic immediacy. Randall, by contrast, gave the assassination a paragraph, which one imagines he regarded as an act of scholarly discipline that kept the focus on his subject's life—and represented a refusal to pander to the biographical mediocrity he lamented in his 1936 survey of Lincoln literature in the *American Historical Review*.

The respective choices of Sandburg/Burns and Randall/McPherson reveal their commitments to different historical traditions that have persisted straight through the twentieth century. Sandburg and Burns belong to a narrative tradition that stresses the artistic, communal dimension to the past. Randall and McPherson place their faith in a detached style of restraint; they reject the excesses and dangers of myth in favor of the verities of fact and evidence. What goes unacknowledged in their work, however, is that fact and evidence have excesses and dangers, too, something that McPherson (C. Vann Woodward's student) is probably more attuned to than Randall was. Restraint, after all, is an artistic choice, too.

Academic history began at the end of the last century as an attempt to create a form that would escape ideological commitments for the sake of objective truth. If nothing else, a century of historical writing, like popular culture, offers ample evidence that ideological commitments, whether of race, class, gender, region, party, or any other kind, continue to have a decisive impact on the shape of history. At the end of the twentieth century, most scholars accept—if not actually practice, or even explore—this truth.

Ironically, some of those who most insistently reject the myth of social science as naive espouse a variety of theoretical approaches that reproduce the faith in method, the cult of expertise, and even the elitism of the social scientists themselves. Although much of this work is distinguished and offers many valuable insights, it cannot became the basis for a truly democratic history that creates usable pasts for historian and citizen alike.[4]

I do not believe, as many scholars continue to profess, that even with all its epistemological or linguistic shortcomings, professional scholarship offers a degree of analytical sophistication unavailable in popular culture (my experiences with the work of people such as Gore Vidal and Randy Newman have taught me that). Nor do professional historians necessarily have more effective research techniques than popular historians (the tenaciousness of a Margaret Mitchell or a Carl Sandburg—and the blind spots of so scrupulous a researcher as Randall—make that clear).

Academic history, almost despite itself, has always offered expressive possibilities. It can be best understood as series of shared conventions: a reliance on primary source documentation; the conscious creation, participation, and reconfiguration of scholarly dialogue; widely acknowledged scaffolding such as bibliography, footnotes, and other forms of citation; even rhetorical patterns such as the use of the topic sentence as a key unit for organizing an argument. Of course, not all historians have accepted these conventions, and any attempt to go much beyond such generalizations—or strictly codify them—is not likely to be useful. This is especially true when one considers the diverse roles performed by public historians—archivists, curators, musicians, and others—who facilitate and mediate contacts between different historical constituencies. Like jazz or the Western, we can have a sense of what history is without being able to precisely define it.

In short, like popular history, professional history is a form of art. This is an obvious assertion, but a necessary one that remains largely unacknowledged. To make it is to rebuke scholars for their hubris for the last century—and to anticipate the opportunities it affords. The challenge facing us in the coming century will be making the most of those opportunities while honoring the obligations of memory.

Notes

Introduction: History as Culture

1. Warren I. Susman, *Culture as History: The Transformation of American Society in the Twentieth Century* (New York: Pantheon, 1984), p. 5. *Culture as History* was the first book I read when I began my graduate training and has been a pivotal influence on my view of history ever since. Readers familiar with Susman's work will no doubt recognize this passage; readers unfamiliar with it are urged to seek it out.

2. Shelby Foote, *The Civil War: A Narrative* (New York: Random House, 1958–1974), reprinted by Vintage in 1986. Foote is also the author of *Shiloh* (1952), an extraordinarily vivid and historically nuanced novelistic account of the battle. It was reissued by Vintage in 1991.

3. The "organizational revolution" is the term Robert Wiebe uses to describe one of the major social developments in the United States during the late nineteenth century. See *The Search for Order, 1877–1920* (New York: Hill and Wang, 1967), especially pp. 111–32.

4. Van Wyck Brooks, "On Creating a Usable Past," *The Dial*, April 11, 1918, pp. 337–41. Brooks's major works include *America's Coming-of-Age* (1915); *The Ordeal of Mark Twain* (1920); *The Pilgrimage of Henry James* (1925); and *The Flowering of New England* (1936). For a description of free-lance intellectual life and its demise, see Russell Jacoby, *The Last Intellectuals: American Culture in the Age of Academe* (1987; New York: Noonday Press, 1989).

5. Examples here include Susman, *Culture as History*; George Lipsitz, *Time Passages: Collective Memory and American Popular Culture* (Minneapolis: University of Minnesota Press, 1990); and Michael Kammen, *Mystic Chords of Memory: Time and Tradition in American Culture* (New York: Knopf, 1991).

6. Examples include Thomas Connelly, *The Marble Man: Robert E. Lee and His Image in American Society* (Baton Rouge: Louisiana State University Press, 1977); Gaines Foster, *Ghosts of the Confederacy: Defeat, the Lost Cause, and the Emergence of the New South* (New York: Oxford University Press, 1987); and Garry Wills,

Lincoln at Gettysburg: Words That Remade America (New York: Simon & Schuster, 1992).

7. Good examples here include John Bodnar, *Remaking History: Public Memory, Commemoration, and Patriotism in the Twentieth Century* (Princeton: Princeton University Press, 1992); and Stuart McConnell, *Glorious Contentment: The Grand Army of the Republic, 1865–1900* (Chapel Hill: University of North Carolina Press, 1992).

8. David Thelen, "Memory and American History," *Journal of American History* (March 1989): 1118.

9. Perhaps the earliest and still most influential expression of this position is Roland Barthes's classic 1957 essay "Myth Today" in *Mythologies,* translated by Annette Lavers (New York: Noonday Press, 1972). More recent formulations include the work of "Birmingham School" theoretician Stuart Hall, especially "Notes on Deconstructing the Popular" in Raphael Samuel, editor, *People's History and Social Theory* (London: Routledge and Kegan Paul, 1981); and Frederic Jameson's widely cited essay "Notes on Deconstructing the Popular," *Social Text* 1 (1979): 130–48. For a particularly clear and concise discussion of myth and ideology in a recent work of cultural history, see the introduction to Richard Slotkin, *Gunfighter Nation: The Myth of the Frontier in Twentieth-Century America* (New York: Atheneum, 1992), pp. 1–26.

10. The most distinguished practitioner of audience-based scholarship (leavened with other approaches) is Janice Radway. Her *Reading the Romance: Women, Patriarchy, and Popular Literature* (Chapel Hill: University of North Carolina Press, 1984) is a classic of popular culture scholarship. Radway's most recent work on the Book-of-the-Month Club, an essay on which is included in Cathy Davidson, editor, *Reading in America: Literature and Social History* (Baltimore: Johns Hopkins University Press, 1989), pp. 259–84, demonstrates the ongoing vitality of her work.

11. In this regard, I am consciously trying to participate in a tradition that includes Constance Rourke, Leslie Fiedler, Greil Marcus, Warren Susman, and others. See Rourke, *American Humor: A Study of the National Character* (New York: Harcourt, Brace and Company, 1931); Fiedler, *Love and Death in the American Novel* (New York: Stein and Day, 1960); Marcus, *Mystery Train: Images of America in Rock 'n' Roll Music* (New York: Dutton, 1975); and Susman, *Culture as History.*

Chapter 1: The Past Keeps Changing

1. Foote's comments also appear in the companion volume to the series, *The Civil War: An Illustrated History,* by Geoffrey C. Ward with Ric Burns and Ken Burns (New York: Knopf, 1990), p. 264.

2. "Revisiting the Civil War," *Newsweek,* October 8, 1990, p. 58; Richard

Zoglin, "The Civil War Comes Home," *Time*, October 8, 1990, p. 78. Both magazines previewed the series in the September 24 issues.

Promotional materials for Burns's lecture tour following the series claimed 39 million people in the United States watched it, a figure also cited in the Spring 1991 *Film Quarterly* review of the documentary on p. 3. Just how many people saw the film—and what exactly it means to have seen it (one installment or the whole series? As background noise or in rapt attention?)—is open to dispute. It does seem fair to say, however, that *The Civil War* occupied a prominent place on the cultural landscape in the fall of 1990.

3. "Civil War Comes Home," p. 78.

4. "Revisiting the Civil War," p. 59.

5. Michael Hill, "A Television Milestone," *Washington Post TV Week*, September 23, 1990, p. 6.

6. "Critics: Series All Blue and No Gray," *Charlotte Observer*, September 30, 1991, p. 1; "Revisiting the Civil War," pp. 61–63.

7. "Revisiting the Civil War," p. 62; Hill, "Television Milestone," p. 10. For Fields's own work on slavery, see her essay "Ideology and Race in American History," in J. Morgan Kousser and James M. McPherson, editors, *Region, Race, and Reconstruction: Essays in Honor of C. Vann Woodward* (New York: Oxford University Press, 1982), pp. 143–78. See also her *Slavery and the Middle Ground: Maryland during the Nineteenth Century* (New Haven: Yale University Press, 1985).

8. Lincoln's comment, which has been widely quoted, is cited by Carl Sandburg in *Abraham Lincoln: The War Years*, Vol. 3 (New York: Harcourt, Brace and Company, 1939), p. 201. For the letter to Fields and another account of the event, see Thomas F. Gossett, *Uncle Tom's Cabin and American Culture* (Dallas: Southern Methodist University Press, 1985), p. 315. Gossett traces Lincoln's comment back to Stowe's daughter Harriet, cited in *The Life and Letters of Harriet Beecher Stowe*, edited by Annie Fields (Boston: Houghton Mifflin, 1897), p. 269.

9. The growth of popular fiction in the early nineteenth century is the subject of a vast and growing scholarship. For an illuminating discussion of the varieties and influence of this writing, see David S. Reynolds, *Beneath the American Renaissance: The Subversive Imagination in the Age of Emerson and Melville* (Cambridge: Harvard University Press, 1988). For a perspective on women writers, who exercised considerable influence in this period, see Nina Baym, *Woman's Fiction: A Guide to Novels by and about Women in America* (Ithaca: Cornell University Press, 1978). For a discussion of the rise of the publishing industry, see Mary Kelly, *Private Woman, Public Stage: Literary Domesticity in Nineteenth Century America* (New York: Oxford University Press, 1985), pp. 3–27. The second chapter of Michael Denning, *Mechanic Accents: Dime Novels and Working-Class Culture in America* (London: Verso, 1987) explains the factors giving rise to "books for the million," while Richard Rubin in *Press, Party, and Presidency* (New York: Norton, 1981) offers a good explanation of the rise and fall of national political

parties in the media. For sectional currents in popular fiction, see William Taylor, *Cavalier and Yankee: The Old South and the American National Character* (New York: Doubleday, 1961).

10. After decades of neglect by literary historians more interested in writers such as Nathaniel Hawthorne and Herman Melville, domestic fiction has recently become the subject of intense interest and debate among scholars. Although there are important variations and alternative tendencies in the genre, it does seem safe to say that domestic novels shared a concern over the individualistic excesses of capitalism, a belief that family and the home acted as a check on such individualism, and the notion that women were uniquely suited to provide the moral guidance and emotional succor necessary for the success of the nation and the realization of postmillennial Christianity. For the half-century spanning the publication of Catherine Maria Sedgwick's *New England Tale* in 1822 and Elizabeth Stuart Phelps's *Gates Ajar* in 1868, domestic fiction was used to argue that a woman's place was in the home—a point they often left the home to make, but one in which the home and the women that ran it were central.

Domestic fiction was not the only genre of women's writing at the time, as Reynolds's *Beneath the American Renaissance* amply attests. However, stories of what he calls "adventure feminists" and others were to a great extent written in the context of—and as a response to—more conventional fiction. See especially pp. 339–51.

11. Marion Wilson Starling, *The Slave Narrative: Its Place in American History*, 2d ed. (1st ed., 1946; Washington, D.C.: Howard University Press, 1988). See particularly Starling's chapters on the slave narrative after 1836 and her discussion of the literary significance of the narratives. For a more recent survey of the form, see Charles T. Davis and Henry Louis Gates, editors, *The Slave's Narrative* (New York: Oxford University Press, 1985).

Although New England abolitionists showed the most interest in reading slave narratives (and writing them on behalf of African Americans), there is some evidence that they were reaching other audiences indirectly as well. A magazine writer in the 1850s lamented that "the whole literary atmosphere has become tainted" with those "literary nigritudes" (Starling, p. 2). Perhaps even more striking, the hugely successful dime novel firm of Beadle and Adams, which published books to be circulated to soldiers at the front, published *Maum Guinea and Her Plantation "Children"; or Holiday Week on a Louisiana Estate* by Metta V. Victor in 1861. The dime novel company was generally known in the years following the Civil War for its Westerns and detective stories, but titles such as *Maum Guinea* and *Black Tom, the Negro Detective* (1893) suggest that at least some stories with racial themes were published. William Wells Brown's novel *Clotelle* (1853) was also published in dime novel format. Henry Nash Smith, one of the first major scholars to study dime novels in his now classic *Virgin Land: The American West as Symbol and Myth* (New York: Vintage, 1950) described them solely as Westerns, perhaps because these were the only dime novels he encountered in his research. Denning, who notes this absence on p. 14 of *Mechanic Accents*, also cites the publication of *Black Tom* and *Clotelle* (on pp. 210 and 26 respectively).

For a discussion of the conventions and issues facing slave women in particular, and the impact of the slave narrative on the subsequent development of fiction by black writers, see Hazel Carby, *Reconstructing Womanhood: The Emergence of the Afro-American Novelist* (New York: Oxford, 1987).

12. Taylor, *Cavalier and Yankee*, pp. 109–13, 146, 157–67. *Cavalier and Yankee* remains the best study of the sectional struggles in antebellum fiction. See particularly pp. 123–55 and 279–94, which trace the development of the plantation novel in the 1820s and 1830s and its transformation under the pressures of abolitionism twenty years later. Central to Taylor's argument is his belief that Southern fiction often unwittingly articulated anxieties that were concealed or forbidden in conventional politics, a premise that continues to inform much popular culture scholarship in other contexts.

13. The alliance between Southern conservatives and antiabolitionist "Hunker" Democrats is a fixture of virtually any discussion of antebellum politics. For a relatively old account of the planter-worker alliance, see Arthur M. Schlesinger, Jr., *The Age of Jackson* (New York: Little Brown, 1941); the subject is handled with more nuance in Sean Wilentz's *Chants Democratic: New York City and the Rise of the American Working Class* (New York: Oxford University Press, 1984). For an insightful discussion of the cultural dimension of the coalition, and its expression in Jacksonian theatre and minstrelsy, see Alexander Saxton, *The Rise and Fall of the White Republic: Class Politics and Mass Culture in Nineteenth Century America* (London: Verso, 1990). The best-known modern study of minstrelsy is Robert Toll, *Blacking Up: The Minstrel Show in Nineteenth Century America* (New York: Oxford University Press, 1974). See also Eric Lott, *Love and Theft: Blackface Minstrelsy and the American Working Class* (New York: Oxford University Press, 1993).

14. On the various theatrical productions of *Uncle Tom's Cabin*, see Toll, *Blacking Up*, pp. 90–97. Though some early versions tried to uphold the antislavery spirit of the novel, satiric minstrel productions quickly became more common.

15. For a superb one-volume rendering of the rise of the Republican party, see Eric Foner, *Free Soil, Free Labor, Free Men: The Ideology of the Republican Party before the Civil War* (New York: Oxford University Press, 1970).

16. For a now classic study on the way these uses were expressed by Northern thinkers, see George Fredrickson, *The Inner Civil War: Northern Intellectuals and the Crisis of Union* (New York: Harper & Row, 1965).

17. The notion of home as battlefield and battlefield as home is discussed at some length in Lyde Cullen Sizer, "A Revolution in Woman Herself: Northern Women Writers and the American Civil War, 1850–1872" (Ph.D. diss., Brown University, 1994).

18. Twain quoted in James Chandler, "The Historical Novel Goes to Hollywood:

Scott, Griffith, and Film Epic Today," in Gene W. Ruoff, editor, *The Romantics and Us* (New Brunswick, N.J.: Rutgers University Press, 1990), p. 247. Chandler's essay provides a provocative study of Scott's influence on U.S. culture and its persistence into the work of D. W. Griffith and beyond.

19. Joel Williamson, *A Rage for Order: Black-White Relations in the American South since Emancipation* (New York: Oxford University Press, 1986), pp. 106, 113. (Condensed from *The Crucible of Race: Black-White Relations in the American South since Emancipation* [New York: Oxford University Press, 1984].)

20. The most important historian to trace the political disenfranchisement of African Americans is C. Vann Woodward. See particularly *Origins of the New South, 1877–1913* (Baton Rouge: Louisiana State University Press, 1951) and *The Strange Career of Jim Crow* (New York: Oxford University Press, 1955; 3d ed., 1974). For the influence of Dixon on Mitchell, see Chapter 2. For an analysis of Dixon's life and work, see Raymond A. Cook, *Thomas Dixon* (New York: Twayne's United States Author's Series, 1974).

21. Stephen Crane, *The Red Badge of Courage* (1895; New York: Penguin Classics, 1985), p. 68.

22. John Higham with Leonard Krieger and Felix Gilbert, *History* (Englewood Cliffs, N.J.: Prentice-Hall, 1965), p. 1.

23. Upper- and lowercase "D." Bancroft was a party insider who enjoyed a career in politics and diplomacy, and Parkman was a New England conservative who later saw the Civil War as a necessary astringent to cleanse the nation of moral impurities and toughen Anglo-Saxon stock. For a discussion of Parkman as a conservative, see Fredrickson, *Inner Civil War*.

24. Quoted on p. 13 of Richard Hofstadter's *Progressive Historians: Turner, Beard, Parrington* (Chicago: University of Chicago Press, 1969), pp. 3–11, 17. The first chapter of Hofstadter's book (which is fascinating for its exploration of intellectual godparents whom he later rejected) is an elegantly synthesized and judicious survey of the field between the end of the eighteenth and the beginning of the nineteenth century. For a case study in early partisan history, see William Taylor's discussion of William Wirt in *Cavalier and Yankee*, pp. 43–71.

25. Thomas J. Pressly, *Americans Interpret Their Civil War* (Princeton: Princeton University Press, 1954), pp. 7–13, 64–66. Pressly's study is a superb account of Civil War historiography from 1860 to 1950.

26. Ibid., pp. 33–37, 47–48.

27. Ibid., pp. 28–51, 73–95 passim, 115–17. In his summary of attitudes from the 1860s to 1880s, Pressly characterizes writers of this period as the "primitives" of Civil War historiography.

28. James Ford Rhodes, *History of the United States from the Compromise of 1850*, 8 vols. (New York: Harper and Brothers [vols. 1–4] and Macmillan [vols. 5–8], 1893–1906). Two additional volumes published in 1919 and 1922 brought the

narrative up to 1909. For a summary of Rhodes's work, see Pressly, *Americans Interpret Their Civil War*, pp. 135–49.

29. Pressly summarizes the Nationalist tradition on pp. 187–92 of *Americans Interpret Their Civil War*.

30. The rise of the academic profession and the class and epistemological foundations girding it have been widely commented upon. Among the works that discuss it in greater or lesser degrees of detail are Robert Wiebe, *The Search for Order* (New York: Hill and Wang, 1967); Burton Bledstein, *The Culture of Professionalism: The Middle Class and the Development of Higher Education in America* (New York: Norton, 1976); Thomas Haskell, *The Emergence of Professional Social Science: The American Social Science Association and the Nineteenth Century Crisis of Authority* (Urbana: University of Illinois Press, 1977); and Frederick Rudolph, *The American College and University: A History* (1962; Athens: University of Georgia Press, 1990).

31. My understanding of the rise of the social sciences has been greatly aided by Dorothy Ross, *The Origins of Professional Social Science* (New York: Cambridge University Press, 1992). For the inability of social scientists to find government jobs and the availability of jobs in the academy, see especially pp. 62–63.

32. Higham, *History*, p. 4.

33. Peter Novick, *That Noble Dream: The "Objectivity Question" and the American Historical Profession* (New York: Cambridge University Press, 1989), pp. 3–5, 56–57. Novick's massive study was singularly illuminating for the present study and is recommended to anyone wishing to understand the development of the discipline over the last century.

34. Novick, *That Noble Dream*, pp. 64–68, 57–60; Hofstadter, *Progressive Historians*, p. 27. Both authors remark on the striking degree of consensus that existed among historians between roughly 1870 and 1900. The persistent power of exceptionalism is a key argument of Ross's *Origins of Professional Social Science*.

35. Hart quoted in Novick, *That Noble Dream*, p. 75. Novick describes Hart as "the teacher and patron of W. E. B. Du Bois and of other black students at Harvard; there was no historian more energetic in promotion of black advance." For descriptions of other "scientific" explanations of racism, see Williamson, *Rage for Order*, pp. 86–90.

36. Lary May, *Screening Out the Past: The Birth of Mass Culture and the Motion Picture Industry* (Chicago: University of Chicago Press, 1983), pp. 43–59. For another excellent survey of early film culture and the place of ethnic groups within in it, see Robert Sklar, *Movie-Made America: A Cultural History of American Movies* (New York: Vintage, 1975).

37. Jack Spears, *The Civil War on Screen and Other Essays* (South Brunswick, N.J.: A. S. Barnes and Company, 1977), pp. 11–12.

38. Richard Schickel, *D. W. Griffith: An American Life* (New York: Simon and

Schuster, 1984), pp. 154–55; Sklar, *Movie-Made America*, pp. 53–54. Sklar points out that Griffith did not, as the director and many later writers claimed, invent these techniques, which were preceded in almost every case by Edwin Porter. He does say, however, that Griffith's recognition of the potential of these techniques and effective exploitation of them justifies the regard he has received.

39. Chandler, "Historical Novel," p. 269; Cook, *Thomas Dixon*, pp. 101–4, 110–11; Schickel, *D. W. Griffith*, pp. 267–68. For Griffith as social reformer, see May, *Screening Out the Past*, pp. 60–95.

40. Schickel, *D. W. Griffith*, pp. 268–69, 298. In the early years of the Wilson administration, at least twenty Jim Crow bills were introduced into Congress. Though most of these failed to pass, Wilson segregated federal eating and rest room facilities by executive order and phased most blacks out of the civil service. See John Hope Franklin and Alfred A. Moss, Jr., *From Freedom to Slavery: A History of Negro Americans*, 6th ed. (1st ed., 1947; New York: Knopf, 1988), pp. 292–93.

41. Ross, *Origins of American Social Science*, pp. 321–22.

42. In *Origins of American Social Science*, Ross in passing notes the connections that link scientism and modernism. "As the name itself indicates, modernism referred to a critical stage in the evolution of modernity and to a problem in historical time. In common usage, the term has come to designate only the aesthetic response to that problem. . . . Both scientism and aestheticism, however, were responding to the crisis in historical consciousness that emerged in Western culture at the turn of the twentieth century" (p. 318).

43. For discussions of Charles Beard's work and influences, see Hofstadter, *Progressive Historians*, pp. 167–356, and Pressly, *Americans Interpret Their Civil War*, 204–14.

44. For discussions of Dunning and his historiographic impact, see Novick, *That Noble Dream*, pp. 68–80 passim, and Pressly, *Americans Interpret Their Civil War*, 231–38. Pressly also discusses Phillips, whose best-known work is *Life and Labor in the Old South* (Boston: Little, Brown, 1929). Phillips is mentioned again in Chapter 4.

45. Pressly, *Americans Interpret Their Civil War*, pp. 257–72. Pressly notes the emergence of what became standard revisionism in the widely overlooked doctoral dissertation of Mary Scrugham, *The Peaceable Americans of 1860–61: A Study in Public Opinion* (New York: Columbia University, 1921).

46. Van Wyck Brooks, *America's Coming-of-Age* (1915; New York: Viking Press, 1930); "On Creating a Usable Past," *The Dial*, April 11, 1918, p. 339.

47. Joan Shelly Rubin, *The Making of Middlebrow Culture* (Chapel Hill: University of North Carolina Press, 1992).

48. Penelope Niven, *Carl Sandburg: A Biography* (New York: Charles Scribner's Sons), p. 422.

Chapter 2: "A Tree Is Best Measured When It's Down"

1. Edmund Wilson, *Letters on Literature and Politics* (New York: Farrar, Straus, Giroux, 1972), p. 610. This oft-quoted sentiment, in a somewhat milder form ("There are moments when one is tempted to feel that the cruelest thing that has happened to Lincoln since he was shot by Booth has been to fall into the hands of Carl Sandburg"), also appears in Wilson's essay on Lincoln in *Patriotic Gore* (1962; London: Hogarth Press, 1987), p. 115.

2. Richard Current, *Speaking of Abraham Lincoln: The Man and His Meaning for Our Times* (Urbana: University of Illinois Press, 1982), p. 40.

3. Gore Vidal, "A Note on Abraham Lincoln," in *The Second American Revolution and Other Essays* (New York: Random House, 1982), p. 273.

4. Hoxie Neal Fairchild, *Religious Trends in English Poetry*, Vol. 5 (New York: Columbia University Press, 1962), pp. 499–500.

5. These works include Sandburg's own *Ever the Winds of Chance* (Urbana: University of Illinois Press, 1983), a sequel to the published autobiography of his early life, *Always the Young Strangers* (New York: Harcourt, Brace and Company, 1953); the memoirs of his daughter Helga, author of *Where Love Begins* (New York: Harcourt, Brace, Jovanovich, 1989), among others; and North Callahan's reissued critical biography, *Carl Sandburg: His Life and Works* (University Park: Pennsylvania State University, 1987). Penelope Niven, the director of the Carl Sandburg Oral History Project of the National Park Service, spent fourteen years gathering, sorting, and analyzing Sandburg's papers, and her *Carl Sandburg: A Biography* (New York: Charles Scribner's Sons, 1991) is likely to remain the standard work for years to come.

6. Louis D. Rubin, "Not to Forget Carl Sandburg," *Sewanee Review* (Winter 1977): 189.

7. Thomas Lask, "Carl Sandburg, 89, Poet and Biographer, Is Dead," *New York Times*, Sunday, July 23, 1967, sec. 1, p. 1.

8. Carl Sandburg, *Abraham Lincoln: The Prairie Years*, 2 vols. (New York: Harcourt, Brace and Company, 1926); *Abraham Lincoln: The War Years*, 4 vols. (New York: Harcourt, Brace and Company, 1939).

9. Sandburg quoted in the *Times* obituary, p. 62.

10. The biographical data cited in the ensuing pages were compiled from a variety of sources, including the *Times* obituary; Gay Wilson Allen's "Carl Sandburg" from the University of Minnesota Pamphlets of American Writers (Minneapolis: University of Minnesota Press, 1972); and Sandburg's entries in *Current Biography, 1940* (New York: H. W. Wilson & Co.) and the *Dictionary of Literary Biography*, Vol. 17, *Twentieth Century American Historians* (Detroit: Gale Research Co., 1986). The most comprehensive source of information on Sandburg's life is Niven's biography, which was published after the early drafts of this chapter had been completed.

11. All of Sandburg's major poetry was published by Harcourt, Brace and Company (later Harcourt Brace & World, Harcourt Brace Jovanovich, and now simply Harcourt Brace).

12. Carl Sandburg to Paula Sandburg, January 30, 1919, in *The Letters of Carl Sandburg*, edited by Herbert Mitgang (New York: Harcourt, Brace & World, 1968), p. 150.

13. For a discussion of the tone of disenchantment in Sandburg's post–World War I poetry, see Niven, *Carl Sandburg*, pp. 354–62. On p. xviii of her preface, she notes that unlike his contemporaries (Hemingway, Eliot) he never served a literary apprenticeship abroad.

14. *Letters of Carl Sandburg*, p. 392.

15. Ibid., p. 298.

16. *Time*, "Books," August 31, 1936, p. 47.

17. "Your Obedient Servant," *Time*, December 4, 1939, p. 84.

18. Figure cited on the back cover of the most recent paperback printing of the one-volume edition of *The Prairie Years* and *The War Years* (New York: Harcourt Brace & Co., 1954).

19. Stephen Vincent Benét, "The Atlantic Bookshelf," *Atlantic*, December 1939, n.p.

20. For full citations on these books and excellent surveys of "The Fictional Lincoln" as well as "The Anti-Lincoln Tradition," see these chapters in Don Fehrenbacher, *Lincoln in Text and Context* (Stanford: Stanford University Press, 1987).

21. *The War Years*, Vol. 2, pp. 332–33.

22. *The Prairie Years*, Vol. 1, p. 15.

23. *The Prairie Years*, Vol. 1, pp. 48, 72; Vol. 2, p. 103. In his essay "The Words of Lincoln," included in both *Lincoln in Text and Context* and the *Abraham Lincoln and the American Political Tradition* collection edited by John L. Thomas (Amherst: University of Massachusetts Press, 1986), Don Fehrenbacher analyzes Lincoln's speech to illustrate how journalistic transcription, grammar, and oral delivery can subtly—and even substantially—affect the meaning of the "House Divided" speech. Consider the difference between "I believe this government cannot endure permanently half slave and half free" and "I believe this government cannot endure, permanently half slave and half free." The first is a rather prosaic observation; the second, with the addition of a comma, takes on grave implications.

24. *The Prairie Years*, Vol. 2, pp. 123–28; Vol. 1, pp. 305–6.

25. *The Prairie Years*, Vol. 2, p. 333; *The War Years*, Vol. 1, p. 7.

26. *The War Years*, Vol. 4, pp. 25, 56; Vol. 2, p. 78.

27. *The War Years*, Vol. 1, pp. 609–13; Vol. 4, pp. 5–7.

28. *The War Years*, Vol. 1, p. xi.

29. Ibid., p. 84.

30. William Stott, *Documentary Expression and Thirties America* (New York: Oxford University Press, 1973). See particularly Stott's preface and Part 1 of the book, which defines and describes documentary as a cultural form.

31. *The Prairie Years*, Vol. 1, pp. 451–66.

32. *The War Years*, Vol. 2, p. 333.

33. For full citations on these books and excellent surveys of "The Fictional Lincoln" as well as "The Anti-Lincoln Tradition," see these chapters in Fehrenbacher, *Lincoln in Text and Context.*

34. Herndon devotes a chapter to the Lincoln-Rutledge affair in *Abraham Lincoln: The True Story of a Great Life* (Chicago: Belford, Clarke & Company, 1889), Vol. 1, pp. 128–42. Herndon tended to undercut Mary Todd Lincoln in his account by paying her backhanded compliments. "She was a very shrewd observer, and discreetly and without apparent effort kept back all the unattractive elements in her unfortunate disposition," he notes in Vol. 2, p. 209. Later in the biography, he quotes an unnamed source who credited her with Lincoln's entry into politics: If she had not been such a difficult woman, he would have spent more time at home and thus would have never developed his astute common touch. See Vol. 3, pp. 432–33.

35. Some of the more notable inquiries into the subject include the appendix of the second volume of James Garfield Randall, *Lincoln the President: Springfield to Gettysburg* (New York: Dodd, Mead & Co., 1945); Richard Current, "Son, Lover, Husband" from *The Lincoln Nobody Knows* (New York: Hill and Wang, 1958); and David Donald, "Herndon and Mrs. Lincoln" from *Lincoln Reconsidered: Essays on the Civil War Era* (New York: Vintage, 1961). Perhaps the definitive work on the subject is John Evangelist Walsh's *Shadows Rise: Abraham Lincoln and the Ann Rutledge Legend* (Urbana: University of Illinois Press, 1993), which makes a compelling case for a romance between the two.

36. *The Prairie Years*, Vol. 1, p. 141.

37. Wilson, *Patriotic Gore*, p. 116.

38. Quotation taken from p. 8 of the January 1929 issue of the *Atlantic.* The December 1928 installment runs from p. 834 to p. 856, the January 1929 section from p. 1 to p. 14, and the February 1929 piece from p. 215 to p. 225.

39. Fehrenbacher, *Lincoln in Text and Context*, p. 258. Fehrenbacher devotes a chapter of his book to "The Minor Affair."

40. Ibid., p. 259.

41. *Prologue to Glory*, in Willard Swire, editor, *Three Distinctive Plays about Abraham Lincoln* (New York: Washington Square Press, 1961).

42. "It was not until I read Carl Sandburg's *The Prairie Years* that I began to feel the curious quality of the complex man. . . . It was Sandburg who guided me back into the Lincoln lore, made me wish to know more of the forces, within and

without, which shaped this strange gentle genius." Sherwood wrote this for the supplementary appendix for *Abe Lincoln in Illinois* (New York: Scribner's, 1939), p. 191.

43. For a lavishly illustrated study of gender issues in the 1930s, and how they were played out in civic culture, see Barbara Melosh, *Engendering Culture: Manhood and Womanhood in New Deal Public Art and Theater* (Washington, D.C.: Smithsonian Institution Press, 1991).

44. James Randall was one of the first to systematically challenge the view of Mary Todd Lincoln as a cross to be borne. Perhaps the most sympathetic recent view is in Jean Baker, *Mary Todd Lincoln: A Biography* (New York: Norton, 1987), which uses a feminist sensibility to explore the roots of her "difficult" reputation.

45. My thinking about the 1930s has been influenced by Warren Susman. See especially his *Culture as History: The Transformation of American Society in the Twentieth Century* (New York: Pantheon, 1984). For a more comprehensive treatment, see Richard Pells, *Radical Visions and American Dreams: Culture and Social Thought in the Depression Years* (New York: Harper & Row, 1973). Pells was also influenced by Susman.

46. This statement is a major premise in Barry Karl, *The Uneasy State: The United States from 1915–1945* (Chicago: University of Chicago Press, 1983).

47. This impulse to try to square the circle—whether in the poor suitor who wins wealth and the girl in screwball comedies, or in the loner who (temporarily) casts his lot with the values of a community in the Western—has been widely noted of films of the 1930s (and U.S. culture generally). For one very good treatment of this phenomenon, see Robert B. Ray, *A Certain Tendency of the Hollywood Cinema, 1930–1980* (Princeton: Princeton University Press, 1985). Like many critics, Ray laments what he considers a lack of real choices in these films, a chronic unwillingness to face irreconcilable differences or make firm ideological commitments. This is not simply a matter of a common strategy that anthropologist Claude Lévi-Strauss attributed to myth generally, but a celebration unique to the United States of the very act of doing so (see p. 64 in Ray, *Certain Tendency*). Although I recognize the weaknesses and evasions intrinsic to such tactics, I cannot altogether share Ray's disappointment, preferring such compromises to a Lincoln who rode roughshod over the law or the oppressive ramifications of living in a society where there was no leadership at all.

48. For an explanation of the term *cultural work* and its ideological functions in popular culture, see Jane Tompkins, *Sensational Designs: The Cultural Work of American Fiction, 1790–1860* (New York: Oxford University Press, 1985).

49. Ibid., p. 110.

50. Alfred Haworth Jones, *Roosevelt's Image Brokers: Poets, Playwrights, and the Use of the Lincoln Symbol* (Port Washington, N.Y.: Kennikat Press, 1974), p. 65.

51. David Donald, *Lincoln Reconsidered: Essays on the Civil War Era* (New York:

Vintage Books, 1963), pp. 14, 16; Jones, *Roosevelt's Image Brokers*, p. 65. The line Roosevelt quoted Lincoln as having asserted, part of some "Fragments on Government," can be found in *Abraham Lincoln: Speeches and Writings, 1832–1858*, edited by Don Fehrenbacher (New York: Library of America, 1989), p. 301.

52. *Abe Lincoln in Illinois* was revived for a New York run in 1993–94, with Sam Waterston in the lead role. (Waterston has become something of a professional Lincoln, portraying the sixteenth president in the television production *Gore Vidal's Lincoln* [1987], in Ken Burns's documentary *The Civil War* [1990], and in this stage production.) The revival of Sherwood's drama in the first year of the Clinton administration suggests the tentative leftward tilt in U.S. political culture in the aftermath of the Reagan-Bush years.

53. *The Letters of Carl Sandburg*, pp. 317–18; a copy of the radio address appears in *Home Front Memo* (New York: Harcourt, Brace, 1943), p. 30.

54. FDR quoted in James McGregor Burns, *Roosevelt: The Lion and the Fox* (New York: Harcourt, Brace, 1956), p. 439.

55. Peter Wyden, *The Passionate War: A Narrative History of the Spanish Civil War* (New York: Touchstone, 1983).

56. William Allen White, editor, *Defense for America* (New York: MacMillan, 1940), p. xvi.

57. FDR quoted in Jones, *Roosevelt's Image Brokers*, p. 93.

58. *Home Front Memo*, p. 34.

59. An excellent discussion of the transition represented by these two painters and their larger cultural milieu can be found in Erika Doss, "The Art of Cultural Politics: From Regionalism to Abstract Expressionism," in Lary May, editor, *Recasting America: Culture and Politics in the Age of the Cold War* (Chicago: University of Chicago Press, 1989), pp. 195–220.

60. Randall, *Lincoln the President: Springfield to Gettysburg*, Vol. 1 (New York: Dodd, Mead & Co., 1945), p. vii.

61. James Randall, "Has the Lincoln Theme Been Exhausted?" *American Historical Review* (January 1936): 270, 294.

62. The fourth volume was completed by Richard Current, who went on to become a major Lincoln historian in his own right.

63. *Dictionary of Literary Biography*, p. 380; *New York Times*, February 22, 1953, p. 61; Randall, review of *The War Years* in *American Historical Review* (July 1940): 917–22.

64. Randall, "Has the Lincoln Theme," p. 294. Becker's essay can be found in *Everyman His Own Historian: Essays on History and Politics* (New York: Appleton-Century-Crofts, 1935), pp. 233–55.

65. James McPherson, *Battle Cry of Freedom: The Civil War Era* (New York: Oxford University Press, 1988), p. 865.

66. Randall, *Lincoln the President: Springfield to Gettysburg*, Vol. 1, p. vii.

67. Ibid., p. viii.

68. James Garfield Randall, *Lincoln the President: Midstream* (New York: Dodd, Mead, 1952), pp. viii, ix, xi.

69. *The War Years*, Vol. 3, p. 666; Randall, *Lincoln the President: Last Full Measure* (New York: Dodd, Mead & Co., 1955), p. 48.

70. Richard Current assures the reader in the preface of the fourth volume that the first eight chapters are "pure Randall."

71. Randall, *Lincoln the President: Last Full Measure*, pp. 48–52.

72. *The War Years*, Vol. 4, pp. 666, 669.

73. *The War Years*, Vol. 3, pp. 539–46.

74. Randall, *Lincoln the President: Springfield to Gettysburg*, Vol. 1, pp. 17, 49, 107, 151, 235. Randall a few years later published *Lincoln the Liberal Statesman* (New York: Dodd, Mead & Co., 1947), a collection of essays. What Randall calls "liberal" there is essentially what he considers "conservative" in *Lincoln the President*.

75. Randall, *Lincoln the President: Springfield to Gettysburg*, Vol. 1, p. 1.

76. Ibid., p. 49.

77. For a good discussion of consensus historians and their impact on the profession, see Peter Novick, *That Noble Dream: The "Objectivity Question" and the American Historical Profession* (New York: Cambridge University Press, 1989), pp. 320–60.

78. *The War Years*, Vol. 1, p. 380; Vol. 2, pp. 4–5; Vol. 3, pp. 579–80.

79. Randall, *Lincoln the President: Springfield to Gettysburg*, Vol. 2, p. 207.

80. Lincoln, *Speeches and Writings*, p. 301.

81. The analysis that follows represents a distillation of a number of sources, including Richard Pells, *The Liberal Mind in a Conservative Age: American Intellectuals in the 1940s and 1950s* (New York: Harper & Row, 1985); John Higham with Leonard Krieger and Felix Gilbert, *History* (Englewood Cliffs, N.J.: Prentice-Hall, 1965); and especially Novick, *That Noble Dream*.

82. The text of Becker's and Beard's speeches were published in the January 1932 and January 1934 editions, respectively, of the *American Historical Review*.

83. For a discussion of the New History and Robinson's role in it, see Higham, *History*, pp. 104–16, and Novick, *That Noble Dream*, pp. 89–92.

84. Novick, *That Noble Dream*, pp. 355–56.

85. Arthur M. Schlesinger, Jr., *The Vital Center* (Boston: Houghton Mifflin, 1949).

86. David Donald, *Lincoln Reconsidered*; Stanley Elkins, *Slavery: A Problem in American Institutional and Intellectual Life*, 3d ed. (1st ed, 1959; Chicago: University of Chicago Press, 1976); Novick, *That Noble Dream*, p. 358.

87. For excellent surveys of recent critiques of Lincoln, see "The Anti-Lincoln Tradition," in Fehrenbacher, *Lincoln in Text and Context*, from which the above quotations were taken, and Richard Current, "Lincoln and Thaddeus Stevens," in

Speaking of Abraham Lincoln. Bennett's piece, "Was Abe Lincoln a White Supremacist?" appeared in the February 1968 issue of *Ebony,* pp. 35–42.

88. Benjamin Thomas, *Abraham Lincoln: A Biography* (New York: Knopf, 1952).

89. Stephen B. Oates, *With Malice toward None: The Life of Abraham Lincoln* (New York: Mentor Books, 1978). However popular it remains—the paperback edition has gone through at least seventeen printings and remains widely available almost twenty years later—this biography has been criticized on a variety of fronts. First, Oates has been taken to task for the unmistakable "Sandburgisms" in some of his descriptions and style (e.g., his use of the present tense at dramatic moments). Even Oates's chapter titles ("Years of Meteors," "Moody, Tearful Night") evoke Sandburg's. For criticism of Oates's style, see Richard Current, "Lincoln Biographies: Old and New Myths," in *Arguing with Historians: Essays on the Historical and the Unhistorical* (Middletown: Wesleyan University Press, 1987), pp. 62–69.

Oates has also been criticized for overstating the degree of Lincoln's identification vis-à-vis the radical wing of the Republican party. Current makes this point in "Lincoln Biographies" (see p. 62 of Current, *Arguing with Historians*). In the bibliographic note to *Battle Cry of Freedom,* James McPherson praises the readability of *With Malice toward None* but considers it an "overcorrection" of Randall's conservatism (p. 866).

Skepticism over Oates's work became outright indignation in the early 1990s amid charges that Oates plagiarized parts of the book from the Benjamin Thomas biography. For a discussion of the case and the issues involved, see Denise Magner, "Professor Did Not Adequately Attribute Material in Book, History Group Says," *Chronicle of Higher Education,* May 27, 1992, p. A15.

90. Examples include George B. Forgie, *Patricide in the House Divided: A Psychological Interpretation of Lincoln and His Age* (New York: W. W. Norton, 1979); Dwight G. Anderson, *Abraham Lincoln: The Quest for Immortality* (New York: Knopf, 1982); and Charles B. Strozier, *Lincoln's Quest for Union: Public and Private Meanings* (New York: Basic Books, 1982). For critiques of this scholarship, see Current, "The Myth of the Jealous Son," in *Arguing with Historians,* pp. 52–60, and Garry Wills, *Lincoln at Gettysburg: Words That Remade America* (New York: Simon and Schuster, 1992), pp. 79–89.

91. Wilson, *Patriotic Gore,* pp. 106–10. For a rebuttal to Wilson (whose analysis was first published in a 1954 *New Yorker* article), see Harry V. Jaffa, *Crisis of the House Divided* (New York: Doubleday, 1959).

92. Lincoln, *Speeches and Writings,* p. 34.

93. William Safire, *Freedom: A Novel of Abraham Lincoln and the Civil War* (New York: Avon, 1988), p. 1399.

94. Gore Vidal, *Lincoln: A Novel* (New York: Ballantine, 1985), p. 279.

95. Ibid., p. 3.

96. Ibid., pp. 357–58.

97. "Gore Vidal's 'Lincoln': An Exchange," *New York Review of Books*, April 28, 1988, p. 58.

Vidal's representation of Lincoln's views on freedpeople rankled a number of professional historians and was only one of a number of problems they found in his work. The opening salvo came from Randall's heir, Richard Current, in a 1986 *Journal of Southern History* article that was published the following year in *Arguing with Historians: Essays on the Historical and Unhistorical*, whose very title evokes Current as a scholarly gatekeeper, soberly examining would-be entrants at the portals of history. Vidal is found wanting.

Current begins the essay by distinguishing between historical fiction such as *Gone with the Wind*, which inserts invented characters into a historical milieu, and fictional history, "which pretends to deal with real persons and events but actually reshapes them—and thus rewrites the past." Current then proceeds to a list of what he considers Vidal's factual and grammatical errors, which he admits is picayune but which the novelist asked for in claiming to have "written from primary sources the way any conscientious scholar would do." This list shades into more substantial criticism, such as Vidal's description of Lincoln still considering colonization as late as 1865. Vidal later pointed out, correctly, that Current himself described this belief in his 1958 book *The Lincoln Nobody Knows*. Current replied, correctly, that he was not endorsing this view but merely presenting one side of an ongoing debate.

Vidal did not actually respond to Current until 1988, when, after the *New York Times* published a critical review of the television miniseries based on the book, he fired off an angry letter to the *New York Review of Books*, claiming the *Times* had willfully tried to discredit him for years. But why did he address the letter to the *New York Review*? Because in the September 24, 1987, issue, C. Vann Woodward had reviewed William Safire's *Freedom*. Woodward, while characteristically mild and even generous, nevertheless wondered why a fictionalized representation of the Civil War was necessary, given the hazards and the notably articulate cast of characters who spoke so eloquently for themselves. (Curiously, he does not ask the same question about historical scholarship.) In any case, in the course of his review Woodward surveyed recent historical fiction, including *Lincoln*, and cited Vidal critics such as Roy Basler and Current.

Vidal's response was combative, even rude, and one is surprised that *he* was surprised that Current would take offense at his remarks. Deploring "the scholarsquirrels" with little better to do than quibble, he went on to argue that although there were some academics who did inspired work—such as David Donald, who reviewed the manuscript of *Lincoln* and gave it his approval—all too many fashioned unimaginative, slavish "hagiography." (For the academic who prided himself on disciplined detachment, this would be the unkindest cut of all.) Current, Vidal writes, has fallen prey "to the delusion that there is a final Truth revealed only to the tenured few in their footnote maze; in this he is simply naive.

All we have is a mass of more or less agreed-upon facts about the illustrious dead and each generation tends to rearrange those facts according to what the times require." For the rest of the exchange, see the *New York Review of Books*, August 18, 1988, p. 66.

One final note. Vidal's attacks on the *Times* prompted a response from reviewer Harold Holzer, a Lincoln authority in his own right. He concluded his reply in the August 18 issue by saying, "Mr. Vidal has convinced himself that he has taken a legend and made of him a man. In reality, he has taken a myth and advanced in its place a countermyth that is as shrouded by misinformation as what it endeavors to revise. Mr. Vidal is the Sandburg of our times." Holzer intended this as a slur and probably saw it as one. In an ironic way, however, Holzer may have noted Vidal's achievement.

97. *New York Review of Books*, April 28, 1988, p. 56.

98. James McPherson's essay appeared in Thomas's *Abraham Lincoln and the American Political Tradition* and was, as well, the title essay in a collection of McPherson's essays published by Oxford University Press in 1990.

99. See, for example, Wills, *Lincoln at Gettysburg*, pp. 144–47.

100. Mark Neely, *The Last Best Hope of Earth: Abraham Lincoln and the Promise of America* (Cambridge: Harvard University Press, 1993). This was the companion volume to an exhibit of the same name held at the Huntington Library in San Marino, California, in 1993–94.

Neely's description of Lincoln as "arch-capitalist" appears on p. 47, though he notes Lincoln's sympathy for labor on pp. 148–49 and the lack of conflict between these two interests before the Civil War. In this way, Neely echoes Richard Hofstadter's classic work of intellectual portraiture, "Abraham Lincoln and the Self-Made Myth," in *American Political Tradition* (1959; New York: Vintage, 1948).

For Lincoln's reluctance as a reformer, see Neely, *Last Best Hope*, pp. 97, 124. Although I regard Neely's view of Lincoln as more conservative than McPherson's, the latter's praise of this volume on the back cover of the hardcover edition of *Last Best Hope* ("a fine study," "penetrating analysis") suggests a lack of fundamental disagreement between the two.

101. Lincoln, "Fragments on Government," in *Speeches and Writings*, p. 301.

Chapter 3: Screening the Book

1. Leslie Fiedler, *What Was Literature: Class Culture and Mass Society* (New York: Touchstone, 1984), p. 211. Fiedler made his argument regarding women characters in *Love and Death in the American Novel* (New York: Dell, 1960). Years later, after he became a champion of popular culture, Fiedler confessed that he found himself "confronting that letter—and candor compels me to admit, find myself still—not

entirely free of ambivalence: an ambivalence reflected in the vestigial scorn I cannot quite repress from the girl from Sacred Heart Academy who *begins* with a high regard for *Gone with the Wind* rather than ends with it (like me) after having passed through an initiation into the world of elitist standards." See pp. 211–12.

2. Page numbers given in the text refer to the Macmillan hardcover edition.

3. *Dictionary of Literary Biography*, Vol. 9, *American Writers, 1900–1945* (Detroit: Gale Publishing, 1981), p. 224; Darden Asbury Pyron, editor, *Recasting: Gone with the Wind in American Culture* (Miami: University Presses of Florida, 1983), p. 1; *Margaret Mitchell's Gone with the Wind Letters, 1936–1949*, edited by Richard Harwell (New York: Macmillan, 1976), p. xxvii. Sales of 28 million copies were widely reported amid the publication of Ripley's *Scarlett* (published by Warner Books) in September 1991.

4. Fiedler, *What Was Literature*, p. 197; Dieter Meindl, "A Reappraisal of Margaret Mitchell's *Gone with the Wind*," *Mississippi Quarterly: The Journal of Southern Culture* (Fall 1981): 414; Moody L. Simms, "*Gone with the Wind*: The View from China," *Southern Studies: An Interdisciplinary Journal of the South* (Spring 1984): 5–7; "Turner, Fonda Steal Show at USSR Debut of GWTW," *Providence Journal*, October 21, 1990, p. 3.

5. Walton A. Litz, editor, *Modern American Fiction: Essays in Criticism* (New York: Oxford University Press, 1963); Virginia Brokaw and Gerhard Stein, editors, *American Historical Fiction* (1958; Metuchen, N.J.: Scarecrow Press, 1986); Edmund Wilson, *Patriotic Gore: Studies in the Literature of the American Civil War* (New York: Oxford University Press, 1962).

6. E. D. Hirsch, Joseph F. Kett, James Trefil, editors, *The Dictionary of Cultural Literacy: What Every American Needs to Know* (Boston: Houghton Mifflin, 1988), p. 120. The entry reads:

"A novel from the 1930s by the American author Margaret Mitchell. Set in Georgia in the period of the Civil War, it tells the story of the three marriages of the central character, Scarlett O'Hara, and of the devastation caused by the war.

"The film version of *Gone with the Wind*, also from the 1930s, is one of the most successful films ever made."

7. Margaret Mitchell to Alexander L. May, July 22, 1938, *GWTW Letters*, p. 215.

8. Nathaniel Hawthorne to William Ticknor, January 1855, in Caroline Ticknor, *Hawthorne and His Publisher* (Boston: Houghton Mifflin, 1913), p. 141. Hawthorne was jealous of the commercial success of novelists such as Fanny Fern, Susan Warner, and Harriet Beecher Stowe, all of whom sold many, many more books than he did. For some comparisons in popularity, see James D. Hart, *The Popular Book: A History of America's Literary Taste* (New York: Oxford University Press, 1950), pp. 92–95.

9. Margaret Mitchell to Thomas Dixon, August 15, 1936, *GWTW Letters*, pp. 52–53.

10. The term is Leslie Fiedler's. Fiedler considers GWTW part of a long literary tradition that extends from Uncle Tom's Cabin through Dixon/Griffith to the television miniseries Roots. See Part 2 of What Was Literature, "Opening Up the Canon" (pp. 143–245).

11. Biographical information on Mitchell's life is widely available from a variety of sources (e.g., The Dictionary of Literary Biography cited above). There are also three biographies of Mitchell: Finis Farr, Margaret Mitchell of Atlanta (New York: Morrow, 1965); Anne Edwards, Road to Tara: The Life of Margaret Mitchell (New Haven, Conn.: Ticknor & Fields, 1983); Darden Asbury Pyron, Southern Daughter: The Life of Margaret Mitchell (New York: Oxford University Press, 1991). Pyron's biography is the most exhaustively researched and analytical of the three and will likely remain the standard work for many years to come.

12. Farr, Margaret Mitchell, p. 17.

13. Edwards, Road to Tara, p. 66.

14. One of the most striking examples of May Belle Mitchell's dual messages to her daughter is her widely cited deathbed letter. "Give of yourself with both hands and overflowing heart, but give only the excess after you have lived your own life," she admonished. Yet Mrs. Mitchell hedged, if not confused, the matter by also saying, "Your life and energies belong first to yourself, your husband, and your children." In that order? Are the interests of all three assumed to be the same? The mother never explained (perhaps she did not know, the product of haughty parents who were equally ambiguous on the matter of gender roles). For an astute analysis of this letter and Margaret Mitchell's relations with her mother, see Pyron, Southern Daughter, especially pp. 90–94.

15. The Atlanta Journal was founded by Mitchell's uncle, Frank Rice, and Atlanta political boss Hoke Smith, a close family friend. Pyron notes this on pp. 142–43 of Southern Daughter, but not the likely corollary that Mitchell was able to get a job at all because she had family connections. Although few would deny that Mitchell was a gifted writer, she clearly had opportunities others did not; her independence—indeed, her feminism, such as it was—was at least some degree dependent on her elite background. For a discussion of this point, see Patricia Storace's review of Pyron's Southern Daughter in "Look Away, Dixie Land," New York Review of Books, December 19, 1991, p. 30.

16. For studies connecting Mitchell to the larger Southern cultural scene, see Darden Asbury Pyron, "Gone with the Wind and the Southern Cultural Awakening," Virginia Quarterly Review (Autumn 1986): 566–87. Such an approach is also central to Pyron's biography of Mitchell, as suggested in its title: Southern Daughter. Also see Louis Rubin, the first contemporary critic to try to recontextualize Mitchell back into her Southern milieu, in "Scarlett O'Hara and the Two Quentin Compsons," included in Pyron, Recasting, pp. 81–104.

17. Edwards, Road to Tara, p. 145.

18. Pyron, Southern Daughter, p. 499; Edwards, Road to Tara, pp. 9–10.

19. The Communist party in the United States was particularly critical of the book and regularly published attacks on it in the *Daily Worker* (one writer was fired after saying something positive about it). For one notable example, see the *Daily Worker* of October 29, 1936. The most visible criticism came from Malcolm Cowley in the *New Republic*, who called it "false in part and silly in part and vicious in its general effect on Southern life in general." *New Republic*, July 15, 1936, pp. 253–54.

20. Margaret Mitchell to Stark Young, September 29, 1936, GWTW *Letters*, p. 66.

21. Margaret Mitchell to Julian Harris, April 21, 1936, GWTW *Letters*, pp. 1–2.

22. Margaret Mitchell to Henry Steele Commager, July 10, 1936, GWTW *Letters*, p. 39. Commager reviewed the book on July 5, 1936.

23. Margaret Mitchell to Susan Myrick, April 17, 1939, GWTW *Letters*, p. 273.

24. Ibid., p. 274. "I do not intend to let any number of troublemakers or Professional Negroes change my feelings toward the race with whom my relations have always been those of affection and mutual respect. There are Professional Negroes just as there are Professional Southerners and, from what I can learn from the Negroes I have talked to, they are no more loved by their race than Professional Southerners are by us." Note that in this passage, "Southerners" are white, whereas blacks are lumped together as "Negroes."

25. Chesnut's work is most fully and revealingly available in *Mary Chesnut's Civil War*, edited by C. Vann Woodward (New Haven: Yale University Press, 1981). For a discussion of the master-slave relationship between women in the antebellum South, see Elizabeth Fox-Genovese, *Within the Plantation Household: Black and White Women of the Old South* (Chapel Hill: University of North Carolina Press, 1988). Fox-Genovese's work was the subject of some controversy after it was published; for some insightful criticism, see Jacqueline Jones, "One Big Happy Family?" *Women's Review of Books*, February 1989, p. 1.

26. Margaret Mitchell to John Temple Graves II, November 12, 1936, GWTW *Letters*, p. 86.

27. Malcolm X with Alex Haley, *The Autobiography of Malcolm X* (1965; New York: Ballantine Books, 1992), p. 32.

28. For a discussion of Mitchell and the Klan, see Helen Taylor, *Scarlett's Women: Gone with the Wind and Its Female Fans* (New Brunswick, N.J.: Rutgers University Press, 1989), pp. 54–62.

29. Margaret Mitchell to Ruth Tallman, July 30, 1937, GWTW *Letters*, p. 162.

30. W. E. B. Du Bois, *Black Reconstruction in America, 1860–1880* (New York: Harcourt Brace, 1935).

On p. 311 of *Southern Daughter*, Pyron emphasizes the degree to which Mitchell was revisionist in her view of Reconstruction. "The wonder is less that the old racial biases pervaded her book than that she challenged the prevailing mythology at all. She did," he states, noting the economic accents in her interpretation that evoke the work of Charles Beard. Pyron also notes that far from idealizing Confederate resistance, Mitchell showed that "good families" had collaborated with the Yankee occupation. These points are well taken, but they hardly alter the overall tone of Mitchell's racial politics.

In a similar vein, Pyron argues that Mitchell's negative portrayal of Prissy has "much more to do with a tense mother-daughter relationship than with racial slurs": As Scarlett is to Ellen, so Prissy is to her own mother, Dilcey. (See *Southern Daughter*, pp. 268–69 and 390–91.) Again, this is an incisive and useful observation, which Pyron makes with great skill. However, the racial politics of creating a whining, incompetent character who is "all nigger lak her pa" (in the words of her own mother) ultimately overwhelms the gender issues involved.

If *GWTW* was a truly revisionist book—and I am arguing that in some ways it was—Mitchell remained a white supremacist. This is one of the major reasons for the book's critical decline, and although hardly a paragon of sensitivity, the movie has had more staying power, in part because it is less obviously abrasive than the novel.

31. Margaret Mitchell to Stanley F. Horn, March 20, 1939, *GWTW Letters*, p. 263; Taylor, *Scarlett's Women*, p. 54. Taylor notes the irony of the research-obsessive Mitchell's decision not to confirm her knowledge of the Klan. She also observes that Mitchell's biographers have failed to explore her anxieties about the Klan and her Catholicism in the 1920s. Taylor speculates that "by placing racial tension between black and white firmly back on the agenda, emphasising its tragic part in the South's history, Mitchell was in some ways fending off the immediate challenges which her only family—and indeed, her own fragile marriageability—were facing in 1920s Atlanta" (p. 62).

32. As noted in the Introduction, a new wave of Southern historians were insisting on the benevolence of the slave order. For a survey distilling and untangling the various historiographic threads on postwar race relations, see the preface of Eric Foner's *Reconstruction: America's Unfinished Revolution, 1865–77* (New York: Harper & Row, 1988), pp. xvii–xxvii.

33. Margaret Mitchell to Sidney Howard, November 21, 1936, *GWTW Letters*, pp. 92–94.

34. *Gone with the Wind: The Screenplay*, edited by Herb Bridges and Terryl C. Boodman (New York: Delta, 1989), pp. 4–6.

35. Richard Harwell, editor, *GWTW as Book and Film* (Columbia: University of South Carolina Press, 1983), p. xx.

36. The reigning expert on the making of *GWTW* is Herb Bridges, who treats the subject in *Gone with the Wind: The Definitive Illustrated History of the Book, the Movie, and the Legend* (New York: Fireside, 1989). He also treats the subject in more compact fashion in "Lights Down, Curtain Up," the introduction to the published screenplay of the film.

37. David O. Selznick to Sidney Howard, January 6, 1937, in *Memo from David O. Selznick*, selected and edited by Rudy Behlmer (New York: Viking Press, 1972), p. 151.

38. *GWTW: The Screenplay*, p. 172.

39. Leonard J. Leff, "David Selznick's *Gone with the Wind*: 'The Negro Problem,'" *Georgia Review* (Spring 1984): 161.

40. Selznick also distinguished between the "old Klan and the Klan of our times" and saw only the latter as bad. See Leff, "Negro Problem," p. 145.

41. According to Patricia Storace, Selznick's representative in Atlanta persuaded him that it would be embarrassing to have blacks in segregated hotels (integrating lodgings were apparently out of the question). Programs for the movie distributed in the South deleted the picture of Hattie McDaniel included in Northern programs. Storace notes Pyron's omission of these striking facts but does not document where she got them. See "Look Away, Dixie Land," p. 31.

42. For fuller treatment of this issue, see Leonard J. Leff and Thomas Cripps, "Winds of Change: *Gone with the Wind* and Racism as a National Issue" in Pyron, *Recasting*, pp. 137–49.

One detail of some interest: According to Storace, one of the few prominent members of the Atlanta African American community who did attend the premiere was the Reverend Martin Luther King, Sr., along with his church choir dressed in "Mammy" costumes. Also attending was ten-year-old Martin Luther King, Jr., portraying a pickaninny. The elder King was censured by the Atlanta Baptist Minister's Union for participating in the benefit for the all-white audience. See Storace, "Look Away, Dixie Land," p. 31.

43. For an analysis of this process and illustrative examples, see Robert Ray, *A Certain Tendency of the Hollywood Cinema, 1930–1980* (Princeton: Princeton University Press, 1985). Less critical or theoretically explicit, but still useful in this regard, is Thomas Schatz, *The Genius of the System: Hollywood Filmmaking in the Studio Era* (New York: Pantheon, 1988).

44. Mitchell was no fan of the New Deal, seeing it as a new version of federal intervention into Southern folkways, and she considered Eleanor Roosevelt "pushy." See Anne Jones, "Margaret Mitchell: The Bad Little Girl of the Good Old Days," in *Tomorrow Is Another Day: The Woman Writer in the South, 1859–1936* (Baton Rouge: Louisiana State University Press, 1981), p. 318.

45. As Elizabeth Fox-Genovese notes, "*Gone with the Wind* as a whole transforms a particular regional past into a generalized nationalized past. In this respect, it contributes to integrating southern history into national history even as it reestablishes the South, with all its idiosyncrasies, as an only slightly special case of an inclusive national destiny." See "Scarlett O'Hara: The Southern Lady as a New Woman," *American Quarterly* (Fall 1981): 391.

46. For an incisive discussion on how this strategy worked in post–World War II U.S. society, see Barbara Ehrenreich, *Fear of Falling: The Inner Life of the Middle Class* (New York: HarperCollins, 1990).

47. Fox-Genovese argues for the triumph of the city over the country in
GWTW, as Tara is transformed from a site of vitality to a site of retreat and in the
process becomes sentimentalized. "With only the slightest exaggeration, it could
appear as the typical house in the country to which busy city-dwellers repair for
rest and refreshment. In this sense, it blends imaginatively with those New
England farm houses that had also once encompassed productive labor." Fox-
Genovese's point is well taken and is especially appropriate for the movie.
However, even in the world of confirmed city-dweller Margaret Mitchell, farming
was still the primary occupation for about half the country in the years in which
she was writing her novel. In addition, although Scarlett herself does not depend
upon it, much is made of Tara as a *working* plantation capable of sustaining those
who live there.

48. The duality in the attitude of the Southern renaissance toward the past and
Margaret Mitchell's place within the movement is ably handled in Pyron, "*Gone
with the Wind* and the Southern Cultural Awakening," pp. 564–87.

49. Margaret Mitchell to Virginius Dabney, July 23, 1942, *GWTW Letters*,
p. 358.

50. Ibid., p. 359.

51. Margaret Mitchell to Herschel Brickell, October 9, 1936, *GWTW Letters*,
p. 75. In the only autobiographical piece she ever published, a brief sketch for the
Wilson Bulletin of September 1936, Mitchell said the novel was about "survival."
She continued:

"What makes some people able to come through catastrophes and others,
apparently just as able, go under? We've seen it in the recent depression. It
happens in every upheaval. Some people survive; others don't. What qualities are
there in those who fight their way through triumphantly that are lacking in those
who go under? What was it that made some of our Southern people able to come
through a War, a Reconstruction, and a complete wrecking of the social and
economic system? I don't know. I only know that the survivors used to call that
quality 'gumption.' So I wrote about the people who had gumption and those who
don't."

The piece is included in Harwell, *Gone with the Wind as Book and Film*,
pp. 37–38.

52. Letter from Pat West quoted in Taylor, *Scarlett's Women*, p. 38.

53. Ibid.

54. The fact that two women could see the same movie and draw opposite
conclusions from it raises the problematic question of how cultural documents are
read. Carlos Ginzburg, in his brilliant *The Cheese and the Worms: The Cosmos of a
Sixteenth Century Miller*, translated by John and Anne Tedeschi (1976; New York:
Viking, 1982), demonstrates how the heretical miller Domenico Scandella could
adapt, subvert, and even completely invert the intended meanings of the books he
read to match his preconceived (and preliterate) assumptions about his world. I
believe a similar process was at work for these women. Just as Scandella formulated

his cosmology in a particular framework within a set of finite ideological options, these women, whatever their differences, clearly focused on the gender dimension to the film they saw. Insofar as we can make interpretations—or even communicate in the first place—one has to believe that culture at least has the potential to conquer solipsism (Pat West, after all, *changed* her mind after seeing the movie, suggesting that the impact of the film at least helped her reorder her conscious priorities). The most lasting works are those that are relevant to a broad audience while at the same time they retain at least some ideological elasticity. This elasticity with regard to gender—a temporal elasticity as well as a spatial one—is central to my argument about the resilience of GWTW in U.S. culture.

55. Discussing the nineteenth-century "woman's sphere," and related ideas such as the "cult of domesticity" and the "cult of true womanhood" (terms that have fallen into disfavor), is a tricky matter subject to much revision by contemporary scholars. The assumptions shaping this description come from Nancy Cott, *The Bonds of Womanhood: Woman's Sphere in New England, 1780–1835* (New Haven: Yale University Press, 1977). The distinction between Northern and Southern womanhood also comes from Cott, in a useful footnote on p. 11. See also Anne Firor Scott, *The Southern Lady: From Pedestal to Politics, 1830–1930* (Chicago: University of Chicago Press, 1970). For the image of Southern womanhood as wrestled with by Southern novelists, see Jones, *Tomorrow Is Another Day.*

56. "Atlanta's debutante group of 1920–21 [of which Mitchell was a member] more or less reflected the current Scott Fitzgerald era—the jazz age—This Side of Paradise," an intimate at the *Atlanta Journal* said later. "It was the fashion to be daring." (Quoted in Pyron, *Southern Daughter,* p. 147.) Malcolm Cowley has noted that the contrast between North and South was one of Fitzgerald's favorite themes; see particularly "The Ice Palace" and "Last of the Belles" (both from 1920) in *The Stories of F. Scott Fitzgerald,* edited by Cowley (New York: Scribner's, 1986). Cowley's comment appears in his editor's note on p. 6.

57. Margaret Mitchell to Julia Collier Harris, April 28, 1936, GWTW Letters, p. 6. Emphasis added.

58. For example, see Margaret Mitchell to Harry Stillwell, June 18, 1936, GWTW Letters, p. 15.

59. After decades of neglect, the impact of the Civil War on Southern women is the subject of a large and growing scholarly literature. Some of the more notable works, listed chronologically, include Mary Elizabeth Massey, *Bonnet Brigades: American Women and the Civil War* (New York: Knopf, 1966); Anne Firor Scott, *The Southern Lady: From Pedestal to Politics 1830–1930* (Chicago: University of Chicago Press, 1970), see especially chapter 4; Suzanne Lebsock, *The Free Women of Petersburg: Status and Culture in a Southern Town, 1784–1860* (New York: Norton, 1985), see particularly Lebsock's afterword; Jacqueline Jones, *Labor of Love, Labor of Sorrow: Black Women, Work, and the Family from Slavery to the Present* (New York: Vintage, 1985), chapter 2; George C. Rable, *Civil Wars:*

Women and the Crisis of Southern Nationalism (Urbana: University of Illinois Press, 1989); and Drew Gilpin Faust, "Altars of Sacrifice: Confederate Women and the Narratives of War," *Journal of American History* (Spring 1990): 1200–1228. Faust's essay is also included in a volume with a number of other notable articles on the impact of the Civil War on women. See Catherine Clinton and Nina Silber, editors, *Divided Houses: Gender and the Civil War* (New York: Oxford University Press, 1992).

60. It is important symbolically that Rhett makes his stand in the West, just as it is important that the locus of the novel is in Georgia and not Virginia. *Gone with the Wind* represents Mitchell's bid to undermine what was a widely perceived Eastern bias in reporting and remembering the war.

61. For a fuller discussion of the racial/sexual dimension of Rhett's character, see Joel Williamson, "How Black Was Rhett Butler?" in Numan V. Bartley, editor, *The Evolution of Southern Culture* (Athens: University of Georgia Press, 1988), pp. 87–107.

62. Pyron, *Southern Daughter*, pp. 153–55.

63. Ibid., p. 117–19.

64. Pyron argues compellingly that Rhett was inspired by the author's mother. In particular, he analyzes how a childhood admonition from May Belle Mitchell worked its way verbatim into Rhett's mouth. Ibid., pp. 265–68.

65. This point is made most concisely in Drew Gilpin Faust, "Altars of Sacrifice." See also Gaines Foster's discussions of the United Daughters of the Confederacy and Confederate memorial celebrations in *Ghosts of the Confederacy: Defeat, the Lost Cause, and the Emergence of the New South* (New York: Oxford University Press, 1987).

66. *GWTW: The Screenplay*, p. 146.

67. Jones, *Tomorrow Is Another Day*, p. 333.

68. Pyron, *Southern Daughter*, p. 380.

69. I am indebted to Roseanne Comacho for this insight.

70. For an illustration of how effectively feminism and racism coexisted in the interwar South, see Kathleen M. Blee, *Women of the Klan: Racism and Gender in the 1920s* (Los Angeles and Berkeley: University of California Press, 1991). See also Joel Williamson's portrait of Rebecca Latimer Felton, the first woman U.S. senator, who literally and figuratively took the place of populist-racist Tom Watson, in *A Rage for Order: Black-White Relations in the American South since Emancipation* (New York: Oxford University Press, 1986), pp. 90–95.

71. Peter Applebome, "Scarlett O'Hara Is Back, and a City Is Again Taken," *New York Times*, September 29, 1991, sec. 1, p. 22.

72. Esther B. Fein, "'Gone with the Wind' Sequel an Astonishing Bestseller," *The New York Times*, October 3, 1991, p. A1.

73. Edwards, *Road to Tara*, pp. viii–ix; Mike Capuzzo, "Tomorrow Dawns for Scarlett," *Providence Journal*, September 26, 1991, p. C1; R. Z. Sheppard,

"Frankly, It's Not Worth a Damn," *Time*, October 7, 1991, p. 72; Eleanor Blau, "Do Scarlett and Rhett Discover Love Anew? A Sequel Reveals All," *New York Times*, September 25, 1991, p. C15.

74. Fein's story in the *Times* included a table of critics' remarks, including Lord's.

75. For an intriguing discussion of women's criteria for successful romance novels, criteria which are coherently articulated—but quite different from dominant literary standards—see Janice Radway, *Reading the Romance: Women, Patriarchy, and Popular Literature* (Chapel Hill: University of North Carolina Press, 1984).

76. Applebome, "Scarlett O'Hara Is Back"; Blau, "Do Scarlett and Rhett Discover Love Anew?" pp. C15–17.

77. See, for example, "Scarlett O'Hara Is Back" and "Do Scarlett and Rhett Discover Love Anew?"

78. Ripley, *Scarlett*, p. 15.

79. Ibid., p. 526.

80. "I'm not going to have a nanny running Cat's [the baby's] life," Scarlett says on p. 720, with her other children ignored back at Tara under her sister Suellen's care.

81. Ripley, *Scarlett*, p. 584.

82. Margaret Mitchell to Herschel Brickell, October 9, 1936, *GWTW Letters*, p. 75; *GWTW*, p. 428; *GWTW: The Screenplay*, p. 138 (this is the last line before the intermission).

83. "I dearly loved his books and re-read them ever so often," Mitchell wrote to Susan Myrick on February 10, 1939, while Myrick was working as a consultant for *GWTW* and Fitzgerald was working on the script. "If anyone had told me ten or more years ago that he would be working on a book of mine I would have been stricken speechless with pellagra or hardening of the arteries or something." *GWTW Letters*, p. 250. Mitchell had also met Fitzgerald as a young man, when she and her brother had given him a ride home when he was stationed in Georgia during the First World War. See Pyron, *Southern Daughter*, p. 77.

Chapter 4: Reconstructing Dixie

1. C. Vann Woodward, "The Irony of Southern History," in *The Burden of Southern History* (New York: Vintage, 1961), p. 170.

2. Slogan quoted in Gaines Foster, *Ghosts of the Confederacy: Defeat, the Lost Cause, and the Emergence of the New South* (New York: Oxford University Press, 1987), p. 3.

3. Two writers in particular have had a major impact on my understanding of popular music—and, for that matter, popular culture in general. Readers familiar with Greil Marcus's *Mystery Train: Images of America in Rock 'n' Roll Music*, 3d ed. (1st ed., 1975; New York: Dutton, 1990) will recognize the thematic and stylistic similarities between this chapter and that book. It was Marcus who first showed me that it was possible to write intelligently and engagingly about popular music, and although I ultimately departed from some of his conclusions and aspects of his style in developing my own voice, this chapter may be seen as an act of homage. Similarly, the work of George Lipsitz—especially *Time Passages: Collective Memory and American Popular Culture* (Minneapolis: University of Minnesota Press, 1990)—has greatly enhanced my understanding of the way popular culture functions in U.S. society. Again, I am in his debt for providing a model of vigorous, insightful cultural criticism.

4. Alexis De Tocqueville, *Democracy in America*, 2 vols., edited by Phillips Bradley (New York: Vintage, 1954), Vol. 2, p. 62.

5. Marcus, *Mystery Train*, p. 98.

6. This pattern is described by David Marc in *Demographic Vistas: Television in American Culture* (Philadelphia: University of Pennsylvania Press, 1984) and *Comic Visions: Television Comedy and American Culture* (Boston: Unwin/Hyman, 1989).

The techno-cultural vacuum described here has remained with us and could seen functioning in two different ways in the rock of the 1980s. The rise of music video early in the decade gave British performers—many of whom had already explored the form and had a supply on hand for the *Top of the Pops* program—an edge that helped trigger a new "British invasion" early in the decade. The other example is compact discs. Compact discs were expensive to buy and develop, and so producers and consumers turned to old favorites, giving performers whose careers were considered over a new lease on life (and, in this case, reinforcing the conservatism of the radio and record industry in the 1980s).

7. Presley then went on to superstardom, where one of his first hit recordings was "Love Me Tender," a song whose music dates back to the Civil War. It was originally known as "Aura Lee," first published in sheet music form in Cincinnati in 1861; the West Point class of 1865 adapted it as "Army Blue." The song has at least three sets of lyrics associated with it. John Hartford's version of "Aura Lee" and background information can be found on *Songs of the Civil War*, produced by Jim Brown, Ken Burns, and Don DeVito (Columbia Records, 1991).

8. Dave Marsh, *Glory Days: Bruce Springsteen in the 1980s* (New York: Pantheon, 1987), p. 90.

9. Ibid., p. 37.

10. "Alan Freed," in Jon Pareles and Patricia Romanowski, editors, *The Rolling Stone Encyclopedia of Rock 'n' Roll* (New York: Summit Books, 1983), p. 205.

11. Indeed, by the late 1960s Motown itself was suspect, an irritating symbol of

black pandering to white taste. By this time, Stax Records, with its more aggressively Southern and unpolished soul sound, had become the label for those in the know. This change and other classic soul music is discussed in Peter Guralnick, *Sweet Soul Music: Rhythm and Blues and the Southern Dream of Freedom* (New York: Harper & Row, 1986). See also Gerri Hirshey, *Nowhere to Run: The Story of Soul Music* (New York: Penguin, 1984).

Ultimately, of course, no music, from rock to rap, has been safe from co-optation. Nothing illustrates this more vividly than the televised images of George Bush's 1988 campaign manager Lee Atwater—the man who so effectively exploited race in his Willie Horton advertisements of the presidential campaign— playing the blues at the president's inauguration in 1989.

12. For an investigation of the Nixon administration's efforts to hamper Lennon, see Jon Wiener, "John Lennon versus the FBI," in *Professors, Politics, and Pop* (London: Verso, 1991). Wiener is also the author of *Come Together: John Lennon in His Time* (New York: Random House, 1984).

13. Grady's speech is included in Paul D. Escott and David R. Goldfield, editors, *Major Problems in the History of the South*, Vol. 2, *The New South* (Lexington, Mass.: D.C. Heath and Company, 1990), p. 72.

14. "Rockabilly," which connotes a mix between rock and hillbilly music, peaked in the late 1950s and is most often associated with performers such as Elvis Presley and Buddy Holly. For a good brief discussion of the form's more obscure practitioners, see Peter Guralnick, "Rockabilly," in Anthony DeCurtis, et al., editors, *The Rolling Stone Illustrated History of Rock & Roll*, 3d ed. (1st ed., 1976; New York: Random House, 1992), pp. 67–72.

15. The most comprehensive source for background on these people and the music they went on to produce is Barney Hoskins's journalistic *Across the Great Divide: The Band and America* (New York: Hyperion, 1993). Much of the following factual information comes from Hoskins. See also Levon Helm's memoir, *This Wheel's on Fire: Levon Helm and the Story of The Band* (New York: Morrow, 1993). A reunited Band, sans Robbie Robertson, also released a respectfully regarded album in 1993, still more evidence of revived interest in the group.

16. "Down to Old Dixie and Back," *Time*, January 12, 1970, p. 43. Robertson, for his part, recalled one club where there were bullet holes in all the walls.

17. Ibid.

18. Ed Ward, "The Band," in DeCurtis, et al., *Rolling Stone Illustrated History*, pp. 431–32.

19. Marcus, *Mystery Train*, p. 55. Baez's version of the song reached number three. This and subsequent chart positions were taken from *The Billboard Book of Top 40 Hits* (New York: Billboard Publications, 1985).

20. Among the books that discuss such issues are W. J. Cash, *The Mind of the South* (New York: Vintage, 1941); Paul Gaston, *The New South Creed: A Study in*

Southern Mythmaking (New York: Vintage, 1973); and Foster, *Ghosts of the Confederacy.* The *Century* articles are cited on p. 69.

21. Regis Debray quoted in Jay Cantor, *The Death of Che Guevara* (New York: Knopf, 1983), p. 573.

22. *Heart Songs* (1909; New York: Da Capo Press, 1983), p. 183.

23. For an examination of Confederate imagery in popular culture, with some discussion of country music, see Thomas Connelly and Barbara L. Bellows, "The Enduring Memory," in *God and General Lee: The Lost Cause and The Southern Mind* (Baton Rouge: Louisiana State University Press, 1981), especially pp. 146–48.

24. Joe Nick Patoski, "Southern Rock" in DeCurtis, et al., *Rolling Stone Illustrated History,* p. 505.

25. Rich Wiseman, "Lynyrd Skynyrd Turns the Tables," *Rolling Stone,* April 22, 1976, p. 20.

26. Tom Dupree, "Lynyrd Skynyrd in Sweet Home Alabama," *Rolling Stone,* October 24, 1974, p. 14.

27. Ibid.

28. Henry Grady quoted in Gaston, *New South Creed,* p. 117; Joel Chandler Harris, editor, *Life of Henry W. Grady, Including His Writings and Speeches* (New York: Cassell Publishing Company, 1890), p. 307.

29. Wiseman, "Lynyrd Skynyrd Turns the Tables," p. 20.

30. Ibid.

31. For a brief sketch of Emmett and the racial politics of minstrelsy, see Alexander Saxton, *The Rise and Fall of the White Republic: Class Politics and Mass Culture in the Nineteenth Century* (New York: Verso, 1990), pp. 165–82. The best-known work on minstrelsy is Robert Toll, *Blacking Up: The Minstrel Show in Nineteenth-Century America* (New York: Oxford, 1974). See also Eric Lott, *Love and Theft: Blackface Minstrelsy and the American Working Class* (New York: Oxford University Press, 1993).

32. *Margaret Mitchell's Gone with the Wind Letters,* edited by Richard Harwell (New York: Macmillan, 1976), p. 8.

33. The Heartbreakers, incidentally, later backed Bob Dylan on tour, taking on the task The Band had performed twenty years earlier.

34. This quotation was taken from Jefferson Davis's message to the Confederate Congress of April 29, 1861, an excerpt from which is published in Kenneth Stampp's anthology *The Causes of the Civil War,* 3d ed. (1st ed., 1959; New York: Touchstone/Simon and Schuster, 1991), p. 154.

35. Marcus, *Mystery Train,* p. 99.

36. Ibid., p. 116.

37. Ibid., p. 114.

38. Ulrich B. Phillips, "The Central Theme of Southern History," *American Historical Review* (October 1928): 30–43.

39. Woodward, *Burden of Southern History*, p. 173.

40. Ibid., p. 5.

41. The medley is available on *This Is Elvis* (RCA, 1981).

Chapter 5: A Few Good Men

1. "Oration by Professor William James," in *The Monument to Robert Gould Shaw: Its Inception, Completion, and Unveiling, 1865–1897* (Boston: Houghton Mifflin, 1897), p. 74.

2. Toni Morrison, *Beloved* (New York: Plume, 1988), p. 191. Morrison based the novel on an actual murder trial in Cincinnati during the years of the Dred Scott controversy.

3. In seeing the political tendencies of popular culture as often ambiguous and indeterminate, my thinking is consonant with a good deal of contemporary cultural theory. For one particularly apt example that discusses Hollywood film of the 1960s, 1970s, and 1980s—a crucial backdrop for this chapter—see Michael Ryan and Douglas Kellner, *Camera Politica: The Politics and Ideology of Contemporary Hollywood Film* (Bloomington: University of Indiana Press, 1988).

4. For a discussion of M*A*S*H as a Vietnam fable, see David Marc, *Comic Visions: Television Comedy and American Culture* (Boston: Unwin/Hyman, 1989), pp. 186–99. (Paul Buhle also collaborated on this material.)

5. Cobb quoted in James McPherson, *Battle Cry of Freedom: The Civil War Era* (New York: Oxford, 1988), p. 835.

6. W. E. Woodward, *Meet General Grant* (New York: Liveright, 1928), p. 372.

7. James McPherson, *The Negro's Civil War: How American Negroes Felt and Acted during the War for the Union* (Urbana: University of Illinois Press, 1982). Woodward is quoted on p. viii.

8. The project is under the editorship of Ira Berlin, Joseph P. Reidy, and Leslie S. Rowland. The volumes are being published by Cambridge University Press.

9. For an extensive collection of letters, affidavits, and other documents relating to black participation in the war, see Berlin, Reidy, and Rowland's *Freedom: A Documentary History of Emancipation, 1861–1867*, Series 2, *The Black Military Experience* (New York: Cambridge University Press, 1982). McPherson's *Negro's Civil War* is a less extensive collection of primary source documents but is arrayed in narrative form. For a treatment of secondary sources, see Joseph Glathaar, *Forged in Battle: The Civil War Alliance of Black Soldiers and White Officers* (New York: Mentor Books, 1991). There is a good brief treatment in Geoffrey Ward, Rick Burns, and Ken Burns, *The Civil War*, the companion volume to the PBS series (New York: Knopf, 1990), pp. 246–53.

10. Benjamin Quarles, *The Negro in the Civil War* (Boston: Little, Brown, 1969), p. 230.

11. Ibid., p. 198; Berlin, Reidy, and Rowland, *Freedom*, p. 14.

12. Glathaar's *Forged in Battle*, for example, deals with the racism black soldiers experienced, but it ultimately emphasizes the "alliance" (the word choice in the subtitle of his book is crucial here) forged by black and white together. Berlin, Reidy, and Rowland's *Freedom*, by contrast, much more forcefully demonstrates the hardships that in many cases overwhelmed the advantages of military service.

13. Berlin, Reidy, and Rowland, *Freedom*, p. 77.

14. Glathaar, *Forged in Battle*, p. 115.

15. The inequality of the Union pay structure is well documented and is discussed in much of the literature on African American soldiers in the Civil War. For one particularly good discussion on this point, see McPherson, *Negro's Civil War*, pp. 193–204.

16. For documents pertaining to fatigue duty, see Berlin, Reidy, and Rowland, *Freedom*, pp. 483–516. For figures on disease and explanations for the disparity between death rates for blacks and whites, see pp. 633–37.

17. Whitfield poem quoted in *Lay This Laurel: An Album on the Saint-Gaudens Memorial on Boston Common Honoring Black and White Men Together Who Served the Union Cause with Robert Gould Shaw and Died with Him July 18, 1863*. Photographs by Richard Benson and an essay by Lincoln Kirstein (New York: Eakins Press, 1973), n.p.

18. For a discussion of *The Big Parade* and the war movie climate of the 1920s, see Michael T. Isenberg's essay in John E. O'Connor and Martin A. Jackson, editors, *American History/American Film: Interpreting the Hollywood Image*, rev. ed. (1st ed., 1979; New York: Continuum Press, 1989), pp. 17–37.

19. "F.Y.I.," *Premiere*, May 1991, p. 15.

20. For a vivid portrayal of the struggles to make the film, see the 1991 documentary *Hearts of Darkness*, directed by Coppola's wife, Eleanor.

21. Pat Aufderheide, "Good Soldiers," in Mark Crispin Miller, editor, *Seeing through Movies* (New York: Pantheon, 1990), pp. 81–111. Aufderheide's essay provided an important intellectual base for the development of views on Vietnam movies in this chapter and in conceptualizing what makes *Glory* different. For another incisive reading of Vietnam movies, see Ryan and Kellner, *Camera Politica*, pp. 194–216, especially 197–205. *Apocalypse Now* is discussed on pp. 236–39.

22. Aufderheide, "Good Soldiers," p. 82.

23. For a complete discussion of the Cimino/United Artists debacle with *Heaven's Gate*, see Steven Bach, *Final Cut: Dreams and Disaster in the Making of Heaven's Gate* (New York: Morrow, 1985).

24. Aufderheide, "Good Soldiers," p. 103.

25. Ibid., p. 111.

26. Edward Zwick, telephone interview, February 4, 1991. Transcript in the author's possession.

27. "Reexamining the Civil War," *Entertainment Weekly*, October 10, 1990, p. 38.

28. Thalberg quoted in Anne Edwards, *Road to Tara: The Life of Margaret Mitchell* (New Haven, Conn.: Ticknor & Fields, 1983), p. 192.

29. For discussions of these and other Civil War films, see John M. Cassidy, *Civil War Cinema: A Pictorial History of Hollywood and the War between the States* (Missoula, Mont.: Pictorial Histories Publishing Company, 1986); and Jack Spears, *The Civil War on Screen and Other Essays* (South Brunswick, N.J.: A. S. Barnes and Company, 1977).

30. Peter Burchard, *One Gallant Rush: Robert Gould Shaw and His Brave Black Regiment* (New York: St. Martin's Press, 1965).

31. Armond White, "Fighting Black," *Film Comment*, January/February 1990, p. 26.

32. Edward Zwick, telephone interview with the author, February 4, 1991; Fields's comment comes from the press kit to the movie.

33. For a treatment of the varied activities that took place on South Carolina's Sea Islands, see Willie Lee Rose, *Rehearsal for Reconstruction: The Port Royal Experiment* (New York: Oxford, 1964).

34. Burchard, *One Gallant Rush*, p. 149.

35. Glathaar, *Forged in Battle*, p. 137.

36. Production notes, *Glory* press kit.

37. For a full discussion of these stereotypes and how they are played out in films produced in the United States, see Donald Bogle, *Toms, Coons, Mulattoes, Mammies, and Bucks: An Interpretive History of Blacks in American Films*, 2d ed. (1st ed., 1973; New York: Continuum, 1989).

38. Pauline Kael, "The 54th," *New Yorker*, December 5, 1989, p. 109.

39. Male gender roles have become a subject of increasing interest in contemporary scholarship. Although it was rarely addressed in any systematic way in the nineteenth century, historians have begun to note how gender suffused the issue of black enlistment for black and white alike during the Civil War. The term *manhood* surfaces again and again in government documents, soldiers' letters, or subsequent memoirs as an aspiration, a concern, or a fact of life. What these people meant by *manhood* varied: For some it connoted freedom, for others responsibility; for some it was a birthright, for others it had to be demonstrated. Yet, however varied their understandings, what is striking is a widely shared sense that the Civil War did indeed mark a watershed for black manhood. For a fuller discussion of this argument, see Jim Cullen, "'I's a Man Now': Uses of Gender for African American Men in the Civil War," in Catherine Clinton and Nina Silber, editors, *House Divided: Gender and the Civil War* (New York: Oxford University Press, 1992).

40. "This was the biggest thing that ever happened in my life," Glathaar quotes

a black soldier in *Forged in Battle*. "I felt like a man with a uniform on and a gun in my hand." See *Forged in Battle*, p. 79.

41. James McPherson, "The Glory Story," *New Republic*, January 8 & 15, 1990, p. 27. McPherson's article also details other minor factual errors, such as the movie's depiction of the Wagner attack as southward instead of northward.

42. Shaw letters quoted in Burchard, *One Gallant Rush*, pp. 44, 36, 67. Jefferson Davis denounced the Emancipation Proclamation as "the most execrable measure in the history of guilty man" but never did vow a war of wholesale extermination, though the Confederate Congress later threatened death to all black soldiers and the whites who commanded them. Because of fears of Northern retaliation, this was never carried out on a major scale, though there were incidents of massacres of blacks (most notably at Fort Pillow in 1864, and probably very often elsewhere as well). The Confederates refused to recognize captured African Americans as full persons exchangeable for one Confederate, resulting in a tragic stalemate when no prisoners were exchanged and thousands died of disease and neglect in Northern and Southern prison camps. See McPherson, *Battle Cry of Freedom*, pp. 566–67, 793–96.

Glory devotes a few scenes to the Confederate death proclamation, and the soldiers are offered an honorable discharge if they choose to leave. As in countless war movies, Westerns, and spy stories whereby men are free to turn down a dangerous mission, none does so.

43. Burchard, *One Gallant Rush*, p. 73.

44. Ibid., pp. 73–74.

45. Edward Zwick, telephone interview with the author, February 4, 1991.

46. Burchard, *One Gallant Rush*, p. 136.

47. McPherson, *Battle Cry of Freedom*, pp. 610–11; Burchard, *One Gallant Rush*, pp. 130–32.

48. McPherson, *Negro's Civil War*, p. 201.

49. Ward, Burns, and Burns, *Civil War*, p. 248.

50. Kael, "The 54th," p. 109.

51. Abraham Lincoln, letter to James C. Conkling, in *Speeches, Letters, Miscellaneous Writings, 1859–1865*, edited by Don Fehrenbacher (New York: Library of America, 1989), pp. 498–99.

52. Roger Ebert, "Morgan Freeman," in *The 1991 Movie Home Companion* (Kansas City: Andrews, McMeel & Parker, 1990), p. 641.

53. Frances E. W. Harper, "Bury Me in a Free Land," in *Complete Poems of Frances E. W. Harper* (New York: Oxford University Press, 1988), pp. 93–94.

54. Glathaar, *Forged in Battle*, p. 139.

55. Luck quoted in Burchard, *One Gallant Rush*, pp. 142–43.

56. For a discussion of memorial efforts on Shaw's behalf, see Kirstein's essay in *Lay This Laurel*.

57. George Fredrickson, *The Inner Civil War: Northern Intellectuals and the Crisis of Union* (New York: Harper & Row, 1965), pp. 155, 161–62. The observation that tributes to Shaw took two basic forms is Fredrickson's, in his provocative and useful chapter "The Martyr and His Friends," which deals with responses to Shaw's death.

58. "Voluntaries" included in *The Complete Writings of Ralph Waldo Emerson* (New York: William H. Wise Co., 1929), pp. 894–95.

59. *Monument to Robert Gould Shaw*, p. 93.

60. *Monument to Robert Gould Shaw*, p. 85.

61. Robert Lowell, *For the Union Dead* (New York: Farrar, Straus, Giroux, 1964), pp. 70–72.

62. Kirstein, in his essay accompanying *Lay This Laurel*, n.p.

63. White, "Fighting Black," p. 26.

64. Stone adopted an Asian woman's perspective in the most recent film in his Vietnam trilogy, *Heaven and Earth*, based on the memoirs of Le Ly Hayslip and released in December of 1993. He described it as "a *Gone with the Wind* kind of Vietnamese story." See *Entertainment Weekly*, August 27/September 3, 1993, p. 74.

65. "Oration by Professor William James," p. 85.

Chapter 6: Patriotic "Gore"

1. Allan Garganus, *Oldest Living Confederate Widow Tells All: A Novel* (New York: Knopf, 1989), p. 266.

2. As many Civil War buffs know, North and South often gave different names to the same battle. In the North, battles were named for local landmarks, and this one was called Bull Run for the creek that ran nearby. In the South, battles were named for the nearest town, e.g., Manassas. In this instance, the Southern name more accurately describes the location of the event, which took place miles away from Bull Run and within the town's borders. First Manassas is what the battle is still called in Virginia, although there is a shopping mall called Bull Run on Route 234.

3. These figures for the Manassas reenactment are given in the press kit from the Prince William County Park Authority, and those for Gettysburg in the *Glory* press kit. Both cases represent fractions of the total number of soldiers who actually participated in those battles. There were about 60,000 men at Manassas (roughly 30,000 on each side), and 175,000 at Gettysburg (100,000 Union and 75,000 Confederate).

4. Jonah Begone, "Differences between Civil War and Revolutionary War Reenacting," *Camp Chase Gazette*, August 1990, pp. 26–28.

5. "Civil War Round Table Organization Guide" taken from a booklet published

by *Civil War Times* magazine in the early 1960s and reprinted by the Civil War Round Table Associates, 1972.

6. For a discussion of the United Confederate Veterans, United Daughters of the Confederacy, and Sons of Confederate Veterans, see Gaines Foster, *Ghosts of the Confederacy: Defeat, the Lost Cause, and the Emergence of the New South* (New York: Oxford University Press, 1987), which includes chapters on Confederate memorial celebrations and changes in them in the decades following 1865.

7. The advertisement ran in a series of issues of *Camp Chase Gazette*, a Civil War reenacting magazine. For one example, see p. 25 of the September 1990 issue.

8. Figures provided by Abraham Lincoln Association president Frank Williams, Providence, Rhode Island, March 5, 1991. The U.S. edition is entitled *Lincoln on Democracy*, edited and introduced by Mario M. Cuomo and Harold Holzer (New York: HarperCollins, 1990).

9. Statistics on round tables are included in promotional materials for the Civil War Round Table Associates and the "Civil War Round Table Organization Guide." The figure of two hundred members and the international chapters are mentioned in passing in the December 1990 *Membership Memo*, pp. 2 and 4.

10. *Camp Chase Gazette*, "Publisher's Note," September 1990, p. 39.

11. Early examples of Civil War reenacting by the GAR, and its political, economic, and social clout, are discussed throughout Stuart McConnell's *Glorious Contentment: The Grand Army of the Republic, 1865–1900* (Chapel Hill: University of North Carolina Press, 1992). See especially pp. 47, 103–4.

12. McConnell, *Glorious Contentment*, pp. 189–93. Fraternization became especially prominent at Blue-Gray reunions that became increasingly common at the end of the century. For fellow feeling that existed during the actual war, see Randall C. Jimerson, *The Private Civil War: Popular Thought during the Sectional Conflict* (Baton Rouge: Louisiana State University Press, 1988), particularly the chapter "The Limits of Sectional Consciousness," pp. 180–237. This issue has also been ably handled by Gerald F. Linderman in *Embattled Courage: The Experience of Combat in the American Civil War* (New York: Free Press, 1987). See especially pp. 236–39.

13. McConnell, *Glorious Contentment*, p. 105. For the fascination with military paraphernalia, see pp. 177–78.

14. Perhaps the best treatment of this subject is in David Glassberg, *American Historical Pageantry: The Uses of Tradition in the Early Twentieth Century* (Chapel Hill: University of North Carolina Press, 1990). For pageantry and the role it played in ethnic communities, see John Bodnar, *Remaking America: Public Memory, Commemoration, and Patriotism* (Princeton: Princeton University Press, 1992).

One ongoing historical re-creation that seems to have links both to pageants and the activities of Civil War reenactors is the annual carnival of Mardi Gras Indians in New Orleans. See George Lipsitz's chapter on this subject in *Time*

Passages: Collective Memory and American Popular Culture (Minneapolis: University of Minnesota Press, 1990), pp. 233–53.

15. For an incisive discussion of Greenfield Village and Colonial Williamsburg, see Michael Wallace, "Visiting the Past: History Museums in the United States," in Susan Porter Benson, Stephen Brier, and Roy Rosenzweig, editors, *Presenting the Past: Essays on History and the Public* (Philadelphia: Temple University Press, 1986), pp. 135–61. Wallace is one of a number of scholars who have noted the absence of class conflict in Ford's village and slaves from Williamsburg. Greenfield Village and Williamsburg are also discussed extensively in Michael Kammen, *Mystic Chords of Memory: The Transformation of Tradition in American Culture* (New York: Knopf, 1991). See especially pp. 342–75.

16. Kammen, *Mystic Chords of Memory*, p. 456; Richard O'Sullivan, "Red Badge Revivalists," *History Today*, December 1987, p. 6.

17. Bodnar, *Remaking America*, p. 214.

18. Ibid., p. 215.

19. Allan Nevins, *Ordeal of the Union*, 4 vols., and *The War for the Union*, 4 vols. (New York: Scribner's, 1947–71).

20. For Nevins's role in the magazine, see Roy Rosenzweig's superb essay on the subject, "Marketing the Past: *American Heritage* and Popular History in the United States," in Benson, Brier, and Rosenzweig, *Presenting the Past*, pp. 21–52.

21. Bodnar, *Remaking America*, pp. 220–26.

22. For discussions of Grant's tenure as chairman of the Civil War Centennial Commission, see Kammen, *Mystic Chords of Memory*, pp. 590–96, and Bodnar, *Remaking America*, p. 211.

23. John Skow, "Bang, Bang! You're History, Buddy," *Time*, August 11, 1986; Herb Phillips, "Playing Soldier: History Hobbyists Relive the Battle of the Blue and Gray," *Travel-Holiday*, August 1989, p. 106.

24. These articles can be found in the July and September 1990 issues of *Camp Chase Gazette*. The latter story, written by an employee of the United States Information Agency, concludes that although secession would not have been a good thing for the Southern states, it would definitely be a good thing for Lithuania. With the explosion of ethnic and regional particularity all over the world in the closing years of the twentieth century, it would seem that Southern secession—an issue that has almost become quaint, even secondary to other factors in Civil War historiography in recent decades—may soon furnish parallels for comparison and contrast in Eastern Europe, the Middle East, Canada, and other areas.

25. Items and estimates provided by Paul Oliveria of the 2d Rhode Island Infantry, Rehoboth, Massachusetts, March 9, 1991.

26. The comments in this section came from a taped and transcribed interview conducted in March 1991 at Jonathan Clarke's house in rural Rhode Island. I also talked with her at a number of reenactments throughout that year and in one-on-

one discussions prior to and following this interview. Notes and transcriptions are in the author's possession.

27. For an account of this case, see Eugene Meyer, "The Soldier Left a Portrait and Her Eyewitness Account," *Smithsonian*, January 1994, pp. 96–104. The woman in question, Lauren Cook Burgess, is the editor of *An Uncommon Soldier* (Pasadena, Md.: Minerva Center, 1994), an annotated collection of letters by a woman who fought in the Civil War.

28. For an elaboration of this position, see the Civil War Round Table Association's *Membership Memo*, Winter 1991, p. 3, which discusses the issue of women in combat roles in reenactments. In the previous issue, editor Jerry Russell noted that a St. Louis round table had finally allowed women to join. "There are good arguments to both sides," he said regarding the men-only policy, and when a woman member of the Civil War Round Table Association wrote him an angry letter in the next issue, he refunded her membership fee. Replying by saying that he personally believes that round tables should be open to all, Russell also asserted the freedom of association. "Some men ARE sexist and have those ridiculous opinions," he wrote. "*And they GET to feel that way*" (emphasis in the original).

29. O'Sullivan, "Red Badge Revivalists," p. 7.

30. McConnell, *Glorious Contentment*, pp. 177–78. As the title of the book indicates, such reconfigurations of memory are an important theme.

31. Ibid., pp. 185–86.

32. Ken Burns, telephone interview with the author, May 9, 1991.

33. McNeill's essay is included in his collection *Mythistory and Other Essays* (Chicago: University of Chicago Press, 1985); the quotation appears on p. 14.

34. Perhaps the first important post–Civil War work that dealt with the subject was Frances Ellen Watkins Harper's *Iola Leroy; or Shadows Uplifted* (1892), a work that sought to remind readers of the unkept promises of the war amid the mounting horrors of reaction at the end of the nineteenth century. The war years represented an important part of Harper's narrative, but the dramatic and political locus of the novel is Reconstruction. In a similar vein, short-story writer Charles Chesnutt dealt with the war occasionally in his fiction, notably, in his famous story "The Wife of His Youth" (1899), yet the war was a backdrop, not a central stage. In the twentieth century, Margaret Walker wrote extensively about the war years in her 1966 novel *Jubilee*, a work that draws on the usable past of the first Reconstruction to illuminate the pitfalls and promises of the second one in the years during which she was writing. Alex Haley's hugely popular *Roots*, by contrast, is much more concerned with the eighteenth and early nineteenth centuries. One of his major characters, Chicken George, is free before the war even begins, and although emancipation does have a major impact on the rest of his family, the story is virtually over by this point. Of course, Haley was writing family history, but one imagines that given the liberties he took in writing the book, he could have focused much more on the Civil War if it had really mattered to him.

Although this hardly amounts to a comprehensive survey of African American popular culture focused on the mid-nineteenth century, it does seem clear that other moments—most notably Reconstruction—were more important to many black writers in the best-known works. This is certainly the case in the most recent major African American historical novel, Toni Morrison's *Beloved* (1987), which flashes back between the 1850s and 1870s.

Conclusion: The Art of History

1. C. Vann Woodward, *"Strange Career* Critics: Long May They Persevere," *Journal of American History* (December 1988): 862. Woodward's piece was part of a forum on *The Strange Career of Jim Crow*, his classic work on post–Civil War race relations (1955; New York: Oxford University Press, 1974).

2. Ken Burns, "Struggling to Hear the Shot That Killed Lincoln," *New York Times*, February 14, 1993, p. H9.

3. James M. McPherson, *Battle Cry of Freedom: The Civil War Era* (New York: Oxford University Press, 1988), pp. 852–53.

4. For further elaboration of a position I regard as consonant with my own, see Russell Jacoby, "A New Intellectual History," *American Historical Review* (April 1992): 405–24. See also Dominick LaCapra's rejoinder, "Intellectual History and Its Ways," pp. 425–29 of the same issue. Taken together, the two articles provide an excellent forum on the role of theory in historical study.

Source Credits

Index

245

While popular versions of the past easily lapse into romance or deliberately occlude complexity, professional historical writing, Cullen notes, usually avoids the sense of personal or communal meaning that characterizes popular history. He identifies behind both forms, however, the presence of ideological issues and presentist involvements that continue to shape Americans' understanding of the Civil War.

ABOUT THE AUTHOR

Jim Cullen is a lecturer in history, literature, and expository writing at Harvard University. He has written for *Rolling Stone, Cleveland Plain-Dealer,* and *Newsday,* as well as several scholarly journals.